Library of
Davidson College

BRITISH POLITICS
AND GOVERNMENT
1951–1970

BRITISH POLITICS AND GOVERNMENT
1951–1970

A STUDY OF
AN AFFLUENT SOCIETY

Mary Proudfoot

FABER AND FABER
3 Queen Square
London

First published in 1974
by Faber and Faber Limited
3 Queen Square London WC1
Printed in Great Britain by
Western Printing Services Ltd, Bristol

All rights reserved

ISBN 0 571 10577 7

320.942
P968b

76-7880

© Mary Proudfoot, 1974

Contents

	page
INTRODUCTION: *July 1945 to October 1951*	9
1 General	9
2 The General Election of July 1945	13
3 The Two Labour Governments from 1945 to 1951	14
4 The Conservatives in Opposition	18
CHAPTER ONE: *The Conservative Government from October 1951 to May 1955*	23
1 The General Election of 25 October 1951	23
2 The Conservative Team	25
3 Constitutional and Administrative Issues	28
4 Economic Issues	30
5 Domestic Affairs	32
6 Defence Policy	35
7 Foreign Policy	37
8 The Commonwealth	48
9 The Opposition	54
CHAPTER TWO: *The Conservative Government from May 1955 to October 1959*	63
1 The General Election of 25 May 1955	64
2 The Conservative Team	66
3 Constitutional and Administrative Issues	70
4 Economic Issues	74
5 Domestic Affairs	77
6 Defence Policy	79
7 Foreign Policy	81
8 The Commonwealth	94
9 The Opposition	100
CHAPTER THREE: *The Conservative Government from October 1959 to October 1964*	105
1 The General Election of 8 October 1959	106
2 The Conservative Team	108
3 Constitutional and Administrative Issues	118

		page
4	Economic Issues	120
5	Domestic Affairs	125
6	Defence Policy	132
7	Foreign Policy	135
8	The Commonwealth	138
9	The Opposition	146

CHAPTER FOUR: *The Labour Government from October 1964 to March 1966* — 153

1	The General Election of 15 October 1964	153
2	The Labour Team	157
3	Constitutional and Administrative Issues	159
4	Economic Issues	160
5	Domestic Affairs	162
6	Defence Policy	165
7	Foreign Policy	167
8	The Commonwealth	169
9	The Opposition	173

CHAPTER FIVE: *The Labour Government from March 1966 to June 1970* — 179

1	The General Election of 31 March 1966	180
2	The Labour Team	182
3	Constitutional and Administrative Issues	189
4	Economic Issues	194
5	Domestic Affairs	205
6	Defence Policy	207
7	Foreign Policy	208
8	The Commonwealth	214
9	The Opposition	218

EPILOGUE — 222

BIBLIOGRAPHY — 226

INDEX — 230

BRITISH POLITICS AND GOVERNMENT
1951–1970

INTRODUCTION

July 1945 to October 1951

SUMMARY	page
1 General	9
2 The General Election of July 1945	13
3 The Two Labour Governments from 1945 to 1951	14
4 The Conservatives in Opposition	18

1 GENERAL

This book is a study of the five Governments which held office in Britain from 1951 to 1970. It is a view, brief and necessarily highly selective, of the two happiest and most affluent decades yet in British history, when the rank and file of the nation really began to enter into its inheritance as a relatively wealthy, literate, liberal and property-owning democracy.

For this achievement both the main political parties, Conservative and Labour, and also the small Liberal group, can claim some credit. Of course problems of all kinds arose in this time and, as it seems to be an established national trait that the British should reflect gloomily on their short-comings and grossly underestimate their successes, most writers have elaborated on the problems and have tended to write off as of little account the achievements. But no one with knowledge of the twenties and thirties ought to be in any doubt as to the movement forward and upward which followed the Second World War. However one chooses to look at these two decades, progress of every kind seems very remarkable indeed. Class by class this was so. The small upper class, well educated and, at their best, trained for a career of service to the State, were no less well educated, and no less disposed to serve than they were before the war. And, now that they were gradually to be relieved of the trappings of an imperial commitment that had become a sham, a burden and something of a bore, they began to devote themselves to more fruitful occupations. The middle groups, prosperous as never before, were now finally freed from the unrealistic dream of the twenties and thirties of a return to pre-1914 conditions. Moreover the working people, the great majority of the nation, found that this time a world war really had not been fought in vain as far as they were concerned. There were hard years, for instance 1951 and 1952, and the subsequent alternations between boom and recession became increasingly disquieting, but the mass hunger, unemployment and hopelessness really were behind them. Increasingly, year by year, for the vast majority, new horizons beckoned. The people were better paid, better housed, better fed and better educated, than ever before.

The British economy certainly had its bad patches. It was beset by balance of payment problems; by stop-go policies; by this, that and the other malaise. But one has only to consider briefly the position between the two wars: the mass economic misery; the General Strike; the dole; the means test; the Special Areas; the spectre of hunger consequent on mass unemployment, to be conscious of the change for the better. Then, the economists had had no glimmer of an answer. Now they, and their masters the politicians, though still very frequently making what turned out to be mistakes, did at any rate begin to bring rather more sophisticated thinking to bear on economic affairs. The problems of the fifties and sixties were the problems of a left of centre liberal and progressive society.

At home, the British were a quiet people in these two affluent decades. Drugs, strikes, sit-ins, demos, mugging and the backlash that all this occasioned, though not unknown at the end of the sixties, belonged essentially to the seventies. In these two decades one should note, for instance, the willingness with which so many, from all parties, moved forward to limit and finally to abolish capital punishment; to liberalize the abortion laws; to provide for the needs of coloured citizens – albeit with increasing misgiving. Later, in the seventies, came shrill cries demanding the reimposition of the death penalty and deterrent prison sentences. The term 'permissive society' then acquired pejorative rather than compassionate overtones. Violence is catching and is not contained by frontiers. Already by the end of the sixties it was coming from so many quarters: from the urban ghettoes of North America; from the war in Vietnam; from Northern Ireland; from the poor and the blacks and the students; from unemployment, inequality and underprivilege all over the globe. Perhaps it came in part, too, from the fairly harmless and childish pleasure that the young found in demos, long hair and protest. It is probable that the often ridiculous over-reaction of their elders in itself gave a cutting, bitter edge to the protests of the young. Certainly it seems that the spectacle of violence brought night after night into every home with a television screen deadened increasingly the capacity of the ordinary man and woman whether young or old to react to atrocity with shock and disgust. The seventies are indeed turning out to be very different from the fifties and the sixties.

However, I have no wish to suggest that the problems of the fifties and sixties were negligible – though they may sometimes seem so – as compared with what had gone before, and with what was to follow after. It is rather that they were the sophisticated problems of a relatively advanced society, from which the threat of primary poverty and all its attendant miseries had largely been removed. *Cathy Come Home* would hardly have made the headlines in the early thirties!

The seminal years were, of course, those of the Second World War. These years, and the changes that they brought to the structure of

Introduction

British society, are outside the scope of this study, although it was then that the foundations of policy for the period under review were laid. In 1945 the electorate, the war behind it, turned its back on Churchill and the Conservative Party which had dominated the wartime coalition Government and returned Labour to power, with a majority of 146 over all other Parties. Labour held 393 seats; the Conservatives 213; the Liberals 12; Communists 2; Commonwealth 1; and others 19. The Conservatives' parliamentary strength was reduced to its lowest level since 1906. They polled only 39.8 per cent of the total vote, as against Labour's 47.8 per cent.[1] 72.7 per cent of the electorate voted. The Labour Party did not quite obtain the support of half the electorate, in 1945, its year of triumph. None the less, the exultation felt in Labour circles is understandable. 'We are the masters now,' declared Lord Shawcross happily.[2] And Dalton writes: 'There was exhilaration among us, joy and hope, determination and confidence. We felt exalted, dedicated, walking on air, walking with destiny.'[3] This electoral verdict was probably surprising to the outside world, and perhaps also to many people in Britain too, although the Gallup poll had, since July 1943, shown an increase of around 6 per cent in Labour's lead over the Conservatives.[4] However, opinion polls were in their infancy, so these figures attracted much less attention than they would today. The reasons for this perhaps gradual, but in the end massive, swing of electoral opinion against a Party which had been in power, with or without minor allies, almost continuously since 1922, is a matter for speculation. Some must no doubt be sought in the politics of the thirties. The Conservatives were probably associated in the public mind in 1945 with the economic crisis of 1931; with massive unemployment; the dole; the means test; and the depressed areas. The Conservative policy of appeasement of the dictators in the thirties was now generally regarded as dishonourable, and, in any case, it had been manifestly unsuccessful. It had not kept Britain out of war in 1939. It had, however, resulted in her entering the war in a state of such unpreparedness that she had, in the initial years, come perilously near to defeat. The Conservatives had thus failed to deliver the goods on the domestic front or on the foreign front. And these were facts which the electorate now remembered.

[1] David Butler and Jennie Freeman, *British Political Facts 1900–1967* 2nd edn., p. 143.
[2] Earl of Kilmuir, Memoirs, *Political Adventure*, p. 137.
[3] Lord Dalton, Memoirs, Vol. III, *High Tide and After*, p. 3.
[4] Mr. Macmillan says that the general view was that the Conservatives would be returned to power by a small majority – something between 30 and 50. He goes on to say, however, that 'as soon as electioneering began in earnest I knew what the result would be.' Harold Macmillan, Memoirs, Vol. III, *Tides of Fortunes, 1945–1955*, p. 31.

Other reasons can perhaps be sought in the experiences of the British people during the war years. A much more egalitarian and united society had emerged, as a result of the shared experiences of 1939–45. Class and educational and material differences had been considerably diminished as the evacuees from the big towns and conurbations were absorbed into the homes and lives of the villages, the country gentry and the small town bourgeoisie;[1] as the young, and even the middle-aged of all classes came closely together in the many-faceted shared experiences of their service lives; as the whole civilian population ate their identical butter, cheese, meat and chocolate rations, and planned and spent their identical clothing coupons, and together suffered the horrors of aerial warfare, and the anxieties and sorrow and uncertainties about their men who fought, up and down the world. The British became a united people – which they had certainly not been in the First World War. In the Second World War the whole adult population, women as well as men, fought for freedom wherever this appeared to be in danger, across the continents of the world, with a unity of purpose probably never before achieved.

There could be no going back, after all this, to the patterns of pre-war Britain. The young men in the forces had been well fed, well clothed and cared for, well educated and made, anyway in part, politically articulate.[2] They returned to civilian life with both a great spread of skills acquired in the course of their service lives and aspirations that their fathers had not dreamt of. Not for them the socially divided, economically backward and unequal, timid, restrictive world of the thirties. Not for them the means test, the wretched housing, the unemployment and the depressed areas. But who this time, was going to build the Brave New World for them? The Liberals had disappeared from view. The Conservatives, who had dominated the thirties were, if for no other reason, clearly unacceptable. Labour seemed the only possible candidate.

At this point it is perhaps desirable to say something about the position of Mr. Churchill, if only because it seemed so odd to many of Britain's friends abroad that the country should at this juncture repudiate the hero who had for so long epitomized the struggle of the whole free world against tyranny. It seems unlikely that the British people ceased, overnight, to feel grateful – though their gratitude was clearly not to be measured in electoral terms. The fact was that the Election in 1945 involved the choice of a political Party and a political programme. In the war years there had been no Parties and no programmes. And Churchill, great national hero though he had been and still was, was not really thought of as a Party man. Indeed, he had never seen himself as

[1] The revelations about life in the poorer sections of the big cities was also a salutary experience. See Dora Ibberson, *Our Towns*.

[2] A.B.C.A. – the Army Bureau of Current Affairs – was specifically intended to bring this about, throughout the forces.

one either. In spite of the formal record, he was not really to be identified with the Conservative Party – and the electors sensed this. Moreover he himself had little to offer, in 1945, that could seriously be described as a political programme. In pre-war days he had changed sides more often than most. Even when he had come out for the Conservatives in 1924 his record, on the domestic front, had not been one to inspire confidence. He had parted with the Conservatives again in 1931 over the issue of dominion status for India. He was not prepared, he had made very clear, to preside over the dissolution of the British Empire. Yet this was one of the many difficult tasks which manifestly now had to be undertaken. Even his attitudes towards foreign affairs in the thirties, right though they turned out to be as far as the Second World War went, would clearly not be wholly suitable for post-war Britain. And there was no evidence to suggest that he was going to revise his views. In fact, there was much to suggest that he was not.

When he first came into the House of Commons as Prime Minister, in 1940, it was the Liberal and Labour M.P.s who had cheered, not the Conservatives. True, he had, after the resignation and death of Chamberlain, become Party Leader. The Conservatives had to provide his team, so he had to be in control. Not for him the Lloyd George role after the First World War.[1] Wisely he decided then to take over the Party; and after the war he was going to stick to it. But, though formally their Leader, he was never really one of them. The Conservatives saw, in him, the man who had won the war and now, perhaps, could win the peace. He saw, in them, the men who could legitimize his leadership. That was all.

2 THE GENERAL ELECTION OF JULY 1945

It seems likely that the General Election campaign in 1945 did little to alter electoral opinion.[2] There can be no doubt that from the Conservative angle it was an unfortunate campaign. Churchill's reference to the Labour Party (with whose senior members he had worked in full harmony since 1940, and whose Leader, Mr. Attlee, had been his deputy) as men of the Gestapo, aiming to establish a socialist dictatorship utterly alien to the British tradition, was clearly not credible.[3] The failure of the Conservatives to make any very specific commitment to the policies set out in

[1] Mr. Macmillan notes: 'He [Churchill] had not forgotten that in the closing years of his career Lloyd George was rendered politically impotent by the lack of any effective party at his disposal.' Memoirs, op. cit., Vol. III, p. 24.

[2] See Nuffield Election Studies, R. B. McCallum and Alison Readman, *The British General Election of 1945*.

[3] '... the use of this terrible word in connection with his opponents was a grievous error.' Macmillan, op. cit., Vol. III, p. 31.

the Beveridge Report of 1943 was a serious omission.[1] Once the war was won, the British electorate had already had more than enough of blood and sweat and tears, and was much more interested in what went on in Britain than what went on at the Potsdam Conference. The man in the street wanted to know what the new line was going to be. The Labour campaign showed that this Party had a line. Labour leaders laid much more stress on the building of a new Britain and much less stress on international affairs. Lord Butler remarks, in his memoirs: 'It would have been better if affirmation of post-war policies had not taken a poor third place to the concentrated exploitation of Churchill's personality and a negative attack on the Labour Party. But the election would probably have been lost in any case.'[2]

3 THE TWO LABOUR GOVERNMENTS FROM 1945 TO 1951

Labour in office was able to make a vastly better showing than in either of its two inter-war minority Governments. There were now able men available who had had experience in the upper reaches of political life during the wartime coalition. They were not new boys now. They were the first of the grammar school generation – very different indeed from the Clydesiders and inter-war working-class trade union M.P.s. The war years had provided wide experience in the kind of government planning that the Labour Party had always advocated. There was clearly an enormous amount to be done; and it looked as though a Labour government was in a better position than the Conservatives to do it.

The overall scarcities suggested to most people, and not only to people in the Labour Party, that fair shares for all could best be achieved by continuing to organize the share-out at government level, anyway for the time being. As to foreign affairs – Churchill had won the war. But now the war was over and victory on the domestic front was what mattered most. So Attlee as Prime Minister and Ernie Bevin as Foreign Secretary had to soldier on, on the foreign affairs front, without much in the way of moral support from an electorate now almost wholly preoccupied with other issues. Between them these two probably did as well as any men could in the new situation in which Britain found herself after the war. Attlee and Bevin played the very few cards remaining in British hands, as far as international affairs went, with courage, skill and imagination. The same could certainly be said on the Commonwealth side. The necessary retreat from empire was begun, most notably in the Far East, with dignity and responsibility; and, for the most part, Britain managed to remain on good terms with her formerly dependent territories. There was no breach with the Americans, even though Americans were not

---

[1] It is ironic to note that Beveridge lost his seat in the 1945 General Election.
[2] *The Art of the Possible*, p. 128.

predisposed to like or trust people who sometimes called themselves socialists. Attlee and Bevin were also good Europeans, deeply concerned with the need to rebuild Western Europe. So far so good. It is difficult to see that the Conservatives could have done much better.

On the domestic front the Labour Government carried on into the peace the tried wartime recipe of a mixed economy, with a public and a private sector, with the Government assuming the overall responsibility for running it. It also took on the not quite so new experiment of what has now become known as the Welfare State. When, precisely, this philosophy became prevalent in British politics it is difficult to say. In the nineteenth century Disraeli, Lord Randolph Churchill, Joseph Chamberlain and many others were all small scale exponents of it in their different ways. The great Liberal Government of 1906 was a much larger scale exponent. And in the inter-war years both the Conservative Governments and the two minority Labour Governments had forged ahead as best they could, hampered though they were by increasingly adverse economic conditions. Thus it could plausibly be argued that Sir William Beveridge, in 1943, was only restating, in larger print and at greater length, principles which every British politician of any standing had accepted for generations.

The Labour Government certainly welcomed, very much more positively than did the Conservatives, the Beveridge principles. It was hampered of course by the severely straitened economic circumstances of post-war Britain, and no doubt this explains in part its moderation. Thus nationalization, so long regarded by Labour Party theorists as the panacea for all evils, was in fact limited to the Bank of England and to public-service type industries. The exception was the Iron and Steel Nationalization Act of 1951 which Attlee threw in late in the day and rather reluctantly, probably as a sop to his left wingers. It was soon to be repealed by his Conservative successors who, however, had no qualms about leaving the rest of these new Acts intact on the statute-book. Nationalization, the Labour Government found, cost money and did not pay large dividends, either in economic or in electoral terms. Taxation was certainly used to launch the Welfare State on Beveridge lines. However, it was not used to effect any far-reaching redistribution of wealth. Government controls were retained over wide sectors of the economy. But these would have been necessary whatever government had been in power both because of overall scarcities of raw materials and because of Britain's many external economic difficulties.

The Labour Government was, in fact, sophisticated, efficient, moderate and quite successful. There was nothing much to quarrel about. Anyway there were probably no other options open. This state of affairs was reflected in the fact that in the five years from 1945 to 1950 the Labour Party did not lose, at a by-election, a single seat won at the General

Election of 1945. At the time of its dissolution in 1950 the Labour majority over all other Parties in the House was 142.[1] Yet it seems probable that the mysterious current of public opinion, which had shown itself in such startling form in 1945, was already moving in the opposite direction, slowly, but surely. The Labour image was becoming less good. The leaders were getting old and tired. They were beginning to quarrel with each other, not only in private but also in public. The British people were getting increasingly tired of the shabby quality of their lives. What had happened to the freedom and prosperity for which they had supposedly fought for seven long years? Was the Labour Party ever really going to deliver the goods? Did it even want to? The public image of men like Sir Stafford Cripps – a vegetarian and a teetotaller – perhaps suggested the reverse. Lord Kilmuir has recorded cheerfully the impact on the Conservatives of this extremely able and upright man: 'Stafford Cripps, austere, punctilious, with occasionally a glacial smile playing unattractively around his prim mouth, was never one of our favourites.'[2] From 1950 to 1951 the image of the Labour Party steadily worsened. Some of the reasons for this are readily apparent. Men like Aneurin Bevan, for instance, had emerged as a capital asset for the Tories. His speech in Manchester in 1948, in which he referred to the deep and burning hatred he felt for the Tory Party, whom he regarded, he said, as 'lower than vermin'[3] was duly noted, by both sides. Lord Kilmuir writes even more cheerfully: 'Bevan rapidly became one of our most effective propaganda weapons, and hardly a week passed without him delivering some unguarded utterance which reverberated around the country to our great advantage.'[4] On the eve of the 1950 Election, the Gallup poll gave the Conservatives a lead of 1 per cent.[5] There was a large turn-out: 84 per cent. The end result was 315 Labour MPs and 298 Conservatives, this solid array being broken only by 9 Liberals. Thus, Labour's majority over all other Parties was reduced to a bare 5. From this time forward, Labour's run-down was swift. Sir Stafford Cripps, now worn out, resigned and a few months later died. It soon became clear that Ernest Bevin could not long remain as Foreign Secretary. He too was a spent force, and Attlee himself had to take over much of the load of Foreign Office work, and handle, as Prime Minister, the programme of rearmament necessitated by the Korean War (South Korea had been invaded by North Korea in July, and Britain had to contribute to the United Nations force set up to repel the invader). Then, Attlee

[1] Ivor Bulmer-Thomas, *The Growth of the British Party System*, Vol. II, p. 188.
[2] Kilmuir, op. cit., p. 146.
[3] *The Times*, 5 July 1948; Macmillan, op. cit., Vol. III, p. 65.
[4] Kilmuir, op. cit., p. 144.
[5] See Nuffield Election Studies, H. G. Nicholas, *The British General Election of 1950*.

made the unfortunate, though perhaps unavoidable, choice of Mr. Morrison as Bevin's successor at the Foreign Office. Morrison was from the right wing of the Party, and was one of Attlee's rivals. But he had neither the physical stamina – he was old and tired – nor the educational background to make anything of this most difficult of all appointments.[1] His handling of the Anglo-Iranian Oil Company dispute revealed the Labour Government caught on the horns of a highly embarrassing dilemma. Oil was of crucial importance to Britain. It seemed that the Iranians were behaving very badly and that a quite small show of force would bring them to their senses. Dalton says that Morrison 'had to be restrained by the Cabinet from embarking on a policy which would have led us to be denounced by the U.N. as an aggressor, almost a rehearsal of what happened to us over Suez six years later.'[2] Certainly it would have been difficult for a Labour Government to argue at that point in time that the Iranians had no right to nationalize their oil industry. The Tories might not have found it so difficult.

But foreign affairs paled into insignificance, as compared with the upheavals on the domestic front. The original ground for the quarrel so soon to convulse the Party for so many years was the proposal by Hugh Gaitskell, Sir Stafford Cripps's successor as Chancellor of the Exchequer, to make a charge for dentures and spectacles, hitherto free under the National Health Service, in order to help to provide the money necessary for rearmament to contribute to the United Nations forces in Korea. Some members of the Parliamentary Labour Party felt that the Government had no mandate for this. Bevan resigned on 23 April and he was followed by Harold Wilson, then President of the Board of Trade, and John Freeman, Parliamentary Secretary to the Ministry of Supply. Thus, men who were then the lively left wingers left the already sinking ship. Attlee was at the same time forced by a duodenal ulcer to go into hospital.

Meanwhile, life in Parliament had become increasingly more difficult with late night sittings, the tiny majority and general unease at home and abroad. The time had clearly come for the Labour leaders to withdraw, have a rest, and reshape their policies. So on 8 September 1951, Attlee made known to his colleagues his decision to request a dissolution. Not all his followers were pleased by the timing. Morrison and Shinwell, for

[1] One official is reported to have remarked, 'Ernie didn't know how to pronounce the places either, but he did know where they were.'

[2] Dalton, op. cit., Vol. III, p. 377. See also Francis Williams, *A Prime Minister Remembers*, pp. 254–5. See also F. S. Northedge, *British Foreign Policy*, pp. 122–6; Eden Memoirs, *Full Circle*, pp. 192–9; Morrison, *Autobiography*, pp. 281–2: 'My own view was that there was much to be said in favour of sharp and forceful action.... In the end we had to abandon any military project.'

instance, who were both away in the States, sent a joint telegram of protest. Morrison apparently thought that it was likely that the Korean War would soon end and that this would be, in some measure at least, an electoral asset. Dalton, probably more correctly, doubted whether the electorate was much interested in issues of war and peace in Korea and he thought that the benefits likely to accrue to the economy would be a long time coming. Be all this as it may, it is clear that Labour embarked on the 1951 October Election at a time when its public image was poor and its self-confidence shaken. Was the Conservative image any better in the autumn of 1951? The answer seems to have been Yes. The Conservatives had made very good use of their years in opposition and they were now in fighting trim.

4 THE CONSERVATIVES IN OPPOSITION

Three factors may explain the Conservative revival. Possibly each of them played some part in it.[1]

In the first place the Conservative Party organization was now on a much sounder footing than in 1945.[2] The political truce of the war years had meant that the Party structure, at the constituency level, had been allowed to fall apart as the Labour Party structure, based on the trade unions, had not. This was serious, and in fact the Rt. Hon. Ralph Assheton, Chairman of the Party Organization from October 1944 to 1946 had forecast, even before the 1945 campaign began, that the Conservatives could not win.[3] Assheton was succeeded as Chairman of the Party Organization by Lord Woolton, the former Minister of Food, who, luckily for the Conservatives, had joined them formally on the very day of their defeat in 1945. Lord Woolton had never been a Conservative. He had been an Independent, with Liberal leanings. He was a well-known public figure and, as a highly successful Minister of Food throughout the most difficult years of the war, his name was a popular and reassuring household word. He enjoyed the full backing of Churchill. His initial impulse was to scrap the whole of the existing Party machine and start again. His second thoughts were probably wiser, namely to concentrate on getting a large increase in active Party members, and in Party funds. In both he was very successful, and, as a result of the vastly improved financial position of the Party, it was possible after the end of 1948 to bring in a rule prohibiting candidates from making subscriptions

---

[1] See J. D. Hoffman, *The Conservative Party in Opposition, 1945-51*, pp. 23 et seq.
[2] Macmillan, op. cit., Vol. III, p. 25.
[3] Bulmer-Thomas, op. cit., Vol. II, pp. 179-84. Samuel H. Beer, 'The British Conservative Party', *Journal of Politics*, 1952.

of more than £25 each to their constituencies, thus ensuring that lack of means should no longer preclude the possibility of standing for a constituency.[1] The door was now wider open to Conservative talent than it had ever been before.[2] The Conservative Party was also much better organized. For instance, at the General Election of February 1950 it had 527 full-time local agents in England and Wales alone, whereas the Labour Party had agents in only 279 constituencies in England, Wales and Scotland. Then, again, Conservative thoroughness over the postal vote was beginning to reap large dividends.[3]

Together with the Woolton elaboration of the Party structure and the increase in its financial resources went a reformation of policy. The Conservative Party Conference of 1946 had made a formal demand for this. But it was a difficult task, for many reasons. The tide was obviously with Labour so that it was no use saying No to the Welfare State. On the other hand, a policy of 'Me Too' is seldom electorally attractive. Then again, Churchill, the Leader, was unconvinced by arguments of the need for change on the domestic front, and very much opposed to giving hostages to fortune in the shape of specific promises. Lord Woolton agreed with him but also felt that it would be dangerous 'to be so vague that the nation could think that the Conservatism that we were expounding would be no different from the Conservatism of the thirties.'[4]

The chief architect of post-war Conservative policy was Mr. R. A. Butler, later Lord Butler of Saffron Walden, and it was under his guidance at the Conservative Research Department that the Industrial Charter of 1947 was formulated.[5] The Industrial Charter accepted most of the Labour nationalization measures. Iron and steel, and road transport had not at that time been nationalized. These were much more contentious Acts, and when they were passed into law the Party at once announced its intention of denationalizing these industries when it was returned to power. However, it accepted in principle a much greater degree of government planning and control than the Conservative Party had ever

[1] '... in the past it has cost a good deal of money to be a Conservative candidate. We cannot afford only to draw our candidates from the people with money.' *1947 Conservative Party Conference Report* (Lord Woolton). See also *Memoirs* of the Rt. Hon. The Earl of Woolton, p. 345: 'I noticed that the organization of the party was weakest in those places where a wealthy candidate had made it unnecessary for the members to trouble to collect small subscriptions.'
[2] See Interim and Final Reports of the Maxwell Fyffe Committee 1948 and 1949.
[3] Nuffield Election Studies, op. cit. (1950), pp. 6–10. 'It is very hard not to believe that the Conservatives owe at least 10 seats to the introduction of the postal vote,' p. 9.
[4] *Memoirs of the Rt. Hon. The Earl of Woolton*, p. 347.
[5] Samuel H. Beer, *Modern British Politics*, pp. 311–17.

before contemplated.[1] It committed the Party to the new financial burdens of the Welfare State legislation imposed by the Labour Government. Needless to say, these new commitments were all stated to be implicit in the Tory tradition inherited from Disraeli and Lord Randolph Churchill. The Conservatives used all available means of mass communication to publicize the new policy, and, according to Party officials, 2,500,000 copies, at 6d each, were sold within the first three months of publication.[2] The Industrial Charter met with considerable opposition from right wing critics within the Party, and it was for some time not certain whether Churchill himself would endorse it. In the end he did, and the Industrial Charter was duly followed up by the Agricultural Charter and other policy statements, including one on Imperial Policy, one on Conservative Policy for Wales and Monmouthshire and one on Scottish Control of Scottish affairs. The pattern gradually became clearer. The Conservative Party began to commit itself both to the full maintenance of the existing social services and to a reduction in taxation. Hopefully, economic growth would make both possible. In place of nationalization, the ideal of a property-owning democracy was put forward. The individual was to come into his own again. But the Conservative Party recognized implicitly if not explicitly, and in spite of its right wingers, that in future management of the economy by one means or another would have to be one of the tasks of government.

The third factor which contributed to the Conservative come-back was their work on the Opposition bench. But this can easily be overstated. Indeed, it may well be that Opposition Parties in the modern State win Elections because of the mistakes made by those in power, rather than because of the attractions of Opposition policies. The Opposition is not in the know and so can seldom speak with authority, especially after a prolonged period in exile. Anyway, there is little time available for it to speak at all, as the Government of necessity controls the House of Commons and the timetable of debates. So it is not surprising that from 1945 to 1950 nothing much happened from the Conservative side. They had little to say and inadequate time in which to say it and the style of their Leader was perhaps unsuited to the new House of Commons. Mr. Macmillan notes that the Churchill speeches were often too long and too stylized to please the M.P.s. There was no longer place for imagination, romance or grandeur. The issues now were bread and butter issues and it took some time for Churchill to realize this.[3]

[1] See Butler, op. cit., pp. 132-49. Lord Butler writes: 'The Charter was... first and foremost an assurance that, in the interests of efficiency, full employment and social security, modern Conservatism would maintain strong central guidance over the operation of the economy, p. 146.   [2] Beer, op. cit., p. 316.
[3] Macmillan, op. cit., Vol. III, pp. 42-3. And see Chapter 3 for his account. of the Parliamentary personalities involved on both sides.

Introduction

However, it was not all loss. As Mr. Macmillan notes, the House of Commons before and immediately after the Second World War was less highly organized and regimented than it is today. The Shadow Cabinet system, adopted by the Labour Party in their long years of Opposition from 1951 to 1964, and subsequently taken over by the Conservatives, was not then the rule. Opposition M.P.s were encouraged to interest themselves in a wide range of subjects, and did so, probably to their great advantage. From March 1950 till October 1951 it was a different story. Labour's overall majority of five (six counting the Speaker) made battles worth while as they had not been in the previous five years.

Perhaps it was in part the apparent failure of British foreign policy that began to tip the balance again towards the Conservatives. The thought may have been that the Churchill team, so splendidly successful in the long, magnificent war years, might set right the kind of mess that Morrison had made at Abadan. Perhaps it would after all be possible to have the best of all worlds: a strong foreign policy; a welfare state in which private enterprise and individual freedom would complement the provisions made for those not able wholly to stand on their own feet; and the leadership of men accustomed and trained to rule. The Conservatives, so the hope went, would better retain the crucial American special relationship; they would be less ready to jettison the Commonwealth, which might, in the future, be Britain's only claim to Great Power status; and, without getting too closely involved, they could give the Europeans a lead. Finally, the Conservatives seemed to be a united as well as a vigorous team. By contrast, the factionalism and the unedifying and almost public bickering of leading Labour politicians seems in the end to have suggested to very many voters that the Labour Party not only did not know how to achieve its goals, but did not even know what its goals ought to be.

What follows is no more than a sketch of the problems of the fifties and sixties, which may, I hope, suggest further areas of study. For instance, in considering Commonwealth issues I have not attempted to give a general account, however brief, but to suggest the range and variety of the problems. Malawi and Tanzania who wanted to go; Gibraltar and Malta who wanted to stay. Nigeria who was too big; Anguilla who was too small. Similarly I have only touched on the major domestic issues and have had to omit altogether some interesting developments, for instance the emergence of Scottish and Welsh nationalism and the much more important issues of Northern Ireland. This latter taxed British nerve and will-power. It stretched the conventional forces which Britain still deployed. But it was not a political issue in the sense that it divided the Parties at Westminster. Nor did it have any clear impact on the electorate.

It may be thought that I have devoted too much attention to defence and foreign and colonial policies. But these were, of necessity, the major preoccupations of one Government after another in the fifties and sixties: how to combine some semblance of strength abroad with affluence at home; how to enable colonial territories to move forward into stable independent statehood, without leaving behind more Congos to tax the international community; how to provide sensibly for the political aspirations of the emerging mini-states. These were the problems which preoccupied British Governments in these two decades perhaps to an even greater extent than did domestic issues.

To forget this fact would be to misread the times. And here, again, the advance in thinking was tremendous. Britain had not been a first-class power in the inter-war years, and she had failed to take account of this. The result had been a series of heavy commitments up and down the world which she was in the end quite unable to honour. Manchuria, Abyssinia, the Rhineland crisis, Austria, Czechoslovakia, Munich, all bear witness to the simple fact that the British did not then understand the limitations which the march of time had placed upon their power and influence in the world. The story after the Second World War was a vastly more creditable one. Power – in the sense of armies, navies, air squadrons and the like backing the red patches on the map – was not theirs. And a series of Prime Ministers and Foreign Secretaries gradually came to recognize this, to many, unpalatable fact. But British influence, based on long years of experience in international affairs, and on the stability and good sense of an established Parliamentary democracy, was very great – from the days of Ernest Bevin to those of Sir Alec Douglas-Home. Britain achieved more, for the peace of the world, as well as for her own advancement in it, since 1945 than she had ever achieved before in the heyday of the 'Great Power' years. Of course the advance was patchy and the set-backs distressing, but there was progress everywhere.

CHAPTER ONE

The Conservative Government from October 1951 to May 1955

SUMMARY	page
1 The General Election of 25 October 1951	23
2 The Conservative Team	25
3 Constitutional and Administrative Issues	28
a The 'Overlord' experiment 1951–1953	28
b The Crichel Down case 1954	29
4 Economic Issues	30
a General survey	30
b Summary of economic developments 1951–1955	30
(i) The financial crisis of 1951–1952	30
(ii) The 1953–1954 boom	32
(iii) 1955	32
5 Domestic Affairs	32
6 Defence Policy	35
7 Foreign Policy	37
a The Anglo-American relationship	37
b The Communist world 1951–1955	39
c Europe	40
d The Middle East	42
e The Far East 1951–1955	46
8 The Commonwealth	48
a General considerations	48
b The Central African Federation	50
c Kenya	52
9 The Opposition	54
a The Labour Party	54
b The Liberals	61

1 THE GENERAL ELECTION OF 25 OCTOBER 1951

The campaign of October 1951 was not an exciting one. There seemed little to choose between the Parties, as far as either domestic or foreign policies went. Both accepted the need to achieve a high and stable level of employment. Both accepted the need to rearm in order to keep the peace. The rearmament necessitated by the outbreak of the Korean war was not an electoral issue. However, the Conservatives made considerable capital out of Morrison's alleged mishandling of the Iranian oil dispute;

and Labour consequently sought to portray the Conservatives as warmongers.

The Conservative Manifesto, entitled 'Britain Strong and Free', stressed the need for stable government for several years and argued that the Conservatives, united, experienced and vigorous, were more likely to be able to provide this than the tired Labour team, now deeply divided and with no new ideas to offer. The Conservatives offered only one really big bait to the electorate – the building of 300,000 new houses a year. The Party Conference at Blackpool in 1950 had insisted on this. The Conservative Leadership had accepted it rather doubtfully, because of uncertainty as to the availability of raw materials. Wisely Churchill, having made the pledge, took it seriously. He chose Mr. Macmillan as Minister of Housing and kept him at this Ministry until October 1954. The target set was duly achieved. The Labour pledge was for only 200,000 new houses, this number being, in their view, the most that could be achieved. In retrospect, it seems that the Labour Party had, ever since the end of the war, been curiously tepid *vis-à-vis* housing problems. This was perhaps because Aneurin Bevan had combined Health and Housing, and his interest had been concentrated on the former.

The Conservatives promised to repeal the Iron and Steel Nationalization Act, and the Road Transport Nationalization Act. The Labour Party made no new proposals for nationalization, but said that they would take over concerns which failed the nation. Not a very exciting prospect, perhaps.[1]

It was not altogether surprising that the two Party programmes were so similar. The times were difficult. Key commodities were in short supply. Britain had few options open, and this was generally recognized. As Churchill was to remark a few weeks later, in a broadcast made to the nation on 5 December 1951, 'There are underlying unities ... far greater than our differences.'

In the end, on October 25th, 82.5 per cent of the electorate went to the polls. The numbers of votes cast for the three main Parties were:

	Votes	Percentage of votes	Seats obtained
Conservative	13,717,538	48.0	321
Labour	13,948,605	48.8	295
Liberal	730,556	2.5	6

With others gaining 3 seats the Conservatives had a small overall majority of 17, although some 230,000 more votes were cast for Labour.[2] Labour votes had tended to pile up in safe Labour constituencies.

[1] Nuffield Election Studies, D. E. Butler, *The British General Election of 1951*.
[2] Butler and Freeman, op. cit., p. 143.

A variety of factors may be viewed as contributing to the Conservative victory. The past nine months had been particularly difficult ones for the Labour Government. The Iranian oil dispute had been hard to handle.[1] The Korean war and rearmament had presented many problems, and certainly gravely accentuated Britain's economic difficulties. Internal quarrelling within the Labour Party had culminated, in April 1951, in the resignations of Messrs. Wilson, Bevan and Freeman on the issue of the N.H.S. charges. This kind of in-fighting always greatly damages a party's image with the electorate. There were other considerations too. The number of Liberal candidates fighting the 1951 campaign had fallen to a mere 109,[2] and this was electorally of considerable advantage to the Conservatives, for, when no Liberal stood, Liberal voters either abstained or divided in the proportion of six to four in favour of the Conservatives.[3] Then, whereas the 1950 Election had been held at a relatively favourable moment as far as the British economy went, in October 1951 storm warnings of a new financial crisis were clearly to be seen. Probably Morrison was right in thinking that it was not a very good time for a General Election from the Labour point of view.

2 THE CONSERVATIVE TEAM[4]

The new Conservative team was, on the face of it, a strong one. Lord Woolton remarks: 'It used to be said that Asquith in 1906 had selected a most brilliant Cabinet of all the talents, but Churchill's new cabinet, with men of the experience of Eden, Salisbury, Macmillan, Butler, Crookshank, with his exceptional knowledge of Parliamentary procedure, and, among the younger men, the brilliance of Macleod and Anthony Head, with the legal strength of Simonds, Maxwell Fyfe and Walter Monckton, the business capacity and knowledge of Oliver Lyttleton, Lord Leathers, and the ex-Governor General Earl Alexander would have stood up against any of its predecessors for personal ability and breadth of experience.'[5] The team was, however, a rather elderly one, the average age being almost sixty.

Churchill, the hero of the free world, was now seventy-seven and had already suffered two strokes, one in August 1949 and another in February 1950. These had, however, been kept from the press. Lord Moran, his doctor, apparently urged him to keep going in political life, fearing that retirement would be damaging to his patient. But Lord Moran also feared, he says, that Churchill was not fully up to the job of being Prime

[1] See Introduction.
[2] As compared with 475 in 1950. Butler and Freeman, op. cit., p. 143.
[3] Nuffield Election Studies, D. E. Butler, op. cit. (1951), p. 242.
[4] See Butler and Freeman (2nd edn.), p. 36, for full list.
[5] See Woolton, op. cit., p. 366.

Minister, and he apparently urged Churchill, even before the 1951 Election, to realize that now he would have to delegate. He couldn't, as in the war, do most of the work himself. But Churchill, always somewhat presidential in style, found it no easier to delegate in the fifties, when he was old and tired and unsure of himself, than he had in the war years. His mind was only alert in patches and there were gaps everywhere in his grip on events.[1] 'The old capacity for work had gone, and with it much of his self-confidence. He forgot figures. Everything had become an effort. Moreover, he was confronted by a whole series of unfamiliar problems.'[2]

Some of the Conservatives were aware of this and full of misgivings from the start. And as time went on, many more became aware of it. But in April 1953, when Eden fell ill, Churchill was resolved to take over the Foreign Office too. Then, in June 1953 came another stroke, which could not, this time, be wholly concealed. At last he was persuaded to resign on 5 April 1955. But it is possible to over-estimate Churchill's weakness. He was still a very great statesman, and it is doubtful whether the Conservatives could, in those years, have found a leader equally acceptable to the nation. Those concerned with the selection of key people in any walk of life will be well aware that no one person combines, at one particular time, all the desirable virtues. Churchill still had very many. And although he clung to office longer perhaps than was desirable, and for reasons some of which seemed rather egotistical he was buoyed up, to the end, by the hope that if he could only stay the course, he could negotiate, at the summit, the treaty that would bring peace to the world. He could do this, as other men could not, he believed. In the end, and under strong pressure from Mr. Macmillan brought to bear in January 1955, he agreed to stand down and let Sir Anthony Eden take over after a spring Election.[3] It is possible that one reason for his reluctance to go was doubt as to whether Eden would be wise enough when crises came. Lord Moran has recorded Churchill's anxiety over Eden's propensity to find fault with the Americans, and in particular with Mr. Dulles, the American Secretary of State. Mr. Dulles's judgement of international issues may not always have been right and Eden's misgivings may have been, on occasions, justified. But none the less it was necessary to remain on friendly terms with the United States, on whose assistance Britain so greatly depended. Possibly Churchill may have seen, as others did not yet, the writing on the wall.

[1] Lord Moran, *Winston Churchill: The Struggle for Survival 1940–1965*, p. 826. There were four strokes between 1949 and 1953: August 1949, February 1950, July 1952 and June 1953.
[2] Moran, op. cit., p. 827.
[3] But Mr. Macmillan notes: 'Now that he has really decided to go, we are all miserable.' Op. cit., Vol. III, p. 556.

The Conservative Team

None the less Churchill treated Eden with the greatest deference, and no other member of the Cabinet knew enough about foreign affairs to offer Eden the stimulus of opposition. Lord Kilmuir comments on this:

> Looking back, I am not sure that his great authority and knowledge of foreign affairs was not a defect in the Government. Winston was determined not to oppose his successor, and none of the other members had the knowledge or experience to question or contradict Eden's policies. I doubt if a Foreign Secretary has enjoyed quite so much independence since Lord Rosebery – in very different circumstances – reigned at the Foreign Office in 1892–94. This entrusting of a vital aspect of government to one man, however competent, was in a sense an abrogation of the rôle of the Cabinet, and in our relationship with Europe in particular it meant that we were bound by Eden's hostile approach to a matter in which he was normally opposed by Churchill, Macmillan and myself at least.[1]

Nor was the Foreign Office Eden's only appointment. He was also Deputy Prime Minister, and even for a few days Leader of the House of Commons. But he had the sense to see, almost immediately, that this last would be an impossibly heavy burden. Churchill replaced him, at his own request, by Crookshank. But the sad fact was that when his great moment came in 1955, Sir Anthony Eden gave the impression of being a little bored with it all. He had had to wait in the wings for too long. Nor was he very well qualified by previous political experience to take over the Prime Minister's office. Lord Moran says that he said on one occasion, in December 1953:

> I wanted to give up the Foreign Office and take some office in the Cabinet which would give me experience of the home front, but Winston has got used to me.... He was so much against my leaving the Foreign Office that I gave in.[2]

However, though there were weaknesses in the Leader and his Deputy, and although the average age of Cabinet Ministers was on the high side, the team as a whole was a good one. And, if something of a one-man band on the foreign affairs front, there was an impressive diversity of talent on the all-important domestic scene. Many were familiar faces; nearly all were rather markedly upper-class faces. Lord Woolton, who had been Chairman of the Party Organization since 1946, and who was one of the main architects of the Conservative revival, became Lord President of the Council, with special concern, as befitted his past career, for Food and Agriculture. Lord Simonds was the new Lord Chancellor. The Marquis of Salisbury held the post of Lord Privy Seal. Lord Ismay went

---

[1] Kilmuir, op. cit., p. 193.   [2] Moran, op. cit., p. 529.

to the Commonwealth Relations Office. Lord Leathers was responsible for the co-ordination of Transport, Fuel and Power. Lord Cherwell became the Paymaster General. Those not already in the ranks of the aristocracy were men who would have been readily acceptable to it. The grammar school generation, which succeeded Sir Alec Douglas-Home in the sixties, had not yet entered into its Conservative inheritance.[1] Inevitably, the Churchill team was criticized as being a 'government by cronies' since so many of its members had worked for Churchill during the war. However, this did give them a background of experience that younger men would not have had.

3 CONSTITUTIONAL AND ADMINISTRATIVE ISSUES

On 6 February 1952 King George VI died. He was succeeded by Princess Elizabeth, who came to the throne as Queen Elizabeth II.

a *The 'Overlord' experiment 1951–1953*

The great increase in the business of government, partly inherited from the war years, and partly a consequence of Labour's predilection for state control, had already resulted in a rearrangement of Cabinet business under the two post-war Labour Governments. Cabinet committees had been Mr. Attlee's response. Now Churchill, confronted with much the same difficulties, sought a solution, not only through the use of Cabinet committees, but also by a more formal grouping of certain departments and areas of government.

Lord Cherwell, whose titular office was that of Paymaster General, was now charged with the co-ordination of scientific research and development. Though reckoned as one of the 'overlords' he had no departments under him. Lord Woolton, whose titular office was Lord President of the Council, was responsible for food and for agriculture. He thus controlled two separate government departments. Like Lord Cherwell, he was an immensely popular and respected figure. Lord Leathers, the third 'overlord' was given the title of Secretary of State for the co-ordination of Transport, Fuel and Power. He, too, was a very old friend and wartime colleague of Churchill. Under this system the Ministers of Agriculture and Fisheries, Food, Transport and Civil Aviation, and Fuel and Power were not in the Cabinet, and their 'overlords' were members of the House of Lords.[2] Not surprisingly this arrangement proved unsatisfactory alike to the displaced Ministers, the Civil Service departments concerned

---

[1] See Kilmuir, op. cit., pp. 190 et seq.

[2] Churchill also tried, unsuccessfully, to persuade John Anderson, later Viscount Waverley, to return to the Cabinet as Chancellor of the Duchy of Lancaster, with responsibility for supervising the Treasury, the Board of Trade, and the Ministry of Supply. But Lord Waverley refused. (Hans Daalder,

and the M.P.s. It was abandoned in 1953.[1] The end of the experiment was precipitated by the illness and resignation of Lord Woolton in November 1952, which was followed by that of Lord Cherwell. In September 1953 Lord Leathers resigned, and the Ministers of Food and Agriculture entered the Cabinet.

b *The Crichel Down case 1954*
This case, relatively unimportant in itself, raised large issues of policy. Briefly, it concerned agricultural land in Dorset, compulsorily purchased in 1937 by the Air Ministry for a bombing range. After the war the land passed into the hands of the Ministry of Agriculture, then the Agricultural Land Commission and finally the Commissioner for Crown Lands, who let it to a tenant, despite the fact that the previous owners had been promised the opportunity to buy it back, and wished to do so. A public inquiry in 1954 revealed that a succession of civil servants had acted in a very high-handed manner in dealings with the previous owners, whose right of repurchase had been brushed aside for what seemed insubstantial reasons.

The case raised an issue about which the public was, in any case, becoming worried, namely the defencelessness of ordinary citizens against civil servants wielding, even now in peace time, enormous powers. Parliament, it was felt, was insufficiently vigilant over these delegated powers. The appointment in 1967 (thirteen years later) of a Commissioner, or Ombudsman, was a minuscule attempt to deal with this enormous problem.

Another issue raised by the Crichel Down case was that of Ministerial responsibility. Was it sensible to press this hallowed convention of the constitution in present circumstances, now that it had manifestly become impossible for any Minister to be aware of all the happenings in the department for which he was responsible? In this case, the answer given was Yes. And Sir Thomas Dugdale, Minister of Agriculture, duly resigned.[2] Again, it seems unlikely that this can be the last word on this

---

Cabinet Reform in Britain, pp. 109–110.) He had been offended at not being called on to play any part in the Election campaign. He had lost his seat in 1950 because of the abolition of university seats by the Attlee Government. He very much disapproved of the 'overlord' concept, both as a former Minister and as a former civil servant. In the end, he accepted a peerage. See also Sir John Wheeler-Bennett, *John Anderson, Viscount Waverley* (1962).
[1] See *The Organization of British Central Government 1914–1956*, edited D. N. Chester, and The Hansard Society, *Parliamentary Reform 1933–1960*, pp. 123–4, also 'The Experiment with Co-ordinating Ministers in the Cabinet 1951–3', *Canadian Journal of Economics and Political Science*, 1955.
[2] R. Douglas Brown, *The Battle of Crichel Down*; Kilmuir, op. cit., pp. 227–8;

issue. Indeed, subsequent Ministers have made, and publicly acknowledged, much more serious 'mistakes', and have not been called upon to resign. The fact was that the Government, in face of considerable public outcry, wanted to make an act of appeasement. And Sir Thomas Dugdale was willing to be sacrificed.

4 ECONOMIC ISSUES

a *General survey*[1]

Mr. Butler, as Chancellor of the Exchequer, was an exponent of what became known, hopefully, as economic liberalism. The Government's declared goal was a gradual ending of government controls and a more or less complete return to the market economy, providing full employment was maintained on Keynesian lines. Recovery, after the ending of the Korean war in 1953, seemed rapid and the boom conditions of 1953-4, due in part to the devaluation of 1949, encouraged Conservatives to think that Mr. Butler's economic liberalism really did work. But the 1955 sterling crisis shattered this easy optimism, and made the boom of 1953 to 1954 look more like good luck than good judgement.

The Government gave top priority to the pledge to maintain full employment, using fiscal and monetary policies to achieve this end. This seemed to Conservatives to be absolutely necessary, in order to dispel the fears of the electorate that Conservative rule meant a return to the conditions of the thirties.

b *Summary of economic developments 1951-1955*

(i) *The financial crisis of 1951-1952* This was at its peak when the Conservatives took office in November 1951. A major cause of the crisis had been the Korean war, and the heavy rearmament programme undertaken by the Labour Government, which imposed a further burden on an already overstrained economy. The mechanics of the sterling area involved a time lag in the impact on the U.K. reserves of the rapid rise in world commodity prices which took place as a result of war conditions. The overseas sterling area had during 1950 made very profitable

---

C. J. Hamson, 'The Real Lesson of Crichel Down', *Public Administration*, 1954; 'Debate on the Crichel Down Case', *Hansard*, 20 July 1954, Vol. 530, cols. 1178-298; D. N. Chester, 'The Crichel Down Case', *Public Administration*, 1954.

[1] See G. D. N. Worswick and P. H. Ady, *The British Economy in the Nineteen Fifties*; A. J. Youngson, *British Economic Growth 1920-1966*; J. C. R. Dow, *The Management of the British Economy 1945-1960*; A. Shonfield, *British Economic Policy Since the War*.

sales of primary commodities at inflated world prices. In 1951 the countries in this area started to spend their enhanced incomes and this involved, to a significant extent, importing goods from outside the sterling area. This in turn led to a run-down of the United Kingdom central sterling area reserves which was exacerbated by a consequential speculative run on sterling. Thus, the current account surplus in 1950 of £300m. became in 1951 a deficit of £400m. Two factors led to the 1951 sterling crisis: (i) growing inflation through overload on the domestic economy and (ii) an unfavourable movement in the terms of trade. These actually became nearly 12 per cent worse in 1951 than they had been in 1950. As imports constituted about one-fifth of Britain's domestic product, a deterioration of the terms of trade by 1 per cent is equivalent to a *drop of* 0.2 per cent in the real value of the G.N.P.

However, the terms of trade began to move decisively in Britain's favour by about 6 per cent between 1951 and 1952 and by a further 6 per cent between 1952 and 1953 thereby increasing Britain's G.N.P. Moreover, the Labour Government had deflated the economy to 'make room' for the rearmament programme and this provided the basis for the Conservative Government's expansion of 1953–5.

So, from the point of view of the electorate, the first years of Conservative Government looked like a planned recovery from Labour's mistakes while in office, though the problems were in fact self-liquidating. This experience gave rise to the view that 'Conservative freedom works'. It did not work for long.

It was unfortunately necessary to increase defence spending from 7 per cent of the national product in 1950 to $8\frac{1}{2}$ per cent in 1951, and to $10\frac{1}{2}$ per cent in 1952. And of course rearmament meant that raw materials generally used for export goods were in even shorter supply. A bottle-neck built up in industries dependent on steel, metal goods, etc. Hence, exports dropped off and the balance of payments deficit increased. It may be noted that rearmament had at this time an expansionary effect in the United States, where the economy was working below capacity, as it had in Britain in similar circumstances in the thirties. But in Britain in 1950 the economy was working at full stretch, so rearmament overstrained resources and used up raw materials needed for the export trade.

The new Conservative Government dealt as best it could with this economic crisis. Stringent measures were taken between November 1951 and March 1952. An attempt was made to cut down imports and the Bank Rate was raised to $2\frac{1}{2}$ per cent.[1] In the March 1952 Budget food subsidies were cut by £160m. (i.e. from £410m. to £250m.). This had the effect of raising food prices significantly and was condemned by the

---

[1] This was the first rise since it was set at 2 per cent in 1932.

unions as an attack on the living standards of working people.[1] The Bank Rate was raised to 4 per cent.

In the course of 1952, the balance of payments surplus rose to £300m.

(ii) *The 1953–1954 boom* Boom conditions made it possible to introduce tax cuts into the 1953 Budget. Mr. Butler as Chancellor of the Exchequer said: 'This Budget is primarily an industrial Budget. Its purpose is to help industry.' Rapid expansion continued throughout 1953, and output rose by 4 per cent. The balance of payments surpluses continued. Unemployment remained low, and the standard of living seemed to be going up. In 1954 it was possible to end food rationing. And the same year saw the beginning of what looked like an investment boom. On 1 January 1955 the *Financial Times* said that 1954 was probably the last of the lean post-war years. The impression of expansion in 1953, 1954 and in the first half of 1955 was partly a consequence of earlier contraction. The devaluation of 1949, the beneficial effects of which were delayed by the Korean war, now at last enabled the Government to expand the economy without the fear of inflationary consequences which would endanger the competitive price of Britain's exports.

It seems, in retrospect, that the boom was genuine enough. But it was caused not, as the electorate then thought, by the Conservative Government's economic liberalism, but by favourable changes in the terms of trade, and in particular by the fall in the world price of raw materials which lasted for two and a half years. It was also a by-product of the 1949 devaluation.

(iii) *1955* By the time the Budget period came along in 1955, things looking considerably less good. Already, in February, the Bank Rate had been raised to 4½ per cent, and hire purchase restrictions had been imposed. There were signs of serious inflation. None the less, the April 1955 Budget took 6d off income tax, and Mr. Butler's thesis was that the February measures to moderate imports and encourage exports had already begun to work and that there was now again room for expansion, hence the tax reductions. This Budget was later denounced as an electioneering Budget (the General Election came in May 1955). Certainly it seemed an unwise one both in the light of the crisis in the summer of 1955 and the second Budget which was necessary in the autumn.[2]

5 DOMESTIC AFFAIRS

Broadly speaking the Conservatives accepted the philosophy of the Welfare State; and they stood by the Party's 1950 undertaking to maintain

[1] The Conservative Election Manifesto had promised that food prices would not rise because food subsidies would not be cut.   [2] See Chapter II.

full employment. The percentage of unemployed was held at just over 1 per cent, except in early 1952 when it was just over 2 per cent.[1] Professor Beer notes that throughout the fifties Conservative Governments maintained very much the same priorities in social policy as had been established by Labour.[2] He points out that, although all incomes were rising, it was not the rich who mainly profited. Welfare expenditure was 13.9 per cent in 1950. By 1959 it had risen to 16.1 per cent.[3] The 'Butskellism' of the 1947 Industrial Charter was still a very real commitment for the Conservatives.

There was, of course, opposition from those Tories who believed that the top priority should be a reduction of taxation to increase business incentive. But, at least until 1955, it was possible to silence them because of the Government's small majority, and the consequent fear of a return to Labour rule. These right wing Tories were to become more influential in the later fifties. But the problem, from 1951 on, was how to cut taxes without also cutting welfare expenditure. 'Growth', that magic word, was thought to be the answer.

The Conservative Government went out of its way to be conciliatory towards the trade unions. For instance, when the question of restoring the 1927 Trade Disputes Act was raised, during the 1951 Election campaign, Churchill said that the Conservative Party had no intention of initiating any legislation affecting trade unions. Sir Walter Monckton, as Minister of Labour, was continually at pains to demonstrate how much the Government valued the co-operation of the T.U.C. The work of the Ministry of Labour was thought of as conciliation. In practice this meant that employers were constantly urged to give way in wage disputes so as to avoid strike action.

Tory popularity certainly increased during the life of this Government, and naturally and notably after the boom years of 1953-4. The culmination came at the 1955 April General Election, when the Conservative majority was increased from seventeen to fifty-nine.

The main achievement, on the domestic front, was Mr. Macmillan's, as Minister of Housing. The election pledge of 300,000 new houses a year was more than redeemed. In 1953, 327,000 houses were built, and in 1954, 354,000. Mr. Macmillan came in for sharp criticism both on the grounds that this was a purely political policy, designed to woo working class votes, and that the materials used were more urgently needed for

[1] These figures may be contrasted with those for the inter-war years, when the average was 14 per cent. They may also be compared with the American post-war average of 5 per cent, Youngson, op. cit. This rough comparison is suggestive, though the U.S. and the British figures are not strictly comparable.
[2] Beer, op. cit., p. 353.
[3] See I. M. D. Little, 'Fiscal Policy' in G. D. N. Worswick and P. H. Ady, op. cit.

industrial development. He defended his policy on the grounds that ill-housed workers were likely to be unproductive workers.[1] He devoted three years of magnificent and ingenious effort as Minister of Housing to the end that more and better and relatively cheap houses should be made available as a matter of first priority, to meet needs which had existed for many decades. At the back of his mind was the idea that rent control, which had long caused so much deterioration in the standard of existing houses, could not be tackled until a large number of additional low-cost houses were available.

As promised in their Election Manifesto, the Conservatives only reversed the nationalization of the iron and steel industry and road haulage. These measures passed into law in 1953.[2] Both were opposed by Mr. Attlee on the grounds that, as a general principle of British politics, governments do not seek the reversal of major actions of a preceding government.[3] It is doubtful, though, whether either of these two measures of denationalization was a matter of much grief to the Labour Party as a whole, now somewhat disenchanted with nationalization.

No effort was made to dismantle the National Health Service, although the charges imposed by Mr. Gaitskell in 1951 were retained, and a prescription charge of 2s was introduced. The National Health Service was to remain Britain's great claim to fame, in the field of the social services. Unpopular though it had always been with large sections of the medical profession, no government would have dared to put the clock back on this one. There is no evidence that the Conservatives had any wish to do so.

The Agricultural Act of 1953 ended the system by which the Ministry of Agriculture bought food, and resold it to distributors. However, British farmers were still assured of guaranteed minimum prices, deficiency payments and other subsidies.

Industrial problems were, of course, at the root of Britain's difficulties in the post-war world. Britain, of necessity, lived by the industrial goods she could produce and sell abroad. After the war great advantages opened up before her, in that so many of her rivals were down and out and needing, as they had needed in the nineteenth century, the capital equipment to start again. But Britain was not in a particularly good position to take advantage of this temporary state of affairs. Her own industries had been starved of new equipment during the war years; she was handicapped by a bottle-neck in the iron and steel industries, made much worse by the rearmament required at the time of the Korean war; she was also handicapped by the trade unions now extremely powerful because, owing to

[1] See Macmillan, op. cit., Vol. III, Ch. XIII.
[2] 1953 The Iron and Steel Act. 1953 The Transport Act. See *Parliamentary Affairs*, 1953, pp. 278–83, for details.
[3] Attlee, op. cit., pp. 214–15.

the high level of employment, employers dared not quarrel with them. The growth of new industries was held back partly because there was no pool of unemployed labour on which they could draw. And labour already in employment lacked mobility because workers had the idea that they had a right to their existing jobs. There was a general reluctance to move, and, as part and parcel of this, a tenacious clinging to restrictive practices, the abandonment of which might force labour movement. There was a steady increase in the demand for consumer goods. But this was satisfied by imports rather than by domestic investment. The Government's 'stop-go' policies were a further difficulty. There was also, undoubtedly, a lack of expertise on the management side.

6 DEFENCE POLICY

One of the handicaps Britain faced probably stemmed from the kind of foreign policy which Britain's leaders and perhaps the British public regarded, at this time, as self-evidently necessary. The assumption was that, no matter what the cost might be in economic terms – and no one attempted these difficult sums – Britain must maintain her pre-war and her wartime role and keep up her Great Power status. This was a commitment which, implicitly if not explicitly, came ahead even of the Welfare State. Indeed, there seems to have been an underlying assumption that unless Britain could stay in the Great Power club, there could be no Welfare State. There were certainly many reasons which persuaded the British of their indispensability if peace was to be assured. The Russian threat loomed large in these years and it was felt to be, and perhaps was, a very serious one, especially in Europe. Not until Stalin's death in 1953 was there any ray of hope for the evolution of a better relationship with the Soviet Union. The Americans were hesitant partners for Britain in the post-war world. Their diplomacy was often heavy-handed and uncertain. Their interests seemed to lie in the Far East rather than in Europe. Britain was dependent on the United States both economically and militarily. But it was difficult to feel that problems of war and peace could safely be abandoned to these inexperienced and temperamental, not to say arrogant, benefactors. The Americans, for their part, were very anxious indeed for Britain to keep up all her commitments. They did not want to be left with the whole world's problems on their plate. All in all, it seemed that so much was at stake everywhere that it was impossible for Britain, poor, but still by far the most experienced and influential world power, to contemplate withdrawal. In Europe, the problem was how to contain what seemed to be the threatened Russian aggression without re-establishing an armed and mighty Germany which could soon, again, pose another threat to the Western European states. In the Middle East the problem was the general one of an awakening

Arab nationalism and, in particular, the policies pursued by Egypt. In the Far East, accepted as mainly an American preserve, the settlement of the Korean dispute had to be achieved. But this was quickly overshadowed by new problems in Indo-China, where the French were confronted with the rising tide of Vietnamese nationalism, linked, so it seemed, with the much greater menace anticipated from Communist China.

It is in this general context that British nuclear policy must be viewed. The 1951-5 Conservative Government followed and developed lines of policy begun by its Labour predecessor. Both Labour and Conservative leaders had from the beginning of the post-war period felt that Britain had to be an independent nuclear power. It is necessary to go back a little way to understand the reasoning behind this argument. In 1946 Congress had passed the MacMahon Act, which ended wartime Anglo-American co-operation in the manufacture of nuclear weapons. So in 1947 the British Labour Government decided to make its own atomic bombs and to build a fleet of V bombers to carry them. These were seen as ordinary weapons to be used in war.[1] In 1952 the first British atomic bomb was exploded, on Montello Island; and in this year the first United States hydrogen bomb was tested.

In the Defence White Paper of March 1955, Churchill announced the decision to manufacture the British hydrogen bomb, as a deterrent.[2] He believed that the existence of these terrible weapons would make the stakes so high that war between the major powers would become impossible.

The military argument was that the British nuclear strike force could be used to defend targets vital to British survival but less vital to the Americans. Churchill also believed that an independent British nuclear deterrent was necessary if Britain was to retain her influence in the world.[3] He wanted to get the MacMahon Act amended but thought that Britain would only be entrusted again with American secrets if she could be seen to be going ahead, on her own.

---

[1] R. Gott, 'The Evolution of the Independent British Deterrent', *International Affairs*, 1963.

[2] Eden says that the decision to manufacture it was taken in 1952. 'After the war, the Labour Government had made the atomic bomb in secret, ingeniously concealing the large sums expended from public and parliamentary gaze. They were certainly right to make the bomb, and they may have been wise to conceal the fact from their followers. We in our turn decided to make the hydrogen bomb in 1952 and so reported to Parliament.' Eden, op. cit., p. 368.

[3] 'Personally, I cannot feel that we should have much influence over their [U.S.] policy or actions, wise or unwise, while we are largely dependent, as we are today, on their protection. We, too, must possess substantial deterrent power of our own.' H.C. Deb., Fifth Series, Vol. 537, col. 1905, 1 March 1955.

The first British hydrogen bomb was exploded on Christmas Island, in 1957. In 1958 the MacMahon Act was amended and Anglo-American collaboration was resumed.

7 FOREIGN POLICY

a *The Anglo-American relationship*
There can be no possible doubt that in the early fifties the overwhelmingly important factor in British foreign policy was the relationship with the United States, whose policies, together with those of the Soviet Union, dominated the post-war world in the fifties. Not, it must be said at once, that this was a particularly happy relationship. Most Americans probably felt, not without justification, that they had done a great deal already, for the Europeans in general, and for Britain in particular, in winning their war for them and in propping up their failing economic structures when peace came. Americans now looked for – and did not always find – some signs of self-help among their protégés. They were in no doubt that the leadership of the free world was theirs. But they did not wish to carry the burdens unaided. For their part, the British found themselves in a difficult position. They had long experience in international diplomacy; and they had continuing commitments up and down the world, which in the most favourable conditions would have been difficult to discharge. Straitened economic circumstances now made these burdens almost impossibly difficult to carry. In these circumstances the wartime link with the United States was necessarily carried over into the post-war years. The British simply could not do without the Americans. They no longer had the economic wherewithal. It is always difficult, with the best will in the world, for the very poor to enter into a close and fruitful relationship with the very rich. And the British/United States relationship at this time was no exception. British scientific and technical skills were valued in America, but once the Americans got hold of the formulae their origin was forgotten. British views on international issues were sought; and then as often as not rejected. British attitudes to colonial and former colonial territories were noted, only to be censured. The relatively liberal British attitude towards neutral countries was considered highly dangerous. The British slant on Communism was regarded as pusillanimous to say the least. And yet neither the Americans nor the British could possibly, in those years, have done without each other. The reasons for this, and the points of particular contact, may be briefly reviewed.

In Europe the Americans were most anxious that the European states should, at the earliest possible moment, take over most of the burden for their own defence by conventional forces against the Soviet Union, thus freeing American forces for the Far East, a part of the world with which they were, and had always been, more directly concerned and interested. This involved, in American eyes, some kind of coming together on the part of the Europeans which might in the end involve the setting up of something like a United States of Europe. Americans felt that British participation, and indeed, leadership, was essential for the achievement of this end. The British view was a rather different one. In these years they looked on European commitments with great reserve.

In the Far East the Americans were ready to play a more active role and required merely British acquiescence. The stage had already been set for this long before 1945. In 1940, for instance, Britain had to tell New Zealand to look to the United States rather than the United Kingdom in the event of a Japanese attack. And subsequently, in the war years, the United States bore the brunt of the Japanese attack in the Far East. In 1951 the Anzus Pact was formed, from which the United Kingdom had been deliberately excluded. Then in 1954 came SEATO in which the United Kingdom did play a role, but a minor one. This was now more definitely than ever an American part of the world, and its inhabitants seemed to recognize this. In these circumstances the Americans found it extremely irritating that the British continued to hold independent – and different – views on Far Eastern problems. Thus, in 1950, Britain recognized the new Government of Communist China, although in deference to the Americans they acquiesced in the Formosan Chinese retaining their seat on the Security Council. But the general British attitude towards the neutral powers in the area was regarded with suspicion. In American eyes at this time there could be no such thing as neutrality. Either a government was for Communism, or it was against it. The British had a different view both of Communism and of the rôle of neutrals, and were unwilling to view world problems in a simple context of black or white. This was bad and confusing, the Americans thought.

In the Middle East too, the differences of emphasis and interests were marked. The Americans were not, as the British, dependent on Middle Eastern oil. On the other hand they were full of anxieties about the spread of Communism; anxieties which on the whole the British, who knew the area very well, did not share. Thus, at the start, different assumptions were made and different objectives were held. These divergencies were greatly accentuated when Mr. John Foster Dulles became Secretary of State in 1953. He and Sir Anthony Eden were as oil and water over a whole range of problems, and the differences between the two men were destined to come to a head in the Suez crisis in 1956–7. However, it was in these earlier years that the seeds of trouble were sown. The Dulles image of Nasser was that of a man trifling with the Communist world, and thus a danger to all right-thinking people. He must be isolated and contained. The Eden image of Nasser was that he was the Hitler of the fifties, and hence that the lesson of appeasement must be remembered. He must be attacked and destroyed. The one man wished to contain Communism by cutting off the economic aid of which Egypt was desperately in need. The other wished for much more positive action. Not containment, but attack. Unfortunately Eden and Dulles came to mistrust each other almost as much as they mistrusted Nasser, their common foe. Churchill was aware of this friction, and it made him very uneasy.[1]

Thus, the British relationship with the United States in the life of this Government may be described as formally friendly, but increasingly uneasy. There would never be enmity between the two, but the special relationship of the war years was showing signs of strain.

b *The Communist world 1951–1955*
In these years the important factor was of course relationship with the Soviet Union. The rest of the Communist world had not yet surfaced. The dividing year was 1953, when Stalin died. Before then there had been great anxiety in Europe, because of Russia's aggressive policies towards the Eastern European countries, and because of her apparent determination to use East Germany to perpetuate and exacerbate European difficulties. The death of Stalin was followed by the revolt in East Germany, which was put down by the U.S.S.R. with all its old ferocity. But the interregnum in the Kremlin none the less gave room for some manoeuvre and Churchill was most anxious to make full use of this. He urged on his reluctant American allies the advantages of a summit meeting, at which Soviet and Western representatives could together discuss the still unresolved issues left over by the Second World War. All that was achieved, however, was the Berlin Conference on Austria in 1954, which led, in the following year, to the signing of a peace treaty with Austria.

It was recognized, of course, that one of the first aims of the Soviet bloc was to weaken the strength and cohesion of the Atlantic Alliance. None the less, the thought was that by a combination of circumstances – the ending of the Korean war, the death of Stalin and the fact that the West had a decisive lead in atomic weapons – it ought to be possible to plan for peaceful co-existence. And when the H bomb came on the scene in 1954 both Churchill and Eden felt that the danger of war had been very greatly reduced.[2] The U.S.S.R. would simply not be able to risk war.

Britain's position *vis-à-vis* China was, in a way, a much more difficult

---

[1] Moran, op. cit., p. 592.
[2] Eden, op. cit., p. 123. 'I was sharply conscious of the deterrent power of the hydrogen bomb.... I do not believe that we should have got through the Geneva Conference and avoided a major war, without it.'

one. The Chinese Communists had won a decisive victory over the Nationalists in 1949, driving Chiang Kai-shek and the rump of his supporters off the mainland to the island of Formosa. In 1950 the British had recognized the new Peking Government in accordance with their established practice of giving *de facto* recognition to new governments however distasteful their policies might be. The Americans, in accordance with their different convention, had refused to do this and continued to recognize Chiang Kai-shek. Britain, anxious not to strain relations with the United States, was thus obliged to 'recognize' two Chinese governments. And the Formosan Government's representative still held his seat on the Security Council, while the Peking Government was not recognized at all by the U.N. Many consequences followed from this entanglement. The British Government, in spite of its representation in Peking, was not able to do much to influence the course of events in China, or in the Far East generally. These were the years of Chinese dependence on the Soviet Union, and there seemed little possibility of driving a wedge between these two dangerous partners. But at least Britain, with her outpost at Hong Kong and her control and influence in many of the surrounding Asian states, was in a better position to achieve a *modus vivendi* than the United States which had, in effect, declared war *à outrance*.

c *Europe*

There seemed to be no possible doubt that the Soviets would exploit to the full any weakness in the position of the Western European allies. The main Russian bargaining counter was East Germany. German reunification, under Russian terms, could be offered as a bait to detach West Germany, recognized by the West as an independent state since 1952, from the allies, and link it with the other East European states already under Soviet control. Therefore it was necessary for the allies to woo West Germany because it was essential to harness her potential industrial might to the defence of Western Europe. It was difficult to do this without arousing European, and, in particular, French fears of renascent German power. With this in mind, the French were very anxious that Britain should come into Europe, to counterbalance the growing might of Germany. The Americans, equally, were most anxious that Britain should take the lead in Europe. For a range of reasons the British themselves were unwilling to do so. Only Churchill had, from the first, seemed to give positive if rather vaguely expressed support to the European idea. Conscious always, and more than most people, of the ever-increasing threat from the Soviet Union, he had unwaveringly, if not very specifically, called for a European front. Hence his 'iron curtain' speech at Fulton, Missouri, in March 1946 when he gave warning of the great divide between Europe and the Soviet Union; and his speech at Zurich in September in the same year, when he talked of European Union, with Britain and the United States acting as outside sponsors. But none the less Britain lagged behind, an enthusiastic member of NATO (which was not, of course, just a European grouping) but a much less enthusiastic supporter of any move towards a supranational Europe in which she herself would be required to play a part.[1] Eden, Foreign Secretary when the Conservatives came back to power in October 1951, seems not to have shared Churchill's enthusiasm. Conservatives as a whole probably thought then in terms of independent Great Power status, based on the Commonwealth and with a special relationship with the United States. The Labour Party at that time shared this view, though for other reasons. They feared commitment to a Europe which seemed, since 1948, to be markedly capitalist in its politics, and thought that the socialist planned economy which they had carefully fostered in England would be at risk in such company. And the fact that British participation was being urged by the United States did nothing much to commend any such schemes to the Labour Party. Further, commitment to Europe was seen as a decisive step away from the Soviet Union, which some Labour Party members would have viewed with regret, even in the Stalin era. In general, the British argued that the movement towards European economic integration was, when all was said and done, a protectionist movement and thus contrary to the principles accepted in the Articles of Agreement of the International Monetary Fund, and in the General Agreement on Tariffs and Trade.

However, when Eden took over as Foreign Secretary in 1951 the hard core of Council of Europe members – the Benelux countries, Federal West Germany, France and Italy were pressing ahead with various plans for functional integration, although between 1952 and 1954 the main current of French opinion was moving against the supranational idea. Gaullists were much opposed, and so were others.

At this point the British, mindful of the need to satisfy the American demand that the Europeans should begin to help themselves, produced the Western European Union Scheme in 1954, which, embodied in what came to be known as the Paris Agreements, was ratified by nine countries.[2] It was agreed to admit the German Federal Republic to

[1] See Miriam Camps, *Britain and the European Community 1955–1963* for a full account of the various attempts made at European integration in the early post-war period.
NATO membership was as follows:
1949 United States, United Kingdom, Canada, Norway, Denmark, Iceland, Italy, Portugal.
1951 Greece and Turkey joined.
[2] United States, United Kingdom, Canada, France, Italy, the German Federal Republic and the three Benelux countries.

NATO; and to make the Brussels Treaty (a defensive mutual assistance pact signed soon after the war by Britain, France and the three Benelux countries) the basis of a new defence arrangement which would be tied in to NATO. The economic facets of the Brussels Treaty were relegated to the already existing Organization for European Economic Co-operation (O.E.E.C.); and the cultural side to the Council of Europe. Germany and Italy were brought in. Eden pledged the retention of four British divisions and an air force contingent on the Continent, to be withdrawn only if the other Brussels Treaty powers agreed. Two reservations were made. These British forces would have to be withdrawn if an acute overseas emergency arose or if their retention in Germany occasioned too severe a financial strain on the British economy. It was clearly not anticipated, however, that this latter would be the case. And no formal arrangements were made for financial reimbursement to Britain for the foreign currency involved.

Eden did well in these negotiations. Fears in France, Germany and the United States were abated, and Britain's own commitment was generous, and indeed was all too soon seen as much too generous. Eden made it clear, however, that even now the British role was to be association with Europe, and not membership. The Europeans were annoyed by this, and so too were the Americans. Britain's future lay in Europe – in the eyes of Europeans and Americans. Only the British themselves did not see it this way. However, Eden found a formula which satisfied all parties, and which certainly led to a relaxation of tension in Europe. Reaction against supranational plans had in any case set in, and Eden's alternative plans saved the day in that he found an acceptable way of achieving German independence, and enabling Germany to make the necessary contribution to European defence. But Eden was, from first to last, aloof from Europe. He merely provided the background diplomatic services required at the time.

d *The Middle East*
In the Middle East difficulties of a quite different kind confronted Britain. Perhaps the toughest of the problems inherited by the Conservatives in this area, in 1951, was the dispute with Iran whose Premier, an anti-Western fanatic named Moussadeg, had nationalized his country's oil industry, and driven out the Shah.[1] The Conservatives were concerned, as the Labour Government had been before them, about the economic consequence of the loss of oil. They also feared that the ruin of the oil industry would result in desperate poverty for the Iranians, and hence the triumph, in that country, of Communism. However, in August 1953 Premier Moussadeg fell from power and the Shah returned. The final settlement was drawn up in July 1954. In March 1955 security for the belt

[1] Eden, op. cit., pp. 192–8.

of states to the south of the Soviet Union was buttressed by the development of the Baghdad Pact, first signed in February between Iraq and Turkey, but open to other states with defence interests in the area. Great Britain joined in April 1955; Pakistan in September and Iran in November. The frontiers of this Pact, the Central Treaty Organization, or CENTO, thus stretched from the Mediterranean to the Himalayas. The thought was that it might become the NATO for the Middle East, and would in fact, link NATO with SEATO, the security pact developed for South East Asia, since Turkey and Britain were also NATO members.

Suez, to the south of the Baghdad Pact area, was a strategic commitment which this Conservative Government, like its Labour predecessor, regarded as ripe for reassessment as far as British policies went. There was general recognition that there must be some cutting back, not only because British interests in the fifties no longer required quite so overwhelmingly strong a presence in Egypt, but also because of the rising tide of Egyptian nationalism.

The essential British interest in Egypt of course remained. Britain still regarded the Canal as a crucial link enabling her to look after her interests, whether commercial or strategic, east of Suez. And she still had great interests to defend, even now that the four Asian dominions had achieved self-government.[1] British interest in Middle Eastern oil was regarded as enormously important and it was generally assumed that this meant the maintenance of military bases of one kind or another. Then, the Canal was an international waterway to be defended at all costs against the shadowy menace of the Communist bloc. The Soviet fleet must be kept out of the Indian Ocean. The Canal was part of a second line of defence, the first line being made up of Turkey and her allies now gradually coming together in the Baghdad Pact.

During the Second World War, Egypt, with whom Britain had a treaty which ran until 1956, had been of crucial importance, because of strategic considerations in North Africa and the Middle East and because of the link it provided, through the Canal, with the Far East. After the war, however, came a wind of change. First, the Egyptians saw Britain's Far Eastern dominions – India, Pakistan, Burma and Ceylon – achieve their independence. Then came the oil dispute with Iran, when a show of strength on the part of Iran forced compromise on Britain, which gave Iranians far-reaching control over the destiny of their own oilfields, hitherto run by foreigners. Why, the Egyptian Nationalists asked, should not the Egyptians, with their much greater national asset of the Canal, do the same? On the British side, too, the wind of change was blowing. The cost of the Egyptian garrison and the whole Canal set-up was very great, and strategic and other considerations now seemed to suggest that the

[1] India 1947; Pakistan 1947; Ceylon 1948; Burma 1948.

Suez link was less vital to Britain's interests than it had been in the past. So, in 1945, the Attlee Government had agreed to negotiate, provided that satisfactory arrangements for the security of the Canal Zone could be made.[1] The negotiations had opened with the then Egyptian Prime Minister, Sidki Pasha, in October 1946, with a view to arranging the partial withdrawal of British forces by March 1947, and the total withdrawal by September 1949. However, in December, these arrangements fell through when King Farouk forced Sidki Pasha to resign.

Part of the trouble then was the Sudan. This territory had been controlled by the Egyptians on behalf of the Ottoman Empire when, after the revolt of the Madhi from the Khedive, who ruled Egypt, Kitchener conquered it in 1898. A Condominium was then created, ostensibly to vest joint control over the country in Britain and Egypt. In fact the Sudan became, to all intents and purposes, a British Protectorate. Continuing and increasing Egyptian concern was felt because whoever controlled the Sudan controlled the upper reaches of the Nile, and thus Egypt's economic destiny. The northern Sudanese were predominantly Arab in race and not unlike the Egyptians. The people of the southern Sudan, however, were primitive African tribesmen, about whom the British authorities felt very protective. The British felt that these people might well, later on, not wish to be absorbed by the Egyptians, who were not noted for their governmental skills or their humanitarian principles.

But in Egyptian eyes the questions of the Canal Zone and the Sudan were linked, and in July 1947 Egypt took her case to the Security Council. A deadlock ensued. Further talks, begun in March 1949 and ending in July 1951 similarly came to nothing. Then in August 1951, the British suggested a regional pact to guard the Canal Zone, which the United States, France and Turkey were willing to join. The Egyptians refused. There seems to have been, at this time, some American sympathy with the Egyptian suspicion that the British were in fact trying to increase Sudanese anxieties, so as to provide an excuse for a continuing British presence. Further disorders in the Canal Zone early in 1952 gave King Farouk an excuse to dismiss his Prime Minister Nahas Pasha. He called in Ali Maher to form a government, thus ending the long domination of the W.A.F.D., or National Party. Meanwhile, army leaders staged a coup which resulted, in July 1952, in King Farouk's abdication.

This change was at first welcomed in Britain, as providing an opportunity to open up new negotiations. King Farouk's government had been corrupt and unstable, and it was hoped that it might be easier to negotiate with his military successor, Colonel Neguib, who was reputedly a friend of the American Ambassador, Mr. Jefferson Caffery. The hope was revived of a defence pact to ensure the security of the Canal Zone. But unfortunately negotiations on the Sudanese question turned out to be

[1] H.C. Deb., Fifth Series, Vol. 423, cols. 784–8, 24 May 1946.

even more difficult than before – possibly because Neguib himself was half Sudanese. He began energetically upon the policy of wooing the people of the northern Sudan. British concern for the primitive African peoples in the three Southern provinces became more acute. However, agreement was at length reached on 12 February 1953, which provided for self-determination at the end of three years, control being exercised in the meantime by a Governor General and a Commission on which the Sudan, Britain, Egypt and Pakistan were represented. Neguib, with his own Sudanese background, hoped to be able to win over the Sudanese political parties by political infiltration. Sir Anthony Eden was determined that the people of the Sudan should be free to make a real choice when the time came.[1]

Negotiations went on over the Canal Zone. In December 1952 the Conservatives decided to shift Middle East Headquarters from Suez to Cyprus, in spite of the fact that Cyprus had no deep-water port. There was a general shift in thinking about the defence line in the Middle East. Reliance came to be placed on the 'northern tier' of Baghdad Pact countries.

Two outstanding questions remained: how the Base could be kept in repair after British troops withdrew; and how it could be reactivated in case of need. The British view was that these conditions could be met if Egypt joined some kind of regional defence pact. This was also the American view. And the Americans were in a good position to exert pressure because they were providing economic aid on a considerable scale to Egypt. India and Pakistan were also interested in safeguarding the Canal route and gave their diplomatic assistance.

Eventually agreement was reached in October 1954, although by this time Neguib was handicapped by his battle with his rival, Nasser. It was provided that the agreement should last for seven years; that British forces should withdraw within twenty months; that in the meantime certain key installations should be maintained jointly by British and Egyptian civilian personnel; and that the base should be reactivated in the event of an armed attack on Egypt, or any other member of the Arab League, or Turkey, in which case Britain and Egypt would consult together. In the meantime Egypt agreed to respect the Constantinople Convention of 1888 regarding freedom of navigation through the Canal.

The Opposition was very critical of this arrangement because of the allegedly poor terms achieved by Britain; and twenty-seven members of the so-called 'Suez Group' of Conservatives voted against their own Government.

Meantime, in November 1954, Colonel Nasser took over from Colonel Neguib.

Other changes, too, took place in the Middle East in these years. In

[1] Eden, op. cit., p. 247.

1952 Ibn Saud of Saudi Arabia died and under his son and successor ties with the West were loosened. In Jordan, the young King Hussein succeeded to the throne in 1953. His was an uneasy throne because two-thirds of the population of Jordan were refugees from Palestine. The North African countries of Morocco and Tunisia were on their way to independence, though this was not granted until 1956. In Algeria, the struggle with France had begun, which was to reach its climax in the years after the French had been dislodged from Indo-China in 1954.

Clearly this was a difficult area. Egypt was at the centre of a newly surfacing world of Arab states and Egypt's relationship with Britain was going to become a major difficulty. Between 1951 and 1955 however, British policy was hammered out with relative success.

e *The Far East 1951-1955*
Britain's problems in the Far East were different in degree if not in kind from her problems in Europe and the Middle East, if only because Britain was there in an advisory capacity rather than as a main participant. This is not to say that the going was easy. Policies throughout South East Asia inevitably turned on the attitude to China. And here, as has been shown, the differences between the British and American viewpoints were very great. It followed that the differences between Britain and America on other issues in South East Asia were also not inconsiderable.

In the first place, American policy towards Japan was difficult for Britain to accept. Japan was to America in the Far East what Western Germany was to some of the Europeans: an ex-enemy to be rehabilitated with all possible speed, so as to help in the cold war with the Communists. The United States signed a peace treaty with Japan in 1951. This was followed by a security pact signed between the United States and Japan, providing for the maintenance of American forces in Japan. But for Britain and also New Zealand and Australia, Japan was an ex-enemy about whom they had bitter recollections. She was also, as Britain knew to her cost in the past, a formidable trade rival. This rivalry was the more serious because Japan was now forbidden by the Americans to enter into trade relations of any kind with mainland China. However, Britain accepted American policy towards Japan, and made little effort to modify it.

Korea was another difficulty. Britain supported the United States in the matter of the Korean war, and the mounting cost of the rearmament necessary for Britain to play even a small part in this American-U.N. venture contributed largely to the financial crisis which the Conservatives inherited when they took office in October 1951.

The subsequent role of the Conservative Government was to attempt to restrain the Americans from pursuing a more aggressive policy which might have brought the U.N. contingent into direct conflict with the Chinese and, above all, to prevent the Americans from using atomic weapons to drive Chinese Communists out of North Korea. The British position was not that the American intervention was a mistake, but that it should be a severely limited operation. Sir Anthony Eden has argued that American action was justified because it aimed at the establishment of a balance of power. Without it, the Communists would have been encouraged to make more ambitious attempts to extend their sphere of influence and thus the danger to peace would have been larger. Aggression must be seen not to pay. 'That was the lesson of Europe in the thirties. It was also the lesson of the Middle East in the fifties.'[1] Eden, in the Korean problem, was working with Dean Acheson, Truman's Secretary of State, with whom he got on well. Long-drawn-out negotiations for an armistice began in Kaesong in 1952 and were subsequently transferred to Panmunjom. On 22 July 1953 an armistice was at last signed and since then an uneasy truce has prevailed. But the immediate result of the Korean war was to make American politicians even more uneasy than they were before about Communist intentions in the Far East, and even more willing to give aid and support to governments half-way willing to stand up to the supposed Communist threat, even when this involved support for a small, unrepresentative minority like the Chinese following of Chiang Kai-shek in Formosa; or former colonial powers like the French in Indo-China.

The three states of what was formerly French Indo-China, Cambodia, Laos and Vietnam, were next on the list for trouble. In these three countries war had been endemic long before the outbreak of the Second World War and, after the French were defeated in 1941 nationalist guerrillas had kept up the struggle against the Japanese. When the Japanese tide receded the peoples of these areas were quite unwilling to receive their former French rulers back again. They were given independence within the French Union in 1946, but this was not enough to satisfy nationalist demands, and these demands were supported, whether overtly or covertly, by the Chinese. So nationalism in this part of the world had from the outset a markedly Communist flavour. For this, if for no other reason, the Americans were anxious to see the French re-established in control. The whole complex issue came to a head in the spring of 1954 when French forces were besieged by local nationalists in the fortress of Dien Bien Phu, in North Vietnam. The American Secretary of State, then Mr. John Foster Dulles, was anxious to relieve the French by combined Anglo-American air support. Eden was firm in his refusal, on the grounds that such action would be repudiated by British public opinion at home, by the Asian neutrals, who, led by India, were beginning to play an increasing role in world politics, and certainly by the Russians and the Chinese. In the end, Eden's views prevailed; Dien Bien Phu fell to the North Vietnamese, and the Geneva Conference was convened in May 1954 with a view

[1] Eden, op. cit., Book I, Ch. 2., p. 28.

to negotiating a political settlement in Indo-China and in Korea. On July 21st an agreement was reached by which Vietnam was divided into a Communist north and a non-Communist south. Laos and Cambodia were established as neutral states.

In the following year a collective defence organization – the South-East Asia Treaty Organization – was set up to try to ensure the collective defence of the area. The organization was composed of Australia, Britain, France, New Zealand, the United States, and three of the Asian states, Pakistan, the Philippines and Thailand. But, because of lack of forces in the area, the defence provided was symbolic rather than real.[1]

In this episode, as in the episode of the Korean war, the British played a very considerable diplomatic role and, largely through British initiatives, a compromise peace was achieved. But the price paid was the anger felt in some American circles at having been frustrated by the too-clever British, who had succeeded in thwarting the desire for war *à outrance* with the Communists and had forced the Americans to compromise with small Asiatic countries who were dabbling dangerously in Communism.

It was in this area that the dangerous rift between Eden and Dulles first began to appear. The Americans disliked the idea of partitioning Vietnam. They wanted, instead, to move Anglo-American forces into Indo-China to help the French. They were more anxious, it seems, for an out-and-out French victory than the French themselves. They favoured direct military action before the meeting of the Geneva Conference; and they wanted SEATO set up before the Conference met. Dulles, in fact, called a meeting of the non-Asian proposed SEATO members without consulting Eden, who sent an angry message to Washington: 'Americans may think the time past when they need consider the feelings or difficulties of their Allies. It is the conviction that this tendency becomes more pronounced every week that is creating mounting difficulties for anyone in this country who wants to maintain close Anglo-American relations.'[2]

The British position was that if the Geneva Conference broke down, both sides would step up participation, and the result might be a third World War.

8 THE COMMONWEALTH

a *General considerations*

These years were not ones of rapid change. The Asian dominions had

[1] Sir Anthony Eden explained the purpose of this pact in the House of Commons on 13 April 1954. It was to be 'something comparable to the NATO organization that exists in Europe.' But Asiatic countries were to be represented, as well as those of European descent. The organization should not be regarded, he said, as 'defence of an obsolete colonialism' (H.C. Deb., Fifth Series, Vol. 526, cols. 969–75, 13 April 1954).   [2] Eden, op. cit., Book I, p. 99.

made their great stride forward into independence under the previous Labour Government and India, Pakistan, Ceylon and Burma were now independent states. Of these, only Burma had left the Commonwealth in 1948. The African dependencies were not yet quite ripe. The winds of change were still only perceptible as a fluttering breeze here and there. However, the conditions of membership of the Commonwealth had become less rigid,[1] and membership still carried quite considerable benefits. The preferential trading agreements which had originated at the Ottawa Conference in 1932 remained, and though perhaps less useful than in the past, they were still of value to countries like Canada, New Zealand, Australia and Ghana, and, of course, to Britain herself. Then, the diplomatic value of membership of the Commonwealth was by no means without attraction, even though the development capital for the under-developed territories had to come, increasingly, from other countries than the impoverished United Kingdom. The early fifties was an age of two great power blocs headed by the United States and the U.S.S.R., and those who wished to make their voices heard on the international stage had to choose their bloc. But even in these years bi-polarity was becoming less marked and, increasingly, dependent Commonwealth countries, as well as the old independent white dominions, began to develop their own slant on the great issues of the time – a slant different both from that of the Anglo-American world, and from that of the Communist states. For one thing, the attitude to Communism itself was different, and decidedly less hostile, in most of the colonial and ex-colonial states. Communism was seen both as a possible ally of nationalism, as in Vietnam; and also, at that time, as an arrangement of society likely to lead to very rapid economic growth. If only for these reasons, there was doubt as to the wisdom of the aggressive anti-Communism enjoined by the Anglo-American world. India, for instance though a member of the Commonwealth, stood out firmly as an unaligned state, not prepared to endorse the policies of either of the two major blocs.

The problems posed by Britain's African territories were complex and extremely difficult. The need to develop towards self-government was evident; and in this regard Africans were no doubt stimulated by Asian advances. But to make these advances in Africa, in under-developed, multi-racial and often mainly tribal societies, was difficult indeed. In some African countries, such as Nigeria, there was deep antagonism between the main tribal groups. In others, such as Kenya and Southern Rhodesia, there was a white settler element. And in these countries the gulf between the white settlers and the Africans made problems associated with constitutional advance seemingly impossible.

[1] At the Commonwealth Prime Ministers' Conference in 1949 a new form of words was developed regarding the Crown, which was henceforth to be 'Head of the Commonwealth'. This meant that republics could remain within the fold.

One line of thought popular in the fifties was that small territories would have to be grouped together in some kind of federal relationship, in order to ensure economic viability, before any idea of independence could be meaningfully entertained.

b *The Central African Federation*

Of these new federations only the Central African Federation properly belongs to this period. The three territories which were to be brought together in this federation were Southern Rhodesia, Northern Rhodesia and Nyasaland. All three had very different past histories. Southern Rhodesia had been a self-governing colony since 1923. It had a large white settler population, and a relatively strong economic base in its tobacco and its coal. Northern Rhodesia was a British colony with a much smaller white population, and considerable mineral resources, for the working of which it was largely dependent on labour coming from Nyasaland, much the poorer of the three where there was virtually no white settlement. The thought was that the union of coal, copper and labour would certainly lead to economic growth. Possible hostility consequent on the growth of white or black nationalism would be muted in a multi-racial society, where blacks and whites would develop in partnership. The British Commonwealth – a multi-racial commonwealth if ever there was one – could give the world a practical demonstration of the possibility of this partnership. The strategic value of a large, economically viable and politically satisfied multi-racial state centrally placed in Africa would be immense. Unfortunately it was not to be. The Africans in all three territories were bitterly opposed to being handed over, as they saw it, to the white settlers of Southern and Northern Rhodesia, and regarded the safeguards built in to the new constitution as wholly inadequate. The white settlers of Southern Rhodesia felt that the provisions made for African participation put their privileged position in jeopardy. They were more sensitive than usual during these years, because of the Mau Mau upheaval then taking place just to the north in Kenya. And white officials in the African areas were scandalized at what seemed to them to be the abandonment of the hitherto generally accepted philosophy of the paramountcy of native interests.

The history of this abortive Federation may be briefly outlined:

When the Conservative Government took office in October 1951 the new Colonial Secretary, Mr. Oliver Lyttleton, pressed ahead with plans that had already been started by the previous Labour Government. In April 1953 a referendum held in Southern Rhodesia approved a proposed federal constitution by a majority of two to one. On 3 September 1953 it came into operation. The thought was that by 1962 the new Federation could become an independent member of the Commonwealth. But meanwhile African opposition steadily increased. There was no wish at all to exchange Colonial Office paternalism for direct exploitation by Southern Rhodesian white settlers. Thus, federation was the hothouse which forced the growth of African nationalism.

The whole issue was debated at length in the Commons on 24 March 1953.[1] Mr. Oliver Lyttelton summarized the Conservative objective as follows:

> We, the British, are seeking to build a society founded upon partnership between the races that inhabit Central Africa.... No future lies in a Central Africa entirely and always dominated by one race or another.... The present scheme provides a framework within which the idea of partnership and the British views about the relations of races, can take root and grow.

Labour's opposition to the Central African Federation scheme as finally hatched, ended what had hitherto been a bipartisan approach to colonial problems. The Opposition argued that federation, as it had worked out, was being imposed on the Africans, who had become very unwilling and suspicious, fearing that the white minority that controlled the government of Southern Rhodesia would in the end control the whole Federation.

In April 1952 African delegates from Northern Rhodesia and Nyasaland had come to England to express to the Colonial Secretary their misgivings over the prominence of Southern Rhodesia. In February 1953 the conference which drew up the scheme for federation was boycotted by the Africans, who were already looking towards West Africa for the patterns of their future development. Labour could not support disregard of African views.

A second and related reason for Labour – and African – misgivings was the lack of adequate safeguards against the abuse of power by European Ministers in control of the federal organs of power. Thus, the 1953 constitution ensured that one-third of the members of the Federal Assembly should be Africans. But a two-thirds majority could amend the constitution. The only safeguard appeared to be the African Affairs Board, which could recommend reservation by the Governor General of any bill discriminating against the African population. This, it was felt, was a wholly inadequate safeguard for the Africans.

There can be no doubt that the setting up of the Central African Federation accelerated the growth of African nationalism, and destroyed the faith of many Africans in British promises of ultimate self-government.[2] Those who set out to form the Federation were full of good

[1] H.C. Deb., Fifth Series, Vol. 513, cols. 658–801.
[2] See Kenneth Kirkwood, *Britain and Africa*; J. M. Lee, *Colonial Development and Good Government*; A. Hanno, *The Story of the Rhodesians and Nyasa-*

intentions. It was perhaps not a venture foredoomed to failure. It did fail because of the inadequate and clumsy handling of African opinion in the early stages; and perhaps because of weaknesses in the Federal constitution. Mr. Oliver Lyttelton's hope that African opposition to the Federation would wither away when the African masses found that federation brought improvement in the social services, etc., proved wholly unfounded.

c *Kenya*
The Kenya story in these years, which centres on the Mau Mau rebellion, may at first sight appear to be a wholly different matter. But there are certain common features. In her thinking on Kenya too, Britain had been impressed by the need for a larger, and possibly federated, territory, on economic grounds. In 1945 a White Paper had set out the desirability of an East African High Commission covering Kenya, Uganda and Tanganyika, with legislative and executive organs. Three years later, in 1948, the High Commission was set up, together with a central Assembly. The Legislative Council in Kenya then for the first time had an unofficial, multi-racial majority.

The next step came in the last two years of the Labour Government, when the Colonial Secretary, Mr. Griffiths, visited Kenya to discuss a revised constitution with all the different racial groups. The position in Kenya was not unlike Southern Rhodesia in that, although the overwhelming majority of the population belonged to a variety of African tribes, between whom there was very considerable diversity, not to say animosity, the pivot of the economy was provided by the white settlers in what were known as the White Highlands. These settlers had, perhaps, a more aristocratic flavour than had their counterparts in Southern Rhodesia, and, under the long leadership of men like Lord Delamere, were more deeply rooted in their country, and showed a greater awareness of its problems. In 1952 the first African member, Mr. Mathu, was appointed to the Executive Council and African and Asian representation on the new Legislative Council was increased. In the same year a Royal Commission was appointed to inquire into land use, industry and development in general. Kenya was an overcrowded country and the white settlers who, over the years, had acquired all the best land, were now demanding full self-government.

In October 1952 the Mau Mau rising broke out and a state of emergency had to be declared. In 1953 Jomo Kenyatta, a member of the Kikuyu tribe and leader of the Kenya African Union, was convicted of being the principal organizer of Mau Mau, and was imprisoned. Fighting continued

---

land; N. Mannsergh, *Documents and Speeches on Commonwealth Affairs 1952–1962.*

until 1956, and the emergency regulations were not ended until 1959.[1]

Mau Mau was a particularly nasty kind of rebellion. Its core was in the ever-restless Kikuyu tribe, and its method was avowedly terrorism. European farmers and their families up and down the White Highlands were murdered, often in the most bestial and terrible manner. And their servants were frequently intimidated into aiding and abetting, or even committing, the crimes. Although the main targets were Europeans, law-abiding Africans were equally at risk. The movement was described in the House of Commons as 'an unholy union of dark and ancient superstitions with the apparatus of modern gangsterism.'[2] At that time it seemed difficult to understand or feel the slightest vestige of sympathy for those who supported it. In retrospect, it can be seen as a part of the bitter, deeply rooted, despairing hatred of many black people for the superior whites who had, as it were, come in on top of them. The whites must be terrorized into leaving Kenya, seems to have been the message. Be this as it may, Mau Mau ended for the time being ideas of regional co-operation, or multi-racial government. But Asians, many Africans and, to their credit, some Europeans remained steadfast in their support for an inter-racial society. It is difficult to determine what lessons the much less violent Africans of the Central African Federation drew from Mau Mau. But certainly the Europeans were served notice of the danger of their position, and, perhaps, of the desirability of keeping control firmly in their own hands. And United Kingdom plans for federating large areas of territory with a view to co-ordinating economic and social development, and for a multi-racial advance towards self-government within the Commonwealth, broke down, as far as Africa was concerned, in the lifetime of this 1951–55 Government, and it was not at all clear what the future could be. The white settler population could not be given full control. The whole inherited and deeply rooted philosophy of trusteeship made that out of the question. But it seemed equally impossible to give support to black nationalism. The African peoples were too backward, divided and inexperienced to make such a move possible. There was not, as in the former Asian dominions, any known tradition of past cultural history, nor was there a sufficiently large and well-established middle or professional class on which to build. None the less, a remarkable feature of the Mau Mau emergency period in Kenya was the unwavering determination of the United Kingdom Government to continue its policy of constitutional development. In April 1954 the Colonial Secretary, Mr. Oliver Lyttelton, announced a new constitution with a multi-racial slant. Africans and Asians could now be elected as ministers, as well as Europeans.[3] African, Asian and European leaders alike deplored Mau

[1] See K. Ingham, *A History of East Africa*.
[2] H.C. Deb., Fifth Series, Vol. 507, cols. 456–553.
[3] Ingham, op. cit.

Mau, and perhaps for this reason developed a common purpose, and even a genunine wish for inter-racial co-operation.

9 THE OPPOSITION

a *The Labour Party*

The Labour Party in Opposition put up a poor showing. Within Parliament, Labour members were deeply and often openly divided over major policy issues, whether foreign or domestic. And the Labour movement outside Parliament provided the nation with an astonishing spectacle of many-faceted strife. The Labour movement has always, and for historical reasons which are beyond the scope of this study, been made up of a federation of groups, all approaching political issues from rather different angles. A united front is at the best of times difficult to achieve. And in Opposition any political party lacks the coherence which the necessity to govern provides in office. So disunity in Opposition was perhaps not so surprising. Nor was the Party strife within the Labour movement in these years anything very new. In the inter-war years, too, both in the two brief periods when Labour ruled as a minority government, and in the much longer years in Opposition, battles of somewhat the same kind had gone on. Ramsay MacDonald and his group of moderates had played the Attlee role against the left wing groups, fumbling after a more meaningful and 'socialist' solution to the nation's problems. Even in the dead thirties, when the National Government, which was really an out-and-out Conservative Government, held almost undisputed sway, the ideological quarrels in the Labour world never quite died down. The war years were the genuinely consensus years. Then came the sweeping Labour victory of 1945 and the great leap forward into a supposedly 'socialist' Britain. In these years, the whole Labour movement massed behind Attlee and his Government, full of enthusiasm and hope. Gradually the hopes faded, partly because the Attlee team, after an initial push forward, got increasingly tired and stale; partly because adverse external circumstances forced so many unwelcome compromises on the two Labour Governments from 1945 to 1951. It was not really surprising that, when the Labour Party went down to defeat in the General Election of 1951, the ensuing period in Opposition should have been characterized by much recrimination and a lot of in-fighting. The structure of the Labour movement made guerilla war easy to wage, and rewarding and absorbing to those who waged it.

The balance of power lay, then as now, with the trade unions, who played a major role in financing the Parliamentary Labour Party, and indeed, to a very large extent, the constituency parties too. The majority of the union leaders were, in these years from 1951 to 1955, as in the past, moderate and pragmatic in their approach to politics. They were not interested in theoretical socialism, and their whole history and training predisposed them to policies of moderation, and *ad hoc* bargaining with whatever political party was in power. Not for these men windy struggles over Clause 4,[1] arguments over German rearmament, or over imperialism in South East Asia. The relevance of this kind of thing to the bread and butter issues with which they were, by long tradition, concerned, was not at that time clear to them. And, if it was not clear to the trade union leaders, still less was it clear to their followers. The rank and file of the trade union movement was apathetic. Indeed, some trade union members probably voted for the Conservative Party. Labour political and economic interests were quite general: no return to the Hungry Thirties; full employment; an end to rationing; and better housing. The articulate and sophisticated Labour voters of the sixties had not for the most part emerged at this time. Where they existed, they were to be found among middle-class activist groups in the constituencies, rather than in the working-class trade union fold.

In the past, the pattern had been that the trade union leaders and the leaders of the Parliamentary Labour Party were in close accord. And this was manifested by the patterns of power shown at the annual Party Conferences, customarily held in September or early October, at different watering places around the coast.[2]

It was at this annual Party Conference, in theory at any rate, that Labour policy was hammered out and agreed on. The Parliamentary Labour Party was, in a general way, supposed to take its line from the Conference. The Conference was customarily attended by a massive trade union representation;[3] by members of the co-operative movement; by constituency representatives; and, of course, by the Parliamentary

[1] Clause 4 of the Labour Party constitution sets out the socialist content of Labour Party objectives, and was drafted by Sidney Webb and adopted in 1918 'to secure for the workers by hand or brain the full fruits of their industry and the most equitable distribution thereof that may be possible, upon the basis of the common ownership of the means of production, distribution and exchange, and the best obtainable system of popular administration and control of each industry or service.'

[2] September 1952 at Morecambe, September 1953 at Margate and September 1954 at Scarborough.

[3] The six largest unions in terms of voting strength were:
(1) Transport and General Workers. This union has nearly as many voters as all the constituency parties put together.
(2) National Union of Mine Workers.
(3) Amalgamated Engineering Union.
(4) General and Municipal Workers Union.
(5) National Union of Railwaymen.
(6) Union of Shop, Distributive and Allied Workers.

Labour Party. The Conference elected, annually, a National Executive Committee, whose business it was to keep a general eye on Labour policy between conferences.[1]

Already in the life of this 1951-55 Government, the old pattern was beginning to change, and there was some uncertainty as to where the seat of power lay. Who gave orders to whom on matters of Labour policy? As the fifties went on, an answer to this question became ever more urgent. All that was established in these years, by Mr. Attlee and his followers, was that it must be left to the Parliamentary Labour Party to decide upon the priority to be given to decisions reached by the Conference.

It may be asked why it was that these three major component parts of the Conference began to draw apart in these years. Why did the trade union leadership begin to move to the left? Why did the constituency representatives become more radical than the Parliamentary Party? Why did the Parliamentary Labour Party continue to be dominated by the moderates?[2]

Some very general reasons may be suggested. As the new pattern of the Welfare State began to emerge, trade unionists took increasing interest in goings-on at Westminster since these now affected them quite directly. The unions had perhaps too little understanding of the great national and international issues of the day. But they saw clearly enough that, for instance National Health Services charges would not be in the interests

---

If these six unions vote together, they control over half the strength of the Conference.

[1] The National Executive Committee was composed of twenty-eight members, and was made up as follows:
(1) The Leader, and – since 1953 – the Deputy Leader of the Parliamentary Party.
(2) The Treasurer, who was elected by the whole Conference.
(3) Twenty-five others:
    (a) twelve members elected by trade unions, from among trade union members;
    (b) one member elected by other affiliated organizations;
    (c) seven members elected by constituency parties;
    (d) five women members.
As a rule, there was a preponderance of M.P.s on the N.E.C. whether trade unionist sponsored M.P.s or others.

[2] See Martin Harrison, 'Trade Unions and the Labour Party since 1945', *Parliamentary Affairs*, Vol. 13, No. 4, 1960, pp. 520-7; R. E. Dowse, *The Parliamentary Labour Party in Opposition*; Emanuel Shinwell, *The Labour Story*; R. T. Mackenzie, *British Political Parties*, 2nd edn., pp. 594-601; *Political Studies*, Vol. V, No. 2, June 1957; R. T. Mackenzie, 'Policy Decisions in Opposition', *Political Studies*, Vol. V, No. 2, 1957; Henry Pelling, *A Short History of the Labour Party*.

of their members. They grasped the possibilities opening up for higher living standards for their members. They probably did not see the limitations which circumstances imposed on all governments alike, whether Labour or Conservative. The constituency representatives were apt to be radical because they too had little understanding of the practical difficulties faced by those in government. And it was in the constituencies that the middle-class intellectuals thought out the theoretical basis of the Labour creed. The Parliamentary Labour Party, on the other hand, was composed of men who had, of necessity, considerable insight into the practical problems of government.

Within the Parliamentary Labour Party there were two main struggles going on, in the period between 1951 and 1955. One concerned the Party Leadership. Many people felt that Mr. Attlee, sixty-eight at the time of the 1951 General Election, ought to stand down and let a younger man take over. Mr. Herbert Morrison, five years younger, was, at any rate in his own opinion, the obvious candidate. He had given long years of stalwart service to the Labour movement, and was one of its most experienced and seasoned workers. Latterly, however, he had not shown himself as a particularly agile politician, and had made a good many enemies, including, it seems, Mr. Attlee himself. He had bungled the important Iranian issue rather badly while he was at the Foreign Office, and many people had come to feel that he did not have the stature required for the Prime Ministership.

In 1951 Mr. Attlee decided to stay on as Leader. Possibly he was influenced by Mr. Churchill's example. He said, subsequently, that he stayed on because Morrison's image at that time was particularly low, and he would not have been elected as Leader. Possibly Morrison would recover his former prestige when the Iranian issue had been forgotten.[1] Morrison, however, alleged that Attlee stayed on in order to dish his chances. He would be too old when the question was reopened and Attlee knew this.[2]

In retrospect, this was perhaps a less important issue than it seemed at the time. It is certainly difficult to believe that Morrison would have provided the Party with very dynamic leadership. He was too near to Attlee in age and in views. When Mr. Attlee finally stepped down in 1955 there was a struggle for the leadership, and Morrison lost to the much younger, better educated and more sophisticated Mr. Hugh Gaitskell.

The second and more interesting struggle going on at this time was that between the small but very vociferous left wing group, led at that time by Aneurin Bevan, and the middle of the road old hands, led by Mr. Morrison. Here there was a real divergence, all across the board, on issues of policy.

[1] Francis Williams, op. cit., p. 255.   [2] *Morrison*, op. cit., p. 293.

Aneurin Bevan was a strange, wayward character, and in many ways, a larger man than any of his motley following. He provided a focal point for a variety of unorthodox left wingers. Lord George-Brown says of him: 'He certainly saw himself as a potential Prime Minister, a greater Lloyd George. He was flattered by all the attention and the publicity he got, but he never commanded that solid backing in the Labour movement which would have been necessary to give him the leadership.'[1]

As far as home affairs went, the Bevanites stood, without equivocation, for what they regarded as pure socialism. This would entail much more nationalization and the phasing out of the private sector. There should be a massive increase in social services, without payment by the consumer, and without selectivity. These policies would be financed by direct taxation, which would have the desirable consequence of a redistribution of national wealth.

As far as foreign policy was concerned, the Bevanites disliked the close relationship with the arch-capitalist power, the United States.[2] They viewed the rearmament of the Germans with great misgiving. The frontiers of West Germany abutted on Russian-controlled territories, with whom the Bevanites wished to maintain friendlier contacts. And in any case, the Western European group of countries, and particularly Germany, were suspect because right wing capitalist governments were in control and, what was even more disconcerting, were doing rather well. Bevanite opposition to British collaboration with the Americans in the development of nuclear weapons was very strong. Finally, the Bevanites viewed the various defence pacts developed by the Tories in collaboration with the Americans, with suspicious dislike. NATO, CENTO, and finally, SEATO, were in their eyes all highly dubious capitalist devices to contain Communism, and prop up – especially in the case of SEATO – wicked old colonialism. The defence pacts tended to perpetuate a *status quo* which any good socialist should want to alter quickly.[3] Also, these capitalist policies cost money, and meant diverting it from the social services to the armaments industry.

Behind these arguments lay the assumption that, whether the electorate wanted it or not, the march towards pure socialism had to go on. Not too much attention should be paid to deviant electoral views as expressed at the 1951 General Election.

[1] Lord George-Brown, Memoirs, *In My Way*, p. 57.
[2] By no means all Labour M.P.s shared this dislike. Denis Healey, for instance, at the Morecambe Party Conference in 1952, described Bevan's views as 'just jingoism with an inferiority complex'. (*Party Conference 1952*, p. 123.)
[3] H.C. Deb., Fifth Series, Vol. 526, col. 971, 13 April 1954 – 'we shall assist in establishing a N.A.T.O. in S.E. Asia for the purpose of imposing European colonial rule upon certain people in that area' (Bevan).

The Opposition

The right wing of the Party – the revisionists, as they came to be known – had quite other views. Attlee and his Government had only just moved out of office, and the thought was that, as the majority against them had been so small, they might easily get back quite soon. Moderate and pragmatic policies were more likely to lead to this than adventurist left wing extremism. The middle ground was the ground that counted in British politics. Attlee himself had no wish for extremism and thought that the electorate had not either. The British people walked, for preference, down the middle of the road; and so did he. Then, of course, he and his colleagues so lately in office, were aware of the necessity for compromise; of the complexity of the problems confronting Britain; perhaps, of the narrowness of the gap which divided the policies of the Tory Government from those of its Labour predecessor. Attlee understood very well that all governments have to respond to the pressures of external circumstances over which they have little or no control. External circumstances did not alter all that much. The options open to the British in the fifties were few indeed. The differences between the Parties had to be dreamt up by the politicians to keep the electorate interested. They did not, and could not, exist in the real world.

The history of the Bevanite movement may be briefly recorded. As already mentioned Bevan had resigned, along with Wilson and Freeman, as Minister of Health, in April 1951, on the issue of the imposition of charges for some of the services offered by the National Health Service. This, at any rate, was the ostensible issue. Certainly Mr. Bevan had personal reasons for feeling disgruntled with Mr. Attlee. He had twice been passed over for high office. Once in 1950, when the Chancellor of the Exchequer's office fell vacant, on the retirement of Sir Stafford Cripps: then Mr. Attlee chose Mr. Gaitskell. Then, in 1951, Mr. Attlee replaced Mr. Bevin by Mr. Morrison at the Foreign Office. When Labour was defeated at the General Election in October 1951, the old 'Keep Left' group in the Labour Party approached these three dissident ex-Ministers, and invited them to join up. The Bevanite group then set up as a party within a party. It held regular meetings; organized the Parliamentary actions of its members; and set out deliberately, as a group, to influence Party policy, and, when necessary, to flout it. The first serious clash with the Party leaders came on 5 March 1952, when fifty-seven Bevanites deliberately defied the Shadow Cabinet's policy on defence and voted against the Party line. A letter had been sent out by Mr. Attlee to every Labour M.P. telling him how he should vote and why. In brief, the policy of the Tory Government should be supported, but doubts should be cast on its ability to carry it out. The immediate consequence of the left wing revolt was the reimposition of the Standing Orders of the Parliamentary Labour Party, which had been suspended since 1945, giving power to the parliamentary committee of the Party to withdraw the whip for indiscipline, and expel a member if he defied the Party line in the Commons.

However, the rebels were encouraged by their success at the Party Conference at Morecambe in September 1952, when Bevanites gained six of the seven constituency seats on the National Executive Committee, and the veteran 'revisionists' Morrison and Dalton, both lost their places.[1] This was important in that, for the first time, the N.E.C. had a majority among its M.P.s whose views did not conform to those of the Parliamentary leaders. At this Conference, however, a vigorous attack on 'Bevanism' came from Arthur Deakin, the trade union leader, who asked 'those within the Party who set up a caucus, to realize that the ordinary rank and file party member or trade unionist has no time for their disregard of those principles and loyalties to which our movement has held so strongly through the whole course of its existence.' Encouraged by this support, Attlee and Morrison decided to order an end to organized groups in the Party, unless these were officially approved. At the election to the Deputy Leadership Morrison won 194 votes to Bevan's 82.

When Parliament reassembled in October 1952, Bevan was persuaded to disband his group and instead to stand for the annual election to the Shadow Cabinet.[2] He was the only one of his group to get in, and he got the twelfth and last place. Quarrelling continued throughout 1953. In September, at the Margate Party Conference, the six Bevanites kept their places on the N.E.C. In the subsequent Shadow Cabinet elections, Bevan moved up from the twelfth to the ninth place. In 1954 came the question of German rearmament, and of the formation of SEATO. It was on this last issue that Bevan resigned from the Shadow Cabinet. He was not prepared to go along with a defence organization in South East Asia designed, he thought, to prop up the colonialist French, and to underscore the rôle of America in encircling Communist China. Mr. Wilson, earlier one of his supporters, succeeded him in the Shadow Cabinet, a matter, of course, for sharp recrimination between rival factions on the left. The next big clash came in March 1955, when the annual White Paper on defence included the announcement that Britain was to embark on producing the hydrogen bomb. Attlee agreed to this; Bevan now outside the Shadow Cabinet, did not. Sixty-two Labour members followed him, and

[1] The Bevanites were: Messrs. Bevan, Driberg, Wilson, Mikardo, Crossman, and Mrs. Castle.

[2] The Shadow Cabinet, elected annually by the P.L.P., consists of eighteen members: six ex-officio, and twelve elected by those Labour M.P.s with seats in the Commons. The ins and outs at these elections reflect the patterns of Labour politics. The six ex-officio members are the Leader and Deputy Leader of the P.L.P.; the Chief Whip in the Commons; the Chief Whip in the Lords; the Leader of the Labour peers; and one elected representative of the Labour peers.

abstained from voting. The Bevanites saw rearmament as wrong in itself and also as a threat to the economy and to the standard of living of workers. The Party Whip was then withdrawn from him, and he came very close to expulsion from the Party itself.

These disagreements within the Labour Party were, of course, damaging in a general way to the Labour cause, if only because the struggle was conducted with malice and spite, and in full view of the public. The *Tribune* and the *New Statesman* reverberated, week after week, with the quarrelling. The leading Bevanite figures were Mr. Crossman, Mr. Mikardo (regarded by Morrison as the organizing brain behind the revolt), Mr. Wilson, Mr. Driberg and Mrs. Castle. It is difficult, however, to dismiss these disagreements as mere bickering, manoeuvring for position, futile disloyalty to the leadership, etc. Both in domestic affairs and on the foreign policy front, great issues were at stake, which went far beyond the clash of personalities involved. Attlee and his 'revisionists' wanted to stick to a moderate line, not very different from that of the Conservatives, perhaps because they thought it the only possible line, in practice, for any British government to take, and perhaps because they sensed that this was what an increasingly middle-class electorate wanted anyway. The Labour Party would simply not win again at the polls, they argued, if it offered a programme inspired by doctrinaire 'socialist' theories. The Bevanites, on the other hand, felt that the electorate should be educated to more enlightened views; and was not disposed to attach over-much importance to the stodgy old middle of the road floating voters who had voted the Party out of office in 1951.[1] The issues about which the Bevanites chose to fight were worth debating. There was at any rate an arguable case for a stouter resistance to American policies in the Far East; for refusing to go on participating in the nuclear armaments race; and for viewing with misgiving the rearmament of West Germany. Utopia had not yet been achieved on the domestic front. Perhaps criticism should be reserved for the methods of the Bevanites, rather than for the issues about which they felt so strongly.[2]

b *The Liberals*

The 1951 General Election and the years following it were the lowest point ever in Liberal fortunes. Only 109 candidates in all could be financed. The Liberals polled only a third of the votes they had polled

[1] He deplored 'the disposition to smooth away the edges of policy in the hope of making it more attractive to doubtful supporters. It is better to risk a clear and definite rejection [by the electors] than to win uneasy followers by dextrous ambiguities.' A. Bevan, *In Place of Fear*.

[2] See N. I. Gelman, 'Bevanism: A Philosophy for British Labour', *Journal of Politics*, 1954, and L. Hunter, 'The Road to Brighton Pier', *Journal of Politics*, 1959.

in 1950 and, apart from Mr. Grimond, only those Liberals not opposed by Conservatives kept their seats. Three seats were lost, and only six Liberal M.P.s were elected.

Churchill, perhaps for old times' sake, offered a Cabinet post to Clement Davies, the veteran Liberal Leader, though it is doubtful that Churchill felt any urgent need for Liberal support. He seems to have believed that the Liberals really ought now to join the Conservative Party. Clement Davies refused the offer, though he pledged Liberal support of the Government, as long as the measures introduced seemed in the Liberal view to be in the interests of the country. He preferred, however, to keep his little group separate. In 1952 Mr. Frank Byers urged the formation of a radical, non-socialist party, thus foreshadowing Mr. Grimond's later proposal. By 1954, improved Party organization brought signs of a revival. Party membership went up by 50 per cent. And, at the Inverness by-election in December 1954, the Liberal candidate came second.

Gradually the thought emerged that, if the Liberals kept their separate identity, they could, both in the country and at Westminster, achieve real influence over the two big Parties by throwing their support now on one side now on the other, as major issues of policy arose. The difficulty was, though, to develop a Liberal political creed, distinctively different from that of either of the major Parties. In the absence of this and of the necessary finance to develop an effective Party organization all over the country, the little Liberal group laboured under seemingly insurmountable difficulties.[1]

[1] See A. Watkins, *The Liberal Dilemma*.

CHAPTER TWO

The Conservative Government from May 1955 to October 1959

SUMMARY	*page*
1 The General Election of 25 May 1955	64
2 The Conservative Team	66
a The Prime Ministership of Sir Anthony Eden, April 1955–January 1957	66
b The Prime Ministership of Mr. Harold Macmillan, January 1957–October 1959	68
3 Constitutional and Administrative Issues	70
a The choice of a Prime Minister	70
b The Cabinet and Suez	71
c Mr. Nigel Nicholson and his constituents	72
d The House of Lords	73
e The Opposition and the Shadow Cabinet	74
4 Economic Issues	74
a General survey	74
b Summary of economic developments 1955–1959	75
c EFTA and the Common Market	77
5 Domestic Affairs	77
a The 1957 Rent Act	77
b The Homicide Act	78
6 Defence Policy	79
7 Foreign Policy	81
a General	81
b The Anglo-American relationship	82
c The Communist world	83
d Europe	83
e The Middle East: The Suez Crisis	86
8 The Commonwealth	94
a General considerations	94
b The Central African Federation	96
c Kenya	97
d Cyprus	98
e Malta	99
f The West Indies Federation	99
9 The Opposition	100

1 THE GENERAL ELECTION OF 25 MAY 1955[1]

Churchill resigned as Prime Minister on 5 April 1955. He declined the offer of an earldom and kept his seat in the Commons. Sir Anthony Eden, for so long the heir apparent, took over as Prime Minister. Barely a week later Sir Anthony announced that Parliament was to be dissolved. The polling date was fixed for May 25th. The circumstances were certainly propitious. The Government had not lost a single by-election since 1951, and it had gained one from Labour.[2] According to the opinion polls it was well thought of, and it had done well in the municipal elections in 1955. It was a quiet campaign and there were no outstanding issues. Meetings were small. Audiences seemed markedly detached, and this in spite of the fact that, for the first time since 1832, no seat was uncontested. Television was, for the first time, used extensively, which perhaps in part accounted for the fall in attendance at meetings. The Conservatives issued a Manifesto, 'United for Peace and Progress'. Eden wrote the preface, and stated categorically that he thought it right that Britain should manufacture the hydrogen bomb, and that it was good to know that the Opposition would support this. As he well knew, by no means all of the Opposition did so. Four days after the date of the Election was announced came the Conservative Budget, prepared by Mr. Butler. Sixpence came off income tax; allowances were increased; and purchase tax was removed from non-woollen textiles, in the interests of the Lancashire cotton industry. Much unfavourable comment was subsequently made about this 'Election Budget' especially after the autumn Budget of 1955. It seemed that Mr. Butler had been willing to take a risk in order to win the Election with, possibly, the thought at the back of his mind that the price could be paid later. But in May 1955 the economic trend was favourable, and it was arguable that the Budget merely underscored this, and, as it were, brought the favourable trend to the notice of the electorate. It was perhaps just bad luck that the good trend was so soon reversed.

The Prime Minister was not a man who enjoyed elections, as he himself admits.[3] Lord Woolton, still Chairman of the Party Organization, was aware of this. However, he arranged that Sir Anthony, presented, though now fifty-eight years of age, as 'this new young Prime Minister', should visit as many constituencies as possible.[4] And it seems that Eden's willingness to do this, and his obvious sincerity, did impress the electorate. Certainly the Conservative record was, by 1955, quite good. The world situation had become much less tense since Stalin's death in 1953. There

---

[1] See Nuffield Election Studies, D. E. Butler, *The British General Election of 1955*.
[2] Sunderland South, 13 May 1953.
[3] Eden, op. cit., p. 278. 'Politicians are of two categories, those who enjoy elections and those who endure them. I belong to the second category.'
[4] Woolton, op. cit., pp. 417-18.

was general demand, in both Parties, for high-level defence talks, not in a mood of desperation, but because it was thought that these might really have some chance of success. And the Conservatives made the necessary arrangements during the Election campaign, thus taking the wind out of their opponents' sails on this issue. It certainly seemed that the Conservatives were in a better position to face the world at the summit than the Labour Party, divided as it was on so many of the main issues of foreign policy. On the domestic side, there was a general sense of increasing well-being in so many of the small ways that matter greatly to ordinary people. The war was well and truly over, and it was nice to be done with the post-war austerities, associated in the public mind, however unfairly, with the Labour Party. Consumer goods of all kinds were pouring back into British homes.[1] And thanks, it seemed, to the Conservatives, there really were homes for them to pour into. England had a new young Queen, crowned in 1953. Everest had been conquered in the same year. The Ashes had been regained. Life for the man in the street was becoming pleasanter, easier and more relaxed. There seemed no good reason to change the recipe provided by the Conservatives.

The Labour Party's Manifesto was not inspiring. 'Forward with Labour' was the motto. But it was not at all clear in what direction the Labour Party would move, if at all. Bevanism showed it as deeply and publicly divided on all the main issues of the day, whether foreign or domestic. The fact was that 'socialism', once a rallying cry to the Labour movement, was now a source of internal dissension and external embarrassment.[2] Nationalization of sections of the chemical and machine tool industry, and re-nationalization of steel and road haulage were talked of. And, at any rate in the case of steel and road haulage, there was widespread Labour support, although this did not always come from the Party Leadership. The Party probably suffered in the eyes of the electorate because of its close links with the trade unions, under whose auspices there had been a newspaper strike, a dock strike and a threatened railway strike. The latter two had occurred during the Election period, and seemed to be a consequence merely of inter-union rivalries.[3] They had been the cause of considerable public inconvenience. Labour seemed to offer nothing that the Conservatives could not provide better. The Welfare State and a managed economy, with a public and a private sector were

---

[1] Cars. Number in private ownership in May 1951 = 2,288, 000
Cars. Number in private ownership in May 1955 = 3,309,000
Number of television sets owned in October 1951 = 1,031,095
Number of television sets owned in April 1955 = 4,580,725
Nuffield Election Studies, D. E. Butler, op. cit. (1955).

[2] L. Loewenburg, 'The Transformation of Labour Party Policy since 1945', *Journal of Politics*, 1959. See also R. T. Mackenzie, *British Political Parties*, 2nd edn., pp. 594–601.   [3] Pelling, op. cit., pp. 114–15.

now common ground with both Parties. As the *Daily Mirror* commented afterwards, Labour lost because its leaders still seemed to be too old, too tired and too weak; because the Labour leadership had been baffled, bewildered and finally betrayed by internal feuds; and perhaps most important of all, because the organization of the Party was rusty, inefficient and pathetically inferior to the new Tory machine. Labour, unlike the Tories from 1945 to 1951, had not made constructive use of its years in Opposition, and it had emerged with nothing new to say.

Be all that as it may, 1955 was certainly a quiet Election. In the end, the turn-out was 76.7 per cent, which was 5.7 per cent less than in 1951. The numbers of votes cast for the three main parties were:

	Votes	*Percentage of votes*	*Seats obtained*
Conservative	13,286,569	49.7	344
Labour	12,404,970	46.4	277
Liberal	722,405	2.7	6

The Tory team now inspired some confidence. The fear that voting Tory would mean a return to the bad old thirties had been finally allayed. The Labour team, by comparison, did not look promising. Yes to the Conservatives was much more emphatic than it had been in 1951. And, for the first time for a century, a Party was re-elected after four years in office, with an increased majority.

2 THE CONSERVATIVE TEAM

a *The Prime Ministership of Sir Anthony Eden, April 1955–January 1957*
As in 1951, though the team looked good at first sight, there was a major weakness not at once apparent. There can be little question that Sir Anthony Eden did not make a good Prime Minister. This perhaps ought to have been predictable. He had been heir apparent for too long. He had never had experience in any high office other than the Foreign Office. He was tense and nervous, and disliked opposition in the Commons. And, from the first, he was in poor health. He seems to have interfered constantly in other Ministers' departments.[1] Some of this was sensed by the electorate. Between the autumn of 1955 and the spring of 1956 the Gallup poll recorded that the percentage of the electorate approving of Eden as Prime Minister fell from 70 per cent to 40 per cent.[2] In the winter of 1955–6 there was a campaign in the press, including the Conservative *Daily Telegraph*, against him. And in January 1956 he had to

[1] Lord Butler refers to '... those innumerable telephone calls, on every day of the week and at every hour of the day, which characterized his conscientious but highly strung supervision of our affairs.' Butler, op. cit., p. 184.
[2] Bulmer-Thomas, op. cit., p. 224.

deny formally rumours that he was about to resign.[1] The weakness was not just on the domestic front, nor was it, as is so often supposed, connected with the Suez crisis. In March 1956, for instance, he made what was generally reckoned as a poor speech on the important issue of the dismissal of General Glubb, then the British power behind the throne in Jordan. In the summer, the Tonbridge by-election, at which the Conservative majority fell from 10,196 to 1,602 provided further evidence of the decrease in support. Popularity, in fact, began to slip away from Eden almost as soon as he took over from Churchill. From the standpoint of the Conservative Party it may have been a good thing that a combination of Suez and ill health brought Eden's term as Prime Minister to an early end.

The Conservative Cabinet, Eden apart, was a strong one. It was the old pack reshuffled of course, but the old pack was decidedly blue-chip. Initially Eden made few changes. Mr. Macmillan took his place at the Foreign Office.[2] Mr. Selwyn Lloyd became Minister of Defence, and the Earl of Home Secretary of State for Commonwealth Relations. In December 1955 there were further changes. Mr. Macmillan became Chancellor of the Exchequer,[3] and Mr. Selwyn Lloyd became Foreign Secretary. This latter appointment may have indicated that Sir Anthony wished, in fact, to be his own Foreign Minister and had found this difficult while Mr. Macmillan was at the Foreign Office. Mr. Butler became Lord Privy Seal, and Leader of the Commons. The most powerful members of the Eden team were Macmillan, Butler and Salisbury.

Sir Anthony Eden resigned after the Suez episode. There seems little doubt that the decision to resign was his own, and that the grounds were ill health.[4] He felt that he could no longer carry the burden of the Prime Ministership, in view of the increasing bouts of incapacitating fever, which were constantly made worse by the nervous strain of office. He did

---

[1] Lord Butler says: 'A flurry of ill-informed excitement in the Sunday papers at the beginning of January prompted him, I think unwisely, to cause a formal denial that he intended to resign to be issued from No. 10.' Butler, op. cit., p. 183.

[2] Lord Kilmuir thinks this appointment was a mistake from Sir Anthony's standpoint. 'The appointment of Macmillan to the Foreign Office ... was a major error of judgement. Macmillan was the last person likely to tolerate interference in the conduct of his department, and Eden should have foreseen that if he wished to retain his deep interest in, and control over, foreign policy, the appointment of a highly talented and individualistic man of Macmillan's capacity and intelligence was hardly the best manner in which to accomplish this. The situation remained difficult until, to everybody's relief, Macmillan left the Foreign Office to replace Butler at the Treasury in December.' Kilmuir, op. cit., pp. 243-4.

[3] Kilmuir, ibid., p. 256. 'He accepted the Treasury on the strict understanding that this was to be regarded as a step towards, and not away from, the Premiership.'   [4] Eden, op. cit., Vol. III, pp. 581-4.

not resign because he felt that he had made a major blunder over Suez; or because he felt increasingly the pressure of unpopularity. Nor did his colleagues wish him to resign. Indeed, they feared that his resignation at that moment might be interpreted abroad as an admission of guilt, and at home as weakness. They did not, it seems, feel guilty or weak. The Suez episode did not make Sir Anthony unpopular in the country. Indeed, opinion polls about that time indicated a sharp rise in his popularity. Be this as it may, his Prime Ministership was a disappointing interlude, damaging to the Conservatives in both their domestic and their foreign policies.

b *The Prime Ministership of Mr. Harold Macmillan, January 1957–October 1959*
The circumstances out of which Mr. Macmillan emerged as Prime Minister are full of interest. The method of selection to be used was far from clear. The two candidates were Mr. Macmillan and Mr. Butler.[1] Both were strong candidates. Mr. Butler had long been regarded as Eden's successor. He had presided over the Cabinet during Eden's absences abroad. He had been the architect of the new conservatism and had built up the policies of the Party during its years in opposition from 1945 to 1951. He was generally regarded as a very able Chancellor of the Exchequer; as a progressive, powerful and forward-looking personality; and as an agile politician. Some on the right wing of the Party may have felt that he was rather too progressive. Possibly some of these same men suspected that he was less than enthusiastic over Eden's Suez policy. But the real disadvantage was perhaps less tangible. He seemed to too many Conservatives to be rather a cold fish. There was a lack of warmth, and a deviousness which sometimes seemed to lead to indecision. It seems that those who came in contact with him did not really like him, although they respected his powerful, analytical mind. He did not attract support, as all politicians must, by whatever means. Mr. Macmillan was a different matter. He too had been, in his time, the architect of a new conservatism. And the progressives, who remembered his line in the later thirties as M.P. for Stockton,[2] and his post-war work at the Ministry of Housing, felt that he too, looked forward. In private life Mr. Macmillan was a publisher. He had had no governmental post until 1940 when he came into the Ministry of Supply. In the war, he had done well in important diplomatic posts in North Africa, Italy and Greece. The impact of Mr. Churchill on him was very great, and it was along Churchillian lines that he learnt to think of foreign affairs.

[1] Lord Salisbury could not be regarded as a candidate, as he was in the wrong House. The arrangement whereby peers could renounce their peerages had not yet been made.

[2] He had been M.P. for Stockton from 1924 to 1929 and again from 1931 to 1945.

In the 1945 landslide he had lost Stockton. But he won Bromley at a by-election in November 1945 and from this time on he had taken particular interest in industrial policies. As to foreign affairs, he shared Churchill's fear of Communist expansion, and Churchill's enthusiasm for the special relationship between Britain and America. (His mother was an American.) In 1951 he entered the Cabinet and, as Minister for Housing from 1951 to 1954, fulfilled the Conservatives' election promise to build 300,000 houses a year. From 1954 to 1955 he was Minister of Defence. Here he apparently resented Churchill's constant interference. In 1955 he became Foreign Secretary under Eden. From December 1955 till January 1957 he had been Chancellor of the Exchequer. He had thus had a varied and very successful Ministerial run-up before getting to the top.

Since the thirties, when he had come under the influence of Keynes, he had been an advocate of planning, and in particular of government spending to relieve unemployment, which was then, of course, regarded in Conservative circles as a very left wing and dubious solution to this intractable problem. In 1938 he had published a book entitled *The Middle Way* in which he recommended, among other things, the nationalization of the coal industry. G. D. H. Cole, reviewing it in the *New Statesman*, had commented: 'it has indeed a great deal in common with the actual policy which a Labour Government might be expected to pursue during its first years of office.' Unlike Mr. Butler it seemed likely that he would be able to carry both wings of the Party with him. He had, as it were, a double image: that of the progressive, and that of the aristocrat. Though of middle-class stock he liked to describe himself as a crofter's grandson. This was not strictly true, although his grandfather was a self-made man, brought up in poverty in Scotland. Mr. Macmillan liked to lay stress on his Scottish ancestry, and carried around with him a photograph of his grandfather's cottage. In fact he himself was brought up in England, and educated at Eton and Balliol. He had then joined the Grenadier Guards. He had married a daughter of the Duke of Devonshire, and he never made any bones about his enjoyment of the grouse moors. He had it both ways. And his warmth and wit and appearance of casual self-assurance seemed to make him a candidate likely to unite the Party, and help it to recover the self-esteem partly lost at Suez. He was a leader, it seemed, that men would like, trust and wish to follow.[1]

Macmillan's team was a rather different one from Eden's. It was not, this time, just a reshuffle of the old pack. Only five of the new Cabinet had served in the wartime coalition Government. Only five had been in the 1951-5 Cabinet.[2] Most of the Macmillan team were younger men who had entered Parliament since 1950. Mr. Butler, whose behaviour in defeat was exemplary, gave loyal service as Home Secretary.

[1] See Anthony Sampson: *Macmillan: A Study in Ambiguity*.
[2] Four, after Lord Salisbury's resignation in March 1957.

Mr. Thorneycroft was the new Chancellor of the Exchequer. Mr. Selwyn Lloyd remained as Foreign Secretary. This latter appointment suggested that Mr. Macmillan was not disposed to put on sackcloth and ashes over Suez, since Mr. Selwyn Lloyd had been Foreign Secretary at the time of the Suez episode.

Subsequent changes in the team were not of great importance. Lord Salisbury resigned in March 1957, in protest against the release from prison of Archbishop Makarios, whom he regarded as responsible for the unrest in Cyprus; and in January 1958 Mr. Thorneycroft, the Chancellor of the Exchequer, and Mr. Birch and Mr. Powell resigned over the Budget estimates.[1] Mr. Heathcoat Amory became Chancellor of the Exchequer. Mr. Macmillan, then embarking on a Commonwealth tour, shrugged off what he described as 'these little local difficulties'.[2] By 1959 he was firmly established in the eyes of the public, as unflappable, urbane, witty, perhaps a little presidential in style. He seems to have managed to be all this, and yet not to have interfered, as Eden had, in the departmental business of his Cabinet colleagues. Mr. Macmillan had, by 1959, become a very good Prime Minister indeed.

3 CONSTITUTIONAL AND ADMINISTRATIVE ISSUES

a *The choice of a Prime Minister*

In 1951 Mr. Churchill seems to have been accepted, without demur, as the natural and inevitable choice of the Conservatives. When he at length retired in 1955, Sir Anthony Eden seemed the obvious successor, and again, no one appears to have questioned this. In 1957, however, it was a very different matter. There could be no balking the fact that there were two candidates – Mr. Macmillan and Mr. Butler. And some one person or group of people had to decide between them. In the Labour Party this would have presented no problems, for the convention of having the Leader elected by the Parliamentary Party was well established. Further, it had been agreed that no politician should accept the Prime Ministership unless he had first been elected Leader of the Labour Party. No such convention existed for the Conservatives. In the past, the Leader had always 'evolved' – with or without the help of the Crown and the outgoing Prime Minister. But the right choice was a far from obvious one in 1957. The Queen – though then young and inexperienced – was, as before, asked to make soundings, and then to choose the Leader. The Queen asked Churchill and Salisbury for their advice, as elder statesmen.

[1] It was rumoured that Mr. Thorneycroft had wanted to introduce a measure of deflation, and that Mr. Macmillan and the rest of the Cabinet refused.

[2] 'I thought the best thing to do was to settle up these little local difficulties and then to turn to the wider vision of the Commonwealth.' Macmillan, *Memoirs*, Vol. IV, *Riding the Storm, 1956–1959*, p. 373.

It is not certain whether she also asked the opinion of the outgoing Prime Minister, Sir Anthony Eden.[1] In any event, it seems that these two asked the opinion of all the members of Eden's Cabinet. They also asked the Chief Whip, Mr. Heath, and the Chairman of the Party, Lord Poole, about back-bench and constituency views. They sought the views of members of the 1922 Committee of back-bench Conservative M.P.s. It seems that although most of the national press, and public opinion generally, had expected that Mr. Butler would succeed, the inner groups consulted overwhelmingly preferred Mr. Macmillan. After the Queen had duly 'chosen' him, the Party elected him as their Leader.

The disadvantages of this informal procedure were the subject of considerable comment at the time. Nothing, however, was done, possibly because most people felt that the circumstances of 1957 were highly unusual, and that in normal times it was likely that the choice would be obvious; possibly because many felt that the choice of a Conservative leader was by convention the prerogative of the Crown. Not until the retirement of Mr. Macmillan in 1963, and his famous hospital-bed efforts to find a new Leader, were the Conservatives finally persuaded of the necessity of finding a more democratic method of selecting the Leader of the Party.

b *The Cabinet and Suez*
The period of office of the 1955-9 Government saw some interesting developments in Cabinet government. The question as to what was now meant by collective responsibility was raised in an acute form by the Suez crisis. It could, of course, be argued that collective responsibility had always been a highly theoretical proposition. Prime Ministers had relied on it when this seemed convenient, and ignored it when it did not. Certainly, since the beginning of Churchill's reign, in 1940, the Prime Minister had either made important decisions by himself, or had relied on the support and counsel of a small inner group of Ministers. Mr. Attlee had followed Churchill's example, in the two post-war Labour Governments of 1945-50 and 1950-1. Mr. Churchill, from 1951 to 1953, had tried to formalize the inner group of Ministers on whom he relied, but without success. Eden's period of office, from 1955 to 1957, was another period of Prime Ministerial supremacy. No one was disposed to challenge these arrangements, on constitutional or any other grounds, as long as everything was going well. What distinguished the Suez episode, and led to a discussion of this issue, was that here a seemingly wilful failure

[1] Lord Kilmuir (op. cit., pp. 286-7) writes: 'I do not know for certain, but am fairly sure, that the advice of Sir Anthony Eden concerning his successor was not invited.' On the other hand, Mr. Robert Blake (*The Times*, 19 October 1963) writes: 'There is every reason to believe, although the contrary is sometimes alleged, that the outgoing Prime Minister's advice was asked.'

to consult the Cabinet as a whole, or even to keep them informed, was associated in the public mind with the pursuit of a mistaken policy. There was, for a time, a strong desire for a reassertion of the traditional doctrine of collective responsibility, as contrasted with the recent series of attempts to govern with small inner groups.

In a way, Suez perhaps provided a ray of hope for the critics, for the wilful Sir Anthony Eden had to resign. But it seems difficult to detect any change in approach on Mr. Macmillan's part from 1957 to 1959. Mr. Macmillan was an extremely able and dominating politician. At all the important occasions in these years, whether 'summit' meetings, conferences on economic affairs, or Commonwealth gatherings, 'Supermac' presided, unruffled, imperturbable, and very much in control. The Suez crisis, for all its traumatic qualities, did nothing to change the trend.

c *Mr. Nigel Nicolson and his constituents*

Another constitutional issue raised during the Suez crisis was the proper relationship between an M.P. and his constituency. Was he obliged to vote according to the wishes of his constituents, or had he the right to follow his own conscience?

In 1952 Mr. Nigel Nicolson had been elected M.P. for Bournemouth, in a by-election. Mr. Nicolson deplored the Government's action over Suez. He joined a group of dissident Tories in the 1922 Committee, and sent a letter to the Prime Minister. He made no public utterance until the military action was over. However, on November 8th he was one of the eight M.P.s who abstained in the vote of confidence. The Bournemouth Conservative Association, which strongly supported Sir Anthony Eden, duly passed a resolution condemning Mr. Nicolson for embarrassing the Government and misrepresenting his constituents. Thus began what turned out to be a two-year struggle between Mr. Nicolson and his local Conservative Party officials. Mr. Nicolson did not resign, nor was he deprived of the Whip. He argued that an important matter of principle had been raised by the local association, and that, if they had their way, the freedom of all M.P.s would be in jeopardy. He tried to enlist support at the Central Office. Mr. Macmillan refused to help him, on the grounds that it was against the Conservative tradition to intervene in matters at issue between a Member and his constituents. The Bournemouth Conservatives at length produced a very right wing alternative to Mr. Nicolson – one Major Friend. Eventually a postal ballot was organized in order to determine whether or not the Bournemouth Conservatives wanted to have Mr. Nicolson as their candidate at the next Election. Mr. Nicolson lost by 91 votes in a poll of 7,433.

Various conclusions could be drawn from this episode. Certainly one would seem to be that M.P.s, in spite of the growing strength of the central Party organizations, could only disregard the expressed wishes of their constituents at their peril. Another was perhaps that, anyway in the Conservative Party, the local organizations might be more prone to right wing views than was the Central Office. Others saw in this episode a strong bid on the part of constituencies to exercise some control over their M.P.s.[1] Yet others thought they saw the beginnings of a back-bench revolt against a Leadership which took so little account of back-bench views.

d *The House of Lords*
Another constitutional issue which came to the fore during the life of this government was the future role of the House of Lords. This issue had lain in the constitutional pending tray since 1911. Now it was brought out again, with a label 'action' attached to it. The business of government had increased very greatly since the end of the Second World War and Mr. Macmillan was less unwilling than most to try to use the Upper House to take some of the weight off the Commons.

Two institutional changes of importance were made in the lifetime of this Parliament. In 1957 peers who attended were allowed to claim three guineas a day for expenses. In 1958 the Life Peerage Act was passed, and in July of that year the first fourteen life peers were appointed, including three women.[2] The intention behind this Act was, no doubt, to introduce more liberal elements into the Upper House. But it seems likely that the change to a more progressive attitude in the House of Lords in fact antedated the introduction of this Act, the practical consequence of which was to enhance the administrative and Party usefulness of the Upper House, rather than to alter its Party balance. For the most part, the life peers fell into two groups – the eminent public figures, and the professional politicians. But it seems difficult to argue that these 'new men' were really responsible for any wind of change blowing through the Upper House, if only because there were too few of them.[3]

However, if the future rôle of the House of Lords was still uncertain, it was clearly not going to be content with tidying up pieces of legislation hastily passed by the House of Commons. Parliamentary draftsmen and civil servants could, and did, take care of this more readily, and more effectively. But it did seem that perhaps the House of Lords could begin to take over from the Commons certain areas of policy-making not directly related to Party policies. Possibly this was because the Lords since 1958 were somewhat more representative than the Commons of some of the élites on whose co-operation the Government depended.

[1] L. W. Martin: 'The Bournemouth Affair', *Journal of Politics*.
[2] See Bernard Crick, 'The Life Peerages Act, 1958', *Parliamentary Affairs*, 1957-8, Vol. II.
[3] J. R. Vincent, 'The House of Lords in the Macmillan Era', *Parliamentary Affairs*, 1966.

The House of Lords was also beginning to show itself as specially concerned with non-Party issues modifying or changing long accepted 'moral' traditions, for example about homosexuality, abortion, capital punishment, etc. Certainly the Upper House seemed to be moving in this direction in the life of the 1955–9 Government.

e *The Opposition and the Shadow Cabinet*
After 1955 it became the practice for the Opposition to allocate members of the Parliamentary Labour Party to specific shadow responsibilities – a practice subsequently adopted by the Conservatives too. It seemed that the election of a Parliamentary Committee or Shadow Cabinet by the Parliamentary Labour Party did not in practice greatly limit the freedom of the Party Leader to allocate front-bench duties as he wished, although it was sometimes alleged that the existence of this Committee inhibited a leader of the Labour Opposition in a way that his Conservative opposite number would not be inhibited. But there were twice as many 'responsibilities' as there were members of the Committee, so that in practice non-committee members were given front-bench duties. And promotion and demotion did not necessarily follow from a member's position on the Parliamentary Committee, which was elected annually.[1]

4 ECONOMIC ISSUES

a *General survey*
The years of the 1955–9 Government were considerably more difficult than the 1951–5 years had been. Then, ready explanations were to hand to account for what was going wrong. It could plausibly be argued that it was merely a matter of recovery after the long years of wartime shortages and, in the view of many, the mistakes of the Labour Government; of adjustment to the changes necessitated by the introduction of the Welfare State; of recovery from the damaging episode of the Korean war. None of these factors could really be held to account for the ups and downs of the economy from 1955 to 1959. Stop-go, in these years, began to look ominously like a permanent characteristic of the British economy. Although the magnitude of the problem was probably not yet appreciated, there was now beginning to be an uneasy suspicion that the real answers had not yet been found.

It was clear that there was also, and for whatever reasons, a change in the direction of Tory economic policy, away from *laissez-faire* liberalism,

[1] The Parliamentary Committee consisted of eighteen elected members: the Leader and his Deputy; the Chief Whip; the Leader of the Labour peers, the Labour Whip in the Lords, and one elected member of the Labour peers, plus twelve others. See R. M. Punnet 'The Labour Shadow Cabinet 1955–64' *Parliamentary Affairs*, 1964–5.

and towards active demand management, by means of fiscal and monetary policy. The debate was not on whether this should happen or not, but on how it should be effected. At this stage there was little understanding of how monetary policy was supposed to work. The appointment of the Radcliffe Committee on the working of the Monetary System is clear indication of these doubts.

The consensus of opinion now among most economists seems to be that Britain ought to have done better in this period. On the credit side there was still more or less full employment. But the overall growth rate was slow, at any rate as compared with many other countries in seemingly similar circumstances. Moreover economic development was bedevilled, on a scale hitherto unknown, by strikes. In 1957, for instance, the highest ever number was recorded, viz. 2,859. These involved the loss of 8,412,000 working days. They were, in part, a consequence of the earlier permissive attitude towards wage increases. Now, the bids for these increases got bigger. In these years it became gradually apparent that a halt would have to be called. The following criticisms were very generally voiced. There was long-term encouragement to invest. But there was a good deal of short-term discouragement, because of fear of inflation and of the possibility of an adverse balance of payments. The business world became hesitant, faced by confused directives and uncertainty about the prospect of steady growth. The Government's particular use of monetary policy, and forms of monetary control such as hire-purchase restrictions and manipulation of the Bank Rate, rather than the direct controls implicit in State management of the commanding heights of the economy, came under increasing fire. Chancellors seemed to seize on monetary policy as a heaven-sent alternative to much more unpopular budgetary policy. As Sir Robert Hall remarked: 'There is... a tendency to speak in magical rather than scientific terms of the use of interest rates and of monetary controls generally. The economy is to be given a potion, or dose, and wonderful results will follow.'[1] Monetary control was increasingly viewed as not effective, and the culmination of this criticism came with the publication of the Radcliffe Committee Report on the working of the Monetary System, in August 1959.[2] It was increasingly obvious that the balance of payments position was still insecure, in spite of the expansion in world trade, and in spite of favourable terms of trade, etc. No one seemed to have any clear idea as to the reasons for this; much less as to a possible solution.

b *Summary of economic developments 1955–1959*
There was, in 1955, a speculative run on sterling, apparently because of rumours during the summer that sterling was to be made fully convertible, with a floating exchange rate. These rumours were denied by

[1] *Economic Journal*, 1959, p. 648.   [2] Cmnd. 827.

the Chancellor of the Exchequer, Mr. Butler, speaking before the International Monetary Fund.

There was a credit squeeze between the summer of 1955 and the winter of 1957. This period saw the end of Tory liberalism under Mr. Macmillan and Sir Edward Boyle, at the Treasury. The aim was now very definitiely to cut back home demand, so that inflation could be stopped, and so that industrialists could concentrate on the export market. There was an autumn Budget in 1955, which came to be known as the 'pots and pans Budget'. And in 1956 there was an early Budget in February, which, among other things, stiffened hire-purchase controls.

The effect of the Suez crisis at the end of 1956 on the domestic economy was surprisingly slight, in spite of the temporary oil shortage. The most striking effect was a flight from sterling, and an I.M.F. loan was necessary to replenish reserves. This was the first time that the I.M.F. stepped in affirmatively, to prevent a sterling crisis.

The summer of 1957 saw a further run on sterling reserves, which fell by £200m. between June and September. The reasons behind this crisis in confidence are unclear. The balance of payments was good, and the domestic economy seems to have been running all right. Among explanations that have been proffered are:

(1) that it was caused by the large wage increases that had taken place in the spring of 1957. This seems to have been the view of the Government;
(2) that it was caused by movements of capital by foreign bankers speculating on the undervalued deutsche mark.

In any event the Government took action and, in September 1957, the Bank Rate was raised to 7 per cent, and other restrictions in investment were introduced. This was the Thorneycroft period of reliance on monetary policies.

In January 1958 Mr. Thorneycroft, Mr. Birch and Mr. Powell resigned, Mr. Thorneycroft being replaced as Chancellor of the Exchequer by Mr. Heathcoat Amory. It was said that the reasons for these resignations was that Mr. Thorneycroft had demanded in the Cabinet that the Budget estimates for 1958–9 should not exceed those of 1957–8. He wished to make price stability the first aim of policy and maintain the current parity of sterling; and, in order to achieve this aim, was ready to envisage sharp deflation. Mr. Macmillan was not.

As 1958 went on stagnation moved into a recessionary phase. There were signs of recession, and there was a marked increase in unemployment. The credit squeeze began to be eased. And, at the end of 1958, the Bank Rate was lowered to 4 per cent.

The 1959 Budget was decidedly expansionist. There was a reduction of 9*d* in the standard rate of income tax. Production expanded rapidly.

Mr. Macmillan became known as 'The Prime Minister of Affluence' and he was able to advise, with some justification, 'You're having it good. Have it better. Vote Conservative.'[1]

c EFTA and the Common Market

It may be convenient to discuss briefly what might be termed economic foreign policy under the general heading of EFTA and the Common Market.

In 1957, a year in which Franco-British relations were a good deal less than cordial, as a result of the Suez débâcle, the Treaty of Rome was signed by the six major European countries,[2] providing for a common market in goods. This was intended, by some at any rate, as a step towards political unification. Britain was, for a variety of reasons, opposed to the Common Market idea, but she did want a wider free trade area in manufactured goods, to include all the O.E.E.C. (Marshall Aid) countries in Western Europe. Negotiations were opened with the Common Market countries early in 1957 and they continued, under Mr. Maudling's auspices, until November 1958 when they broke down, largely as a result of French opposition. Britain then began to build up a rival organization, which became known as the European Free Trade Area. The EFTA countries were Britain, Norway, Sweden, Denmark, Austria, Portugal and Switzerland. The intention was that this should be a temporary arrangement, to keep the seven countries together, while they were negotiating with the Six. EFTA was, however, not a particularly good bargaining tool, as there was relatively little trade between the E.E.C. and the EFTA countries. The EFTA organization had no supranational overtones, and the EFTA countries retained their autonomy vis-à-vis the outside world. This meant that Britain's Commonwealth Preference arrangements were not affected. The economic arrangement was, however, of limited value to Britain, as there were no powerful industries in the EFTA countries which could provide a competitive thrust to British industry, and the population of the EFTA group was only roughly half that of the Common Market group. However, as a result of EFTA, the valuable Scandinavian market did become more readily accessible to British goods.

5 DOMESTIC AFFAIRS

a The 1957 Rent Act

One of the most important, and most controversial, pieces of legislation

---

[1] See Nuffield Election Studies, D. E. Butler and R. Rose, *The British General Election of 1959*, p. 22.

[2] France, Germany, Italy, Belgium, the Netherlands and Luxembourg.

passed by this government was the Rent Act of 1957, introduced by Mr. Henry Brooks, Minister of Housing. This Act removed 810,000 houses from rent control, and allowed for rent increases for the 4.3 million still controlled. Much heat and fury was expended by the Labour Party in attacking this Act, which, it alleged, was a 'landlord's charter' directly contrary to the interests of the working population. The Government, on the other hand, argued that the fact that rents had been held to the 1939 level had meant that millions of houses had fallen into disrepair, since landlords, unable to raise rents, had had no incentive to maintain, much less improve, their properties. Thus an ever-increasing number of existing houses became unfit to live in. Since the end of the First World War there had been, more or less continuously, a shortage of cheap housing. Both political parties had found that willingness to put capital into their construction was a first-class electoral asset but an economic liability, in that capital so used provided no direct return. While there was an absolute shortage of housing in the country, some diversion of capital resources could be defended. But by 1955, the Conservatives argued, this was no longer the case. If old houses were kept in repair and fully used there would no longer be any shortage. But there was in the 1957 Act no compulsion on the landlord to spend the increased rent on the upkeep of his property.

Be this as it may, it seems that there was no spectacular rise in rents after 1957. Most controlled houses were still let at less than £1 a week, and one quarter at less than 10s.[1]

But there can be little doubt that, in spite of all the Tory arguments, the Act was a very unpopular one.

b *The Homicide Act 1957*
The attitude of the public towards capital punishment had been slowly changing, since the end of the First World War, and in the twenties and thirties various small pressure groups had worked, to no avail, for its abolition. In 1947-8 a more formal attempt to get abolition on to the Labour Party programme failed. In the early fifties, however, a variety of events combined to change the attitudes of many politicians and of the educated public. In 1953 came the Report of the Royal Commission on Capital Punishment,[2] which had been set up in 1949 to consider not its abolition, but its limitation. But the Report implied serious doubts about the merits of capital punishment at all. And in 1954 the chairman, Sir Edward Gowers, announced his conversion to abolition. Public opinion about this time was roused by three sensational murder trials (Bentley; Evans and Christie; and Mrs. Ruth Ellis). All of these ended in hanging;

[1] See A. J. Youngson, op. cit., pp. 222-4, and H.C. Deb., Fifth Series, Vol. 567, cols. 1362-478, 28 March 1957, for third reading debate.
[2] Cmnd. 8932.

and in all of them there was suspicion either of a miscarriage of justice or of undue severity. There then emerged a new pressure group, well financed, and led by Victor Gollancz and Arthur Koestler, known as the National Campaign for the Abolition of Capital Punishment. Public opinion polls, from then on, began to show a trend away from support for hanging.[1] It became evident that there was now a group of Tory backbenchers who also belonged to the abolitionists' group. In the autumn of 1955, Sydney Silverman, a Labour M.P., introduced a Bill to suspend capital punishment, but it only got as far as a first reading. To assuage its own back-benchers, the Tory Government then brought in a Bill which retained the death penalty, but modified the law of murder. The abolitionists then moved an amendment to suspend the death penalty for five years. The Government wanted this amendment to fail and therefore allowed a free vote. However, 48 Tories voted for it, and the amendment passed by 293 votes to 262. Finally, the Government gave Silverman's Bill facilities and Government time. A free vote was allowed at all stages, and, in July 1956 the Bill was passed by the Commons. It was rejected by the Lords. There were then two courses open to the Government: either to invoke the Parliament Act, and give Mr. Silverman facilities to reintroduce his Bill; or to bring in a Government Bill, retaining hanging but amending the law of murder. The second alternative was adopted, it seems because the Government felt that it was undesirable that a coalition of back-benchers should make the running in important social issues. So, during the summer recess, a Government Bill was drafted which made concessions towards the abolitionists, but still retained the death penalty. In March 1957 the Homicide Act became law.[2]

6 DEFENCE POLICY

In the life of this Government, the issue of nuclear defence versus defence by conventional weapons became, perhaps for the first time, a matter of general and public concern.

Defence by nuclear weapons was not a new policy. The nuclear road had first been trod by Mr. Attlee, in the Labour years in the forties. It was under his auspices that the Atomic Research Centre had been established at Harwell in 1945. And his Government had decided, in 1947, to manufacture British atom bombs, and build a fleet of V bombers to carry them. Britain's first atom bomb had been tested in 1952.

In March 1955, Churchill had announced the Conservative Government's decision to manufacture a British hydrogen bomb.[3] He thought

[1] J. B. Christoph: 'Capital Punishment and British Party Responsibility', *Political Science Quarterly*, 1962.
[2] See *Annual Register, 1957*, p. 500, for the main provisions of this Act.
[3] H.C. Deb., Fifth Series, Vol. 537, col. 1905, 1 March 1955. See also R.

that only by manufacturing a British H bomb would Britain establish enough equality in the Anglo-American partnership to be entrusted again with American scientific secrets, from which Britain had been excluded by the MacMahon Act of 1946. The first British hydrogen bomb was tested in 1957, five years after the United States had tested theirs. And in 1958 the MacMahon Act was amended, to allow disclosures about atomic weapons to countries which had already achieved substantial atomic weapon technology.

So far so good. But the development of an independent British deterrent did, of course, involve costly duplication of American effort, which Britain in the fifties could ill afford.

The arguments in favour of an independent British deterrent were various. It was feared by many people, in both the Conservative and Labour Parties, that the United States might not be willing to use her atomic weapons to attack Russian bases, if only Europe was threatened. Once the U.S.S.R. had developed the means of attacking the United States, the United States would not risk a nuclear reprisal. As long as there were American forces in Europe, and American bombers in Britain, all might be well. But who could tell how long this would be? With the development of intercontinental ballistic missiles, a new mood of isolation might sweep over the United States. Britain and Europe might then be left in the lurch.

At this time Britain was not contemplating the development of a close defence relationship with the European states. So the question at issue was simply a British independent deterrent, to ensure the safety of targets vital to the survival of Britain.

There were other arguments, too. To have the bombs was the only way, it was thought, for a small, but advanced nation to retain Great Power status. And without this status Britain could not use her influence to keep the peace. As Mr. John Strachey, Labour M.P., said in the House of Commons on 17 April 1957, the question was whether Britain had 'the will and the nerve to preserve itself and its enormous influence for good in the world.'[1]

These kinds of arguments were palatable to many Labour M.P.s because it had always been felt that out-and-out dependence on the United States, a right wing capitalist power if ever there was one, was very undesirable. Thus, Mr. Gaitskell had argued in the House, on 1 April 1957: 'Our party decided to support the manufacture of the hydrogen bomb ... because we did not think it right that this country should be so dependent ... upon the U.S.A.'[2]

Gott, 'The Evolution of the Independent British Deterrent', *International Affairs*, 1963. [1] H.C. Deb., Fifth Series, Vol. 568, col. 2036, 17 April 1957. [2] H.C. Deb., Fifth Series, Vol. 568, col. 71, 1 April 1957.

Mr. Noel-Baker, at the autumn Labour Party Conference in 1957, said: 'Unilateral disarmament would mean surrendering Britain's influence in the struggle to demilitarize the world.' Even Mr. Aneurin Bevan, the leader of the left in the Labour Party, said at this same Conference, that unilateral nuclear disarmament would send a British negotiator 'naked into the Conference Chamber'. Only if Britain herself had the bomb could she press effectively for world nuclear disarmament. She could, as a third force, exercise a moderating influence on both the United States and the U.S.S.R. The belief in Britain's mission in the world was very strong; and it was certainly not confined to Conservative circles.[1]

The Defence White Paper of 1957 gave what was perhaps the first indication that some costing of all this was going on. The defence budget was to be reduced, it was now said, by concentrating British resources on nuclear weapons, and cutting back on conventional forces. Thus, the British commitment to NATO was reduced; and it was announced that National Service would end in 1960. The British were served notice that they could not have it both ways. The Government had had, in effect, to choose between the nuclear and the conventional methods of defence, and it had chosen the former.

Gradually, opposition began to build up. The Campaign for Nuclear Disarmament (C.N.D.) and the Aldermaston marches started in 1958, for instance. On the whole, however, the policy of the independent British nuclear deterrent can really be described as bipartisan in these years. And neither the Conservative Party nor the Labour Party seems to have had much inkling that, all other considerations apart, on economic grounds alone the policy might be impossible to sustain, even if conventional defences were cut back. Still, the 1957 White Paper did indicate that the process of costing was beginning.[2]

7 FOREIGN POLICY

a *General survey*

If the costing was beginning in defence matters, it does not seem to have been taken much into account where issues of foreign policy were concerned. After the Suez episode of 1956–7 it was, it is true, generally accepted that independent international action by Britain would not in future be feasible. But the fact that this limitation stemmed from economic decline does not seem to have been understood. The assumption, noted in the previous chapter, that Britain must maintain her Great Power status was, if anything, even more strongly held in the life of this

[1] See L. D. Epstein, 'Britain and the H Bomb', *Review of Politics*, 1959.
[2] See F. S. Northedge, op. cit.; Eden, op. cit., Vol. III; K. Younger, *Changing Perspectives in British Foreign Policy*.

Government than it had been in the years from 1951 to 1955. Mr. Macmillan, who succeeded Sir Anthony Eden as Prime Minister in 1957, clearly still thought of Britain as one of the great powers.

b *The Anglo-American relationship*
The Suez episode was the big issue, in these years. This will be discussed under the heading of the Middle East. But it may be noted that the Anglo-American relationship probably would have been uneasy even if the Suez crisis had never occurred. As I have said, Mr. John Foster Dulles, President Eisenhower's Secretary of State, and Sir Anthony Eden were as oil and water. And because of this Eden's relationship with Eisenhower was cool, too, for Eisenhower relied greatly on Dulles. Dulles found Eden too clever by half; and Eden found Dulles devious, pompous and self-righteous. It seemed to the British that the United States was obsessed by the fear of Communism, but was unwilling to take the necessary steps to check the Russians. Thus, for instance, the United States refused to accede to the Baghdad Pact, which was intended as the northern tier of defence for the Middle East against the U.S.S.R., although fully supporting the principles which lay behind it.[1] Britain was concerned less with the ideology of Communism, about which she was much less fearful than the Americans, than with practical problems relating to the lessening of tensions in Europe which might avert the danger of Russian aggression. Thus, throughout this five-year period, Britain was more ready than in the past to contemplate rearrangements in Europe likely to lead to a *détente* with the U.S.S.R. But she was still not disposed to go into Europe and take the lead in building up a European power bloc, as the United States seems to have wished.

American policies in the Far East continued to give cause for anxiety in Britain. In 1958, for instance, the Chinese Government in Peking began to indicate its intention to take over the tiny off-shore islands of Quemoy and Matsu, which lay between Formosa and the mainland, and which were still held by the Formosan Chinese Nationalists. The United States

[1] See Eden, op. cit., Vol. II, p. 336. 'In recent years the United States has sometimes failed to put its weight behind its friends, in the hope of being popular with her foes.'

A Treaty had been concluded between Iraq and Turkey in February 1955, which was open for accession to any member state of the Arab League, or any state concerned with the peace and security of the Middle East. The U.K., Pakistan and Iran acceded in 1955. In 1957 U.S. representatives became members of the economic and military committees, although the U.S.A. did not accede to the pact. Iraq ceased to take part in arrangements relating to the pact, after its revolution in 1958, and formally withdrew in March 1959. In August 1959 the organization and its headquarters were established in Ankara.

immediately threw a protective cover over these little islands, and, for a time, it looked as if this might be a *casus belli*.[1] It would have been one wholly unacceptable to British public opinion. The British, unlike the Americans, had given formal recognition to the Peking Government in 1949 and were now most reluctant to become embroiled in American attempts to bolster the Formosan Government-in-exile of Chiang Kai-shek. However, the Communist claims were dropped, and the crisis passed. But it was generally and uneasily felt in Britain that American policies in Asia were unwise and not in accord with British interests.

c *The Communist world*
British efforts to achieve a *détente* with the U.S.S.R. gathered strength, and there was some easing of tensions. Britain was very anxious to negotiate, despite American misgivings. Mr. Macmillan, who, after he became Prime Minister in 1957, was virtually his own Foreign Secretary, saw himself, as Mr. Churchill and Sir Anthony Eden had before him, as the mediator between East and West. And Moscow, now, seemed anxious to talk.

In July 1955 a summit conference was held at Geneva, which unfortunately achieved little.[2] It was followed by a Foreign Ministers' conference in November 1955. In April of 1956 Mr. Bulganin and Mr. Krushchev visited the United Kingdom and some useful talks took place. It was hoped that these might prove to be the beginning of closer and more normal diplomatic links between the two countries.

In November 1956 there was a sharp decline in cordiality because of the Soviet take-over in Hungary and because of Russian policy at the time of Suez. And in 1958 the second Berlin crisis drove a further wedge between the two countries. However, in 1959 Mr. Macmillan visited Moscow and despite the failure to reach agreement on Germany some progress was made.[3] In the summer of 1959 there was another Foreign Ministers' conference at Geneva.

The British Government's effort was, from first to last, to relax tensions, thus enabling East and West to co-exist peacefully. Moscow, too, seemed to wish this.

One of the few tangible achievements in the life of this Government, as far as relationships with the Communist world went, came in May 1955, with the signing of the Austrian Peace Treaty.[4]

d *Europe*
The possibility of relaxing tensions between East and West depended

[1] See Wilfrid Knapp, *A History of War and Peace 1939–1965*, pp. 242–3.
[2] Eden, op. cit., Vol. III, Book II, Chs. 3 and 4.
[3] Sampson, op. cit., Ch. 9.
[4] Eden, op. cit., Vol. III, Book III, pp. 289–96.

very largely, in these years, on finding some solution to the German problem. For Britain, as for France and the other European states, this was a very delicate matter. The increasing wealth and stability of the new West German federal state[1] was essential to the NATO alliance, and to any future Western European grouping. But the Russians viewed the emergence of a strong West Germany with the utmost misgiving. There were other cross-currents here. In the near future West Germany was clearly going to become a formidable trade rival for Britain. And one of the reasons why West Germany was able to compete against Britain so successfully was thought by many to be that she was not much burdened by the need to provide for her own defence, since Allied troops took care of most of this. It seemed an unfair advantage. But to require West Germany to defend her own frontier unaided would have meant permitting large-scale German rearmament. And this would have immediately re-awakened the worst Russian fears, to say nothing of those of the French.[2]

There were other difficulties too. The West Germans, understandably, wanted first and foremost the reunification of their country. Hence East Germany was a pawn of first-class importance in the hands of the U.S.S.R. In Western eyes the danger was that West Germany might be detached from Western Europe by the bait of unification with East Germany, under more or less overt Communist auspices.

Britain was an uncompromising opponent of a united Germany after the Second World War, fearing that this would enable Germany again to play off West against East, and thus regain her old and terrible power. This fear seems to have been, if anything, more strongly held in Labour circles than among the Conservatives. In Labour eyes, the Germans had been Nazis during the war. Now they had turned into right wing capitalists; and very successful ones at that. The practical demonstration of the profitability of capitalism was naturally disconcerting to the Labour Party. Equally disconcerting was the fact that West Germany was generally seen as the protégé of the United States.

On the other hand, in the American view, the West Europeans would never be able to stand on their own feet, *vis-à-vis* the Communist world, without the West Germans, with their great wealth of raw materials and skilled manpower. Anyway, it was easier for the Americans to get on with the West Germans than with the French. Americans resented what they regarded as ridiculous French pretensions to 'Great Power' status. And wartime recollections of their troubles with the arrogant young

---

[1] The German Federal Republic was formally recognized as an independent sovereign state by the allies in 1954.

[2] See Hans von Herwerth, 'A German View', *International Affairs*, 1963. (Hans von Herwerth was the German Ambassador in London from 1955 to 1961.)

Capitaine de Gaulle remained vividly in the minds of many. Thus, in the American view, West Germany must be built up large, as the cornerstone of the new Europe.

The Germans were glad to co-operate with the Americans, and willing enough to be a corner-stone in the Western alliance. But naturally they did not wish to eliminate the possibility of reunification with East Germany. And they were always fearful lest their American and European allies might force them to do just this. And of course the Americans and their allies were always apprehensive lest a disgruntled West Germany might in the end turn again to the East.

It thus came about that Germany and the problem of German reunification was a major obstacle in the way of an East–West *détente*. And it sometimes seemed to the British that West Germany was the one European country which wanted to maintain the Cold War indefinitely. In the face of this dilemma the British Government was inclined to favour some kind of disengagement for the whole area of central Europe. The Warsaw Pact powers and the NATO powers might both withdraw, in some measure it was felt, from central Europe. In October 1957, Rapacki, the Polish Foreign Minister, suggested at the General Assembly that an atom-free zone might be created in Germany and Poland. Unfortunately these efforts were complicated both by the virulent anti-Communist crusade waged by Senator McCarthy in the United States and by Britain's very strained relations with the French after Suez. In any case, the French were less dependent on Britain, and hence less ready to listen to her advice, after 1958, when West Germany entered into a close relationship with France, and the era of friendship between Presidents Adenauer and de Gaulle began. West Germany was less than enthusiastic about disengagement. She feared that this would lessen the chance of German reunification. She was also fearful on security grounds. However, in 1957 the Berlin Declaration, made by the United States, Britain, France and West Germany, officially adopted disengagement as a policy, although it was coupled with the idea of German reunification by free elections. But the very next year came the Berlin crisis, triggered off by a Soviet note in November 1958 threatening to hand over Russian-held East Berlin to East Germany, unless West Berlin was made a Free City, and Western troops were withdrawn from it.

The existing British relationship with Europe was of course wholly changed by the Treaty of Rome, signed in 1957 by the six E.E.C. countries.[1] This treaty involved, for the Europeans, formal economic obligations and, it then seemed, a progressive merging of sovereignty. Britain was not prepared to join, for a variety of reasons. But she recognized that a formidable economic bloc had been set up, which would further limit her future exploitation of European markets. She recognized,

[1] See p. 77, footnote 2.

too, that a political bloc was in the making, and that the United States, so much concerned with the issue of European solidarity, might come to prefer this bloc to Britain.[1]

e *The Middle East: the Suez Crisis*[2]

The Middle East was an unquiet area in these years. The Russians and their satellites were showing an increasing interest in it. Britain was in process of withdrawing from it. She had agreed, under the terms of the 1954 Anglo-Egyptian Treaty, to evacuate the Suez Canal Zone and give up the British military base there. In return, Nasser had agreed to uphold the 1888 Constantinople Convention which recognized the right of the Suez Canal Company to operate the Canal until the expiry of the concession in 1968. Britain was the largest single user of the Canal, and British shipping accounted for 28 per cent of the ever-increasing tonnage passing through it. Three-quarters of the ships passing through the Canal belonged to NATO. Britain held 44 per cent of the shares of this great international company.

Nasser, though certainly not a Communist, conceived a general mistrust of British policy in the area, and in particular of the defence agreement known as the Baghdad Pact, to which Iraq, Turkey, Britain, Pakistan and Iran belonged. He saw this pact as a British attempt to re-establish political hegemony, and was unimpressed by the British view that a 'northern tier' of defence against Communism was desirable. On the contrary, he was quite ready to take arms and economic aid from Soviet or Soviet controlled states, as well as from Western sources.

The Suez crisis began, in a sense, in 1954 when Colonel Nasser, who had aspirations to leadership in the Arab world, had taken over from Colonel Neguib. Under his influence, so it was thought by Sir Anthony Eden, the young King Hussein of Jordan in March 1956 dismissed Colonel Glubb from his position as adviser and mentor to Jordan.[3] This was a direct blow to Britain's influence in the Arab world, and one which caused Eden great concern. Nasser offered to replace the British subsidy to Jordan (£6om. per annum) with one from Egypt, Syria and Saudi Arabia. But Eden knew that if anyone was going to pay, it would be the U.S.S.R. Eden made one of his less successful speeches in the House on this occasion. It was duly noted as a sign that he was slipping.

It also happened that there was at that time some difficulty with Egypt over the project for building the Aswan dam, an ambitious scheme to

---

[1] See Younger, op. cit.
[2] See F. S. Northedge, op. cit., pp. 218–41; Eden, op. cit.; A. Nutting, *No End of a Lesson: The Story of Suez*; L. Epstein, 'Partisanship in the Suez Crisis', *Studies in British Politics*, ed. Richard Rose; T. Robertson, *British Crisis: The Inside Story of the Suez Conspiracy*; H. Thomas, *The Suez Affair*.
[3] Eden, op. cit., Vol. III, p. 348.

improve the irrigation of the Nile Valley, and develop hydro-electricity. Britain, France, Germany, the United States and the World Bank were all involved. The total cost, over a period of sixteen years, was estimated at about $1,300m. The terms suggested for the loan were not entirely acceptable to Egypt, especially as the U.S.S.R. began to make overtures for the contract on easier terms. Britain and the United States were doubtful for other reasons. Nasser had shown clearly that he was no friend to the West, and this dam, which would be of immense economic value to Egypt, would eventually put her at the head of all the Arab states. Other Arab states friendly to the West wondered why help on such a massive scale should be given to Egypt. And increasingly, the Foreign Office and the State Department began to wonder too, and became doubtful of the wisdom, on economic as well as on political grounds, of this large undertaking. On July 19th, Mr. Dulles, with an uneasy and half isolationist Congress behind him, abruptly withdrew the American part of the offer; and as a result of this decision the loan from the World Bank was also cancelled, for the two transactions were linked. The British were informed, but not consulted. Within a few days they, perforce, followed suit. Thus began the Suez crisis. It seems that the Americans had little or no idea of the political crisis that their action would precipitate.

On July 26th Nasser responded to the withdrawal of the loan by nationalizing the Suez Canal. He hoped, he said, to use the Canal dues in place of the loan. This move had probably been planned for some time, to gain prestige in the Arab world, and the Aswan dam issue very likely merely provided the necessary excuse. The Suez Canal was a long-established and very important international waterway, and this was a unilateral attempt to take it over. In early August British and French troops were mobilized, in case armed intervention should be required. The French were, of course, shareholders in the Canal; and they had, or thought they had, an interest in toppling Nasser because Nasser was, in their eyes, the power behind the revolt of the Arabs in French Algeria.

Throughout August and September various attempts were made at the international level to negotiate with Nasser for the re-establishment of some kind of international control of the canal, and a Suez Canal Users Association (S.C.U.A.) was set up. By the middle of October, Nasser seemed ready to make some concessions. However, on October 29th Israel invaded Egypt, hoping, presumably, to strike at a moment when Egypt was in hot water with Britain and the United States. Unrest between Egypt and Israel was, of course, endemic. On October 30th the British and French, as the powers mainly concerned for the safety of the Canal, sent an ultimatum to both the Egyptians and the Israelis, to withdraw ten miles from the Canal. On October 31st Nasser refused to comply with this, and in consequence Alexandria and the Egyptian airfields were bombed by the British. A Franco-British force sailed from Malta and landed at Port Said on November 5th. The United Nations Security Council condemned this action as aggression, and, led by Mr. Dulles, called for a cease fire. On November 8th the Franco-British force withdrew, and a U.N. emergency force moved in.

The above is, in brief outline, the record of what, indisputably, happened. Since Suez meant, both at the time and afterwards, so many different things to so many different people, it may be useful to analyse some of the issues further.

In the first place, why did Eden mount the attack on Suez at all? Sir Anthony said that he thought it essential to separate the Israeli and Egyptian troops if a major war in the Middle East was to be averted. The United Nations might, he accepted, have been a more suitable law enforcement agency. But the U.N. had not troops in the area and was not prepared, whereas the British and the French had troops readily available, and were prepared. His first object was to keep the Canal open. He had not inconsiderable sympathy with the Israelis,[1] and he disliked Nasser very much, as a latter-day Hitler. It seems that Mr. Gaitskell, too, had this view of Nasser. Thus, speaking in the House of Commons on 2 August 1956, Mr. Gaitskell had said 'It is all very familiar. It is exactly the same that we encountered from Mussolini and Hitler in those years before the war.'[2] Mr. Gaitskell gave, in this August debate, his reasons for opposition to Nasser: that the Canal was a major international waterway, and that it was therefore undesirable that it should be in the hands of one state; that the manner of the nationalization, without warning, negotiation, or discussion made it quite unacceptable to the international community; and that it appeared to be part of Nasser's struggle for mastery in the Middle East. As to the use of force, Mr. Gaitskell went on to say 'There has been much talk in the press about the use of force in these circumstances. . . . Obviously there are circumstances in which we might be compelled to use force in self-defence or as a part of some collective measures.' He did say, however, that he thought it would be very important for Britain to act in accordance with the U.N. Charter, and with the approval of the Security Council and the Assembly. Thus Middle Eastern foreign policy seemed to be, in August 1956, and after the Egyptian seizure of the Canal, remarkably bipartisan. Mr. Dulles, too, was talking big, in August, to the effect that Nasser should be forced

[1] Eden, op. cit., Vol. III, p. 523. 'I thought then, and I think now, that the Israelis had justification for their action. It is at least a grim possibility that they would not be a free nation today had they not taken it. The marked victim of a garotter is not to be condemned if he strikes out before the noose is round his throat.'

[2] H.C. Deb., Fifth Series, Vol. 557, col. 1613 et seq., 2 August 1956.

to disgorge the Canal, etc.[1] He also feared that Nasser was part of a Russian plot to take over the Middle East. However, whatever his sympathies, it seems that Dulles intended merely to hold Egypt and Israel apart. It seems likely that Eden really wanted, in any case, to take military action against Egypt, after the nationalization of the Canal and that the Israel-Egypt war merely provided him with the necessary pretext. He had learned, he thought, the lessons from the thirties regarding appeasement. This time the tyrant must be stopped in his tracks, before it was too late. Eden was particularly sensitive about the Canal Zone because of the criticism which had come from the 'Suez Group' Conservatives in 1954, when he had first negotiated British withdrawal from the base. He had then assured his critics that Nasser really could be trusted. Now he felt betrayed.

Was there 'collusion'? i.e. did Britain, France and Israel 'plan' the Israeli-Egyptian war, in order to provide the Anglo-French forces in the area with the necessary pretext? This was widely suspected at the time, because the Anglo-French action followed so rapidly on the Israeli attack; and subsequently French and Israeli Ministers made 'revelations' and various books appeared purporting to be based on interviews with those concerned. Eden denied this at the time.[2] In his memoirs, published in 1960, he said that he had a shrewd suspicion that Israel might attack, and that he had discussed with the French what to do if this happened. But he had, he stated emphatically, no foreknowledge of the Israeli attack on Egypt. Indeed, what the Government had most feared was an Israeli attack on Jordan, with whom Britain had a treaty of alliance. In 1967 Mr. Anthony Nutting, who was then Minister of State at the Foreign Office, and who resigned over this issue, although without giving any reasons at the time, published his book, *No End of a Lesson*. Here he seemed to provide chapter and verse for the charge of collusion.

According to those who claim that there was collusion, the idea was first put forward by the French on 14 October 1956. Eden was interested

[1] On 31 July 1956, in a letter from President Eisenhower to Eden, he wrote that it was important to negotiate, but that force could not be ruled out. See Herman Finer, *Dulles over Suez*, pp. 90-1. See also Eden's account (op. cit., p. 437) of a meeting held in London on August 1st between Mr. Dulles, M. Pineau, Foreign Secretary of France, and Sir Anthony Eden. Eden reports Dulles as saying, 'A way had to be found to make Nasser disgorge what he was attempting to swallow ... we must make a genuine effort to bring world opinion to favour the international operation of the Canal.... It should be possible to create a world opinion so adverse to Nasser that he would be isolated. Then if a military operation had to be undertaken it would be more apt to succeed.'

[2] H.C. Deb., Fifth Series, Vol. 562, cols. 1457-8, 20 December 1956. 'To say ... that Her Majesty's Government were engaged in some dishonourable conspiracy is completely untrue, and I most emphatically deny it.' See also Nutting, op. cit., p. 164.

because he had, ever since the seizure of the Canal, been looking for an excuse to attack Egypt.[1] The background to this was that, in September, the Israelis had already asked the French to help them fight a defensive war. Eden was at first reluctant to become embroiled, because of the fear of compromising relations with the Arab states, and especially with Jordan. However, on October 16th Eden, Selwyn Lloyd, Mollet and Pineau met at the Hôtel Matignon in Paris; and Eden then agreed, with the proviso that Great Britain and France should appear to be reacting to, rather than taking part in, an Egyptian-Israeli war. On October 18th Eden told at least some members of his Cabinet what he planned to do. On October 24th the Secret Treaty of Sèvres, formalizing these agreements, was signed, between France, Britain and Israel.[2] It seems that Eden himself at no time met the Israeli leaders.

The crucial question, in all this tangled web, would seem to be not what Eden knew or did not know, but whether Israel was given advance information as to Franco-British plans. If so, Israel would certainly have been encouraged to attack. And this would perhaps justify the charge of 'collusion'.

From the accounts available, it seems that the French were much more committed to this plan than the British. They seem to have been continually urging it on Eden. The French and the Israelis, according to most of the evidence, made the running, and then told the British. Once action started, the French were for pushing on, as quickly as possible. The British were hesitant. And the climbing down, when it came, was done by Britain.

An interesting question is the extent to which the Cabinet was consulted. Opinions evidently differ. But most writers seem to believe that very few Cabinet Ministers were fully in the picture, and that the Cabinet was only informed briefly, because Eden feared opposition. Eden himself says rather cryptically that 'the Cabinet were kept in touch with our work'.[3] Mr. John P. Mackintosh says: 'When President Nasser took control of the Suez Canal on 26 July 1956, a Cabinet Committee was formed the next day to prepare counter-measures. It consisted of Mr. Butler, Mr. Macmillan, Mr. Selwyn Lloyd, Mr. Head, Mr. Lennox-Boyd and Lord Salisbury, and its task was "to work out plans day by day to put our policy into effect."' Probably not too much can be made of this. As Mr. Mackintosh goes on to note, the procedure was not different in any important respect from the way in which Chamberlain had planned and executed British policy in the late summer of 1938.[4] It seems agreed that on October 30th, the Cabinet was simply told that an ultimatum had been sent.

Whether or not even the Cabinet Committee was in agreement with

---

[1] Nutting, op. cit., Ch. X. [2] T. Robertson, op. cit. [3] Eden, op. cit., p. 432.
[4] John P. Mackintosh, *The British Cabinet*, p. 436.

Eden's policy to the bitter end must remain a matter for speculation. However, Mr. Macmillan, when *Full Circle* was published in 1960, went on record in the House of Commons, as saying, in answer to a question from Mr. Noel Baker: 'I was, and am, glad to share the full responsibility which I took at that time with a leader for whom I feel the deepest sense of loyalty and respect.' There seems no reason at all to doubt that Mr. Macmillan, then Chancellor of the Exchequer, really did whole-heartedly support Eden.[1]

It has been widely surmised that Mr. Butler's position was somewhat different. Mr. Gerald Sparrow, a personal friend of Butler's, has stated that he opposed the resort to force, and that at one time he considered resignation, but that he did not resign because he feared that this would bring down the Government.[2] If this is so, he gives in his memoirs no indication at all of holding any such opinions. He says that speculation against sterling caused the Chancellor of the Exchequer, Mr. Macmillan, to urge disengagement.[3] Professor Daalder also comments on the existence of an inner group. But he adds: 'Practically all members of the Cabinet and of the Conservative Party in Parliament agreed to the Suez policy, however, and in most cases probably heartily approved it.'[4]

It is interesting to speculate on why Eden withdrew when he did, leaving a relatively simple military operation incomplete. There were, of course, different reasons and combinations of reasons, and there is difference of opinion as to which were paramount.

There was certainly a run on sterling, and the need for an immediate American loan to avoid devaluation necessitated compliance with American views.[5] Some have talked of back-bench and/or front-bench revolt. Eden himself says that there were reports at the time of a dissident minority in the Conservative Party in the Commons; and that he knew that there had been contact 'between one or two members of our Party and the Opposition leaders.' He says that this did not influence him. Condemnation by the U.N. was expected. But the sharpness and generality of the opposition was not. The attacks of the Opposition in Parliament were also expected; but again the strength of the attack seems not to have been foreseen. In the House of Commons in August Gaitskell had, after all, declared himself as not opposed to the use of force.

---

[1] Anthony Sampson, op. cit., Ch. 7.
[2] G. Sparrow, *R.A.B. Study of a Statesman*.
[3] 'Speculation against sterling, mainly in the American market... had an even profounder effect (than censure by the U.N.) on the Chancellor of the Exchequer, Harold Macmillan, who switched almost overnight from being the foremost protagonist of intervention to being the leading influence for disengagement,' Butler, op. cit., p. 194.
[4] Hans Daalder, *Cabinet Reform in Britain 1914–1963*, p. 123.
[5] Sampson, op. cit., Ch. 7.

American opposition was undoubtedly one of the crucial factors, linked as it was with the gathering sterling crisis. American opposition was probably in part related to the coming Presidential Election in November. President Eisenhower and Mr. Dulles wanted to appear as men of peace; and they both had their eye on the Russians.[1] But Dulles, for all his disagreements with Eden, had talked so much of the possibility of having to force Nasser to 'disgorge' the canal, that his final stand must have been a bitter blow to Eden. Russian threats were vague, and were probably not taken too seriously. It is doubtful whether they were, in themselves, a serious factor, in persuading the British to withdraw. Eden himself gives as his reason for withdrawing the fact that the U.N. was, at an early stage, ready to take over responsibility. This is the Kilmuir view too, although Lord Kilmuir does not deny that Suez was a tragedy for Britain: 'Through Nasser's importunity, Dulles's deviousness, and Russia's machinations, the bitter tragedy of Suez was born.'[2]

After the event Eden, Macmillan and other Conservative leaders tried to give the impression that the war had been a kind of victory, in that it had resulted in the creation of a U.N. force, and in that the United States became, because of the Suez crisis, alert to the danger of a power vacuum in the Middle East.[3]

Outwardly, the Conservative Party presented a very nearly united front. The only two Ministers who resigned were Mr. Anthony Nutting and Sir Edward Boyle. Eight 'left-wing' M.P.s abstained in the vote taken in Parliament on November 8th. But on the right of the Party the thought was that Eden had not gone far enough and that he had lost his nerve at the crucial moment.[4] On the whole, however, the Tory Party remained remarkably united. The adverse effect on the Government's popularity in the country was short lived, partly, no doubt, because the Labour Party failed to take full advantage of the situation. According to the opinion polls Eden's personal popularity had been waning before Suez and during the crisis it actually increased.

The Labour Party was, of course, united in its condemnation of the

[1] 'The simple desire of Mr. Eisenhower to be re-elected on a peace platform and the maddening twists and turns of Mr. Dulles's legalistic mind were less important than the fears of the United States that any forcible action against Egypt would incite the Arab world to regard or even call in Russia as their ally.' Butler, op. cit., p. 196.

[2] Kilmuir, op. cit., p. 279.

[3] Kilmuir, op. cit., p. 279. 'The United States and the Americans woke up with a jolt from their vague illusions, and moved swiftly from the realm of fatuous resolutions to that of positive action. The arrival of the U.N. force marked the beginning of a new era in world government. The U.S. were forced to make a major change in their passive attitude towards the Middle East.'

[4] In May 1957 eight right wing M.P.s resigned the Whip when the Government accepted Nasser's terms for the Canal.

Government's action, and kept up a continuous stream of attack throughout the crisis. Mr. Gaitskell, in a B.B.C. broadcast, called on Eden's followers to depose him; and Lord Kilmuir has recorded that the scenes in the House of Commons were the worst since 1911. The attack culminated in the debate on November 8th when the Labour Party tried unsuccessfully to persuade disaffected Tories to join them.

Undoubtedly, the relationship between Britain and the United States was worsened by the Suez episode. In his memoirs Eden is bitter about Dulles, because of his duplicity and change of front, for Dulles had led Eden to believe that he would not, in the last resort, be opposed to a show of force. Thus Eden felt a sense of shocked betrayal after Dulles's speech of September 13th.

In general, the effects of the Suez misadventure were surprisingly small. The damage done to the Anglo-American alliance was easily and swiftly repaired by Mr. Macmillan. But Suez was important in a more enduring way, in that, from then on, it was apparent to British statesmen, and, indeed, to the world at large, that Britain could no longer take independent action in the face of American or U.N. disapproval. In a sense, there was nothing new here. This had been true at least since 1945, although a succession of British statesmen had tried to avoid recognizing this. Damage more particularly associated with Suez was, perhaps, that a taint of colonialism still attached, or was thought to attach, to the British attitude. British statesmen seemed to be implying that they thought the Egyptians a backward people, lacking the necessary skill to run the Canal themselves. This implication was, of course, offensive to African and Asian countries generally, and to the Commonwealth in particular. In any case it turned out not to be true.

Suez certainly resulted in some considerable loss of British prestige in the Middle East; and this has been a continuing factor ever since. And it made for a sharp deterioration in the British relationship with France. This deterioration was to have far-reaching consequences.

The Suez episode was a splendid opportunity for the moralists. Long ago, in the inter-war years, Etienne Mantoux, a young French economist, had noted what he described as 'mea culpism' among the British. While other nations enjoy blowing their own trumpets, the British, at any rate since 1918, have loved to bewail their wickedness. Suez was a splendid occasion for all this. Collusion with Israel; 'gunboat diplomacy'; disregard of the U.N.; failure to consult the Cabinet; breach with the United States, on whose goodwill Britain necessarily depended. All these charges could be, and were, made. It is doubtful, though, how many of them can really be sustained. As to collusion, no doubt the Israelis were aware of how the thinking went, in British and French circles. As to gunboat diplomacy, it is difficult to believe that this would have been held against Eden if he had succeeded in preventing Nasser from grabbing an international waterway which certainly didn't belong to Egypt. As to the U.N., the impossibility of working with, as opposed to talking in, this body was well known. The Russian veto was only one of many obstacles. As to the Cabinet, any student of British institutions will be aware that Cabinet government cannot now mean, if it ever did, that every decision taken in every department is subject to close scrutiny by the whole Cabinet. The time factor alone would preclude this. As to the breach with the United States, it would be most unfair to pin the whole blame for this on to Eden. Since 1945 British relations with the United States had been difficult at best.

The conclusion would seem to be that, while there may be little particular ground for the moralists the whole escapade must be regarded as a blunder. The Eden policy may have been defensible in theory. Different people hold different views on this. But it was certainly executed with a striking lack of diplomatic finesse. There was insufficient awareness of likely repercussions to it up and down the world. To embark on a military adventure of this kind, and then not carry it through, was to make the worst of all worlds.

8 THE COMMONWEALTH

a *General considerations*

In the previous chapter it was noted that the wind of change in the Commonwealth was no more than a fluttering breeze, felt here and there in the years from 1951 to 1955. In the life of the 1955–9 Government the breeze became distinctly more perceptible and both England and her remaining dependencies became more generally ruffled by it. The British Government now began to speed up its plans for withdrawal from Empire, although the speed-up didn't become a headlong rush until after 1959. It may be of interest to consider the thinking which lay behind the policy of more rapid withdrawal. It must be understood, however, that the policy itself was not new. What was new was the timetable.

Many decades back, in the nineteenth century, it had been recognized that direct British rule over great stretches of undeveloped territory up and down the world was not practicable. The first response to this problem had been indirect rule, through existing native authorities. This had turned out, even in the period between the two wars, to be impossible in the great Asian dominions of the Crown, if only because many of the most strongly entrenched native authorities were much more reactionary than the British. It also came to be regarded as unnecessary, because in the Asian dominions an educated professional class of civil servants was there, ready to take over and provide good government for the British wards, as the British understood this term. Could not similar élites be trained in the African and other dependencies, given time and effort? This was the genesis of the radical new deal for Africa planned by the Attlee Government after 1945. The invitation went out to the educated African, who had hitherto been excluded in favour of traditional chiefs, to come into junior political and administrative partnership with the British, initially through democratic local self-government. There followed the move to begin to Africanize the government services, develop co-operatives and trade unions, and lay the foundations for mass education. But these were plans for an independent Africa which might materialize in the twenty-first century, not the twentieth. The necessary social, economic and educational advance of the African masses could not be achieved overnight, so the thinking ran in Whitehall. Just as the common people of Europe had moved slowly forward, decade by decade until they were ripe, perhaps by 1918, to enter into their inheritance, so now the African masses must begin this slow progress towards self-government. For Britain to contract out of her responsibilities before power could be transferred to a responsible and educated class able to carry on in the British tradition seemed, to most Englishmen, utterly irresponsible. Maybe Britain should never have undertaken the burdens of Empire. But, having once done so, she could not abdicate until she could hand over in the knowledge that her wards were now able to look after themselves adequately. Britain would have to stay in Africa for a long time, and there could be only a slow and gradual devolution of power.

But it was not possible for Britain to stay in Africa for a long time. And the existing small, educated élites, using techniques of mass communication hitherto unknown, managed to politicize African masses in one country after another with a speed which made the official time-table seem hopelessly out of date. Thus the masses became politically conscious long before social and economic progress could provide stability.

The rise of nationalism in Africa had become apparent in 1949, at the time of the Accra riots, in the Gold Coast. In 1951 Mr. Nkrumah had been swept into power. Six short years later, in 1957, Britain had to recognize the independence of the Gold Coast, henceforth to be known as Ghana. Ghanaian society was relatively sophisticated, as African societies went. There was no white settler element, and the economy was fairly strong. This forced march to independence had, not surprisingly, an immense impact on political thinking all over Africa, and, indeed, beyond Africa. What the Gold Coast nationalist leaders could do, others thought they could do too, all over the African continent. The British policy of slow advance towards material betterment; towards mass literacy; towards the training of a responsible political élite, working, perhaps, towards a Westminster type of democratic society, was seen as hopelessly outdated. African nationalism had found a short cut – or so it seemed.

Other reasons, too, prompted the British to move faster. One was certainly the attitude of the United States. Before the Suez crisis the Americans had thought that, on the whole, the best way to exclude Communism from Africa was the continuation of European, and in particular British, colonial rule. After Suez, different thinking came to prevail in Washington. Very many Americans were, after all, by tradition, anti-colonialist. They liked to forget the strong imperialist strand in their own history. And it was felt that, in the new world of United States supremacy, European colonial rule was inappropriate. The African continent was more likely to turn to America as its leader, if America resumed its original anti-colonialist stance.[1]

Another, and more pressing factor caused a change in British thinking, and that was, quite simply, violence. Increasingly it came to be realized that the choice was between keeping to the time-table, which would involve maintaining colonial rule by force for a period of time, or conceding more or less immediate independence. Britain had neither the economic strength nor the political will to go on with the policies necessary to contain violence. The sense of imperial mission, of responsibility for dependent peoples; of the impossibility of good government, as Britain understood this term, until there was a minimum of material prosperity, and a responsible and educated political and administrative élite – these ebbed away, and gradually the feeling grew that the Africans had better be left to go to hell their own way, since this was what most of them seemed to wish. The one sizeable retarding factor was the white settler element in countries like Kenya and Southern Rhodesia.

It would, of course, be a mistake to oversimplify this picture. For instance, while many African groups were making it clear that the attainment of British-type political institutions was not their goal, in the West Indies the desire to duplicate the whole paraphernalia of government on the Westminster model was embarrassing for, perhaps, the opposite reasons. There was something more than faintly farcical in the desire prevalent in these little islands to copy all the expensive trappings of Westminster. British West Indies seemed to want only to be more English than the English.[2]

b *The Central African Federation*
In these years the failure of the federal principle to provide a solution to the problems of nationalism in multi-racial societies began to be apparent for all to see in the Central African Federation, consisting of Southern and Northern Rhodesia, and Nayasaland. Here, it became increasingly obvious that African nationalism, and the political aspirations of the

[1] K. Kirkwood, *Britain and Africa*.   [2] See J. M. Lee, op. cit.

white settlers of Southern Rhodesia were as oil and water. No common needs drew these groups together. On the contrary, they moved further and further apart. The existence of the Federation accelerated the spread of militant African nationalism, especially in Nyasaland after Dr. Banda returned in 1958. But 1957, the year in which Ghana received her independence, was probably the critical year. By the London Agreement signed in April, sizeable concessions were made to Sir Roy Welensky's mainly white Federal Government, in that it was announced that, at the review of the Federal Constitution to be held in 1960, Britain would consider granting dominion status to the Federation. The Africans got the impression that the Federation was there to stay, and that there was nothing they could do about it. Then came the Constitutional Amendment Act of 1957, by which among other things the British Government agreed not to amend or repeal any Federal Act. In the light of this agreement the African Affairs Board came to be seen as a very ineffectual safeguard for African interests. In 1958 came a new Electoral Act, which was the cause of further ill will among the Africans, because it seemed still further to entrench the electoral supremacy of a small group of white men.

Finally, disturbances broke out in all three territories, which were almost as decisive in their effects on the C.A.F. as Mau Mau was in Kenya. In Nyasaland the disturbances were such as to cause the British Government to appoint the Devlin Commission to inquire into the cause of the unrest. The Devlin Report, when published, drew attention to the opposition of an overwhelming majority of Africans to the Federation; and to the fact that something perilously like a police state had been established in Nyasaland, in order to counter the activities of the Congress Party, led by Dr. Banda.

The criticisms explicitly made of the whole official handling of the African opposition to the Federation caused the Government to appoint the Monckton Commission, in July 1959, to review the Federal Constitution. By 1959 the end of the C.A.F. was in sight.[1]

c *Kenya*

In Kenya the Mau Mau rebellion continued, although by 1955 the worst was over. However, large numbers of British troops were still necessary, to protect Europeans and those of the Kikuyu tribe who had not succumbed to Mau Mau. Mr. Tom Mboya's African Congress Party was now beginning to demand much more far-reaching measures of self-government. The British resolve to remain in control, necessitating, as this did, the taking of repressive measures, was increasingly denounced

---

[1] See Kirkwood, op. cit. See R. L. Watts: *New Federations*. Also House of Commons Debate on *Report of Devlin Commission*. H.C. Deb., Fifth Series, Vol. 610, cols. 317-444, 28 July 1959.

in Third-World type countries; and in England, debate was triggered off by the Hola Camp incident. It seems that on 3 March 1959, eleven Mau Mau detainees in this prison camp died. On May 6th the coroner's finding was that these men had died as a result of beatings by African warders, after they had refused to work. The findings of the inquiry set up to investigate this incident marked a decisive point in the discussion about British policy in Africa. On the one hand, there was open political controversy over the handling of the Mau Mau terrorists – the large number of terrorists executed; the treatment of hard-core prisoners at camps like Hola; the behaviour of individual military officers, etc. But at a more general level, Mau Mau was seen not only as a problem in Kenya, but as the kind of problem Britain was only too likely to encounter in future elsewhere in British Africa. Increasingly, the problem was seen as one of resources. British military resources had already been seriously stretched by events in Malaya. It looked now as though vast investment capital would be needed for the economic and social development of countries like Kenya, if the hitherto accepted policy was to be maintained. When African leaders began demanding immediate independence, the mood in informed circles in England may have been something akin to relief.

d *Cyprus*
Cyprus was another trouble spot for the British, in the life of this Government; here, the problems posed were, if anything, even more intractable than those of Africa. Cyprus had been bought by Britain in 1875, because of its strategic value as a Middle East base. The majority of its inhabitants were Greeks; but it was adjacent to the Turkish mainland, and had a large Turkish minority. The island of Cyprus had never belonged to Greece. However, in 1955 a campaign of terrorism against Britain was started by a left wing organization in the island known as EOKA. The objective of this organization was not independence but union with Greece, or 'enosis'. EOKA, whose members embarked on a campaign of terrorism against both the British and the Turks, was supported actively by left wing groups in Greece, and by the Orthodox Archbishop Makarios. At the U.N. the demand was for self-determination for the people of Cyprus.

However, the large Turkish minority, strongly backed by the Turkish Government, was bitterly opposed to any such solution. The future of the Turkish minority in the island would, the Turks argued, be very gravely at risk if 'enosis' took place – and it was in any case a very unsuitable solution for an island far from Greece, but closely adjacent to the Turkish mainland. The Turks wanted the *status quo* preserved, or else a partition of the island.

The value of Cyprus, from the standpoint of the British Government, was not what it had been. The Suez episode in 1956 had shown that bases in the eastern Mediterranean were of diminishing strategic value. Cyprus looked like a liability which any British government might now wish to be relieved of.

By 1959 all three parties to the dispute gave up their original claims, and, under an agreement reached in February 1959 at Zurich, it was decided to establish a Republic under the auspices of the Commonwealth. Turkey was persuaded to accept this solution partly because the United States offered a bilateral treaty, which was, in effect, a defensive military alliance. This took care of Turkey's fear of the U.S.S.R., and of the Communist left in Greek and Cypriot politics, and this at a time when the 1958 revolution in Iraq had seriously weakened the Baghdad Pact.[1]

e *Malta*
The little Mediterranean island of Malta presented, in these years, problems of a rather different kind. Unlike some others, the Maltese at that time knew on which side their bread was buttered. They feared the run-down of the British naval dockyards, on which their economic prosperity, such as it was, was almost wholly dependent. They had not the slightest wish to leave the shelter provided by their British connection. On the contrary, they saw their interests best served by a much closer link. They wanted integration with Britain, and Maltese M.P.s at Westminster. The desired end would have been economic integration, and thus, the Maltese hoped, the achievement of a very much higher standard of living. This scheme, which came under active consideration in 1955, was finally shelved, as Maltese demands became ever more extreme. The British got cold feet as they thought of the many other little island dependencies who might in the future make similar claims. The balance of power in the House of Commons might, at some future date, again lie with small groups of overseas M.P.s, with no real stake in British politics, other than the votes they could offer with which to buttress their bargaining position. The memory of Parnell, and the growing knowledge that the British economy could not afford to support the Maltas of the British Empire as integral parts of the new Welfare State, finally put paid to the plan for Maltese integration. An alternative of 'dependent Commonwealth' participation in a reformed House of Lords was never actively pursued.

f *The West Indies Federation*
Another federation encouraged, though not directly sponsored, by the British Government in these years was that of the British West Indian islands. Some form of closer association between the islands had long been considered desirable, although the West Indian Royal Commission

[1] Eric Barker, 'Settlement in Cyprus', *Parliamentary Quarterly*, 1959.

of 1939 had expressed some doubts as to the feasibility of this policy.[1] However, a number of common services between the islands had grown up over the years.[2] And, since the end of the Second World War, political awareness, and demands for self-government became increasingly pressing. In 1947 the then Colonial Secretary, Mr. Arthur Creech-Jones, convened a conference at Montego Bay, Jamaica, to consider the possibilities of closer association. The Conference recommended a loose Federation. Finally, the British Caribbean Federation Act was passed by Parliament in 1956, and the new federal constitution came into force in January 1958.[3] The Federation seemed a good solution to West Indian problems. In the climate of opinion of the late forties and fifties, it seemed ludicrous to try to develop all the paraphernalia of self-government in each tiny, separate island. Anyway to the outside observer, the similarities between the islands were very great. The racial make-up was much the same throughout the islands, with the exception of Trinidad, which had a large East Indian minority. The problems, whether economic, social or political, seemed very much the same.

But the Federation was not a success. The two large islands, Jamaica and Trinidad, wanted independence in their own right, and did not wish to shoulder the burden of 'carrying' the more backward small islands. Each island had evolved its own separate identity, and was fiercely determined to keep it, whatever the cost. In a curious way, each island felt a proud and close identity with the United Kingdom, but no identity at all with neighbouring British islands. The West Indians had never been a sea-going people, and communications between the islands, even those adjacent to each other, had never been close. There was, further, as it turned out, no great economic advantage to be gained by federating. All the islands produced much the same tropical agricultural crops, so that their economies did not complement each other.

9 THE OPPOSITION

In some ways, the Opposition did better in this period than it had done in the years of the first post-war Conservative Government from 1951 to 1955. It might, perhaps, have done better still if the right lessons had been learned from the 1955 defeat. They were not. Wilson, appointed by the N.E.C. to inquire into the reasons for the Conservative victory, put

---

[1] Cmnd. 6607.

[2] For example, in 1919 a West Indies Court of Appeal had been set up. In 1924 the Imperial College of Tropical Agriculture was founded in Trinidad. In 1940 a Comptroller for Development and Welfare was appointed.

[3] The Bahamas, Bermuda, the British Virgin Islands, and the two mainland territories, British Guiana and British Honduras, preferred to stay out of the Federation.

it all down to the rust and deterioration of the Labour Party machine.[1] The veteran Mr. Shinwell was probably nearer the mark when he observed that given the right policies and effective leadership, organization would have followed.

However, the leadership problem was now resolved. Attlee, who had lingered on after two General Election defeats, at length retired in December 1955. He may have felt that, after the Labour Party's September Conference at Margate, Gaitskell's reputation was sufficiently assured to get him the Leadership. It does seem that Attlee did not like Morrison, and did not for various reasons think him a suitable Leader, and so was prepared to stay on himself until he was sure that Morrison would be generally regarded as too old to succeed him. Gaitskell was Dalton's protégé as well as Attlee's;[2] and both these prominent Labour politicians thought it very important for Labour to have a much younger man as Leader, a man, as Attlee put it 'born in this century'. The results of the Leadership election at the end of 1955 were as follows:

Gaitskell	157
Bevan	70
Morrison	40

After his defeat, Morrison resigned as Deputy Leader and was replaced by James Griffiths, and he says, himself, that the whole episode hurt him very much.[3] Dalton in his memoirs, says he thought that Morrison should not have stood for the Leadership at all. He should, however, have stayed on as Deputy Leader, and put his experience at the service of the younger man. If he had, this would have been a very popular move, and he would have continued to occupy an important position in the Party hierarchy. Continuity was important, and Morrison's resignation made it impossible to achieve this.[4]

Hugh Gaitskell, the new Leader, was a man of the centre and the nominee of the trade unions.[5] Born in 1906, he had been educated at Winchester and New College. He got a First in P.P.E.,[6] and then taught economics in London. In the thirties he had favoured rearmament, and

[1] Bulmer-Thomas, op. cit., Ch. 44.
[2] See Dalton, op. cit., p. 429. 'Towards this most exceptional young man I decided that I would do my best to deflect the leadership.'
[3] Morrison, op. cit., pp. 304–5.
[4] Dalton, op. cit., pp. 434–5. 'It would have been a very big thing to do, and he was not quite big enough to do it.'
[5] George-Brown, op. cit., p. 80. 'Hugh was elected by the Parliamentary Party as the Leader always is, but he owed his support to the backing he was given by the old hard core of the great Unions.' See Stephen Haseler, *The Gaitskellites*.
[6] Philosophy, Politics and Economics.

had opposed Munich. In the war he had worked under Dalton, who remained always his staunch supporter. He first entered Parliament in 1945, and was first a Parliamentary Secretary, and then Minister of Fuel and Power. He handled the 1949 financial crisis during Cripps's illness. In 1950 he became Chancellor of the Exchequer.

As Leader of the Opposition from January 1956, he made no concessions to his militant left wingers. They had to make peace with him as best they could. Perhaps they had come to see that a continuing split in the Party might lose them yet another Election; perhaps they hoped for office if Gaitskell became Prime Minister.

The Suez crisis later in 1956 helped to draw the Party together, anyway temporarily, although Gaitskell's own attitude was a little suspect because he had, in his August speech, appeared to agree with the need to use force to free the Canal, if this turned out to be the only way to get it back. Anyway, the Party was at one in the angry and uproarious scenes in the Commons in November 1956. But foreign policy issues are never of interest for long to a British electorate, and Suez proved no exception to the rule.

As Bevan had come third in the autumn 1956 elections to the Shadow Cabinet, Gaitskell offered him the Shadow Cabinet Foreign Secretaryship after Suez. He hoped, no doubt, to muffle Bevan's bitter opposition by accepting him into the inner circle. And, in September 1957, at the Brighton Conference, Gaitskell persuaded Bevan to oppose a left wing resolution calling for unilateral disarmament, on the grounds that he was the Party spokesman on foreign affairs and so could not oppose the Leadership. Hence there followed Bevan's improbable speech arguing that it would not be right to send a Labour Foreign Secretary 'naked into the conference chamber'. This seemingly happy and perhaps rather inconsequential ending to the Bevan feud augured well for Labour's future. Unfortunately, however, other problems were soon to emerge, to confront the moderate Labour Leadership with even greater difficulties. In 1956, for instance, Frank Cousins emerged for the first time, as head of the T.G.W.U. The unions under his influence began moving steadily to the left of the Parliamentary Party, thus upsetting the long established balance of power in the Labour movement. Up till now, the unions had obligingly paid the piper, without attempting to call the tune. But by 1959, the General and Municipal Workers were voting for unilateral nuclear disarmament; and Frank Cousins was campaigning actively to get the official Party defence policy changed. The old cracks reopened. C.N.D. was launched; and the demand grew for unilateral renunciation of the H bomb. By 1959, the official Labour policy on defence was the formation of a non-nuclear club, and, in Europe, disengagement. By this Gaitskell meant a large neutral area, from which armed forces would be withdrawn, both by NATO and by the Warsaw Pact Powers.

Why did Labour fail to unite as an Opposition, despite Conservative difficulties from the middle of 1956 till 1958, when so much seemed to be going their way? Perhaps their dilemma was that they feared the electoral consequences of advocating a further dose of socialism. It was hard in that seemingly affluent society, to make socialism seem an attractive alternative. Yet they had no other alternative to offer. Suez; misgovernment in the Central African Federation; the Hola camp incident; even the 1957 Rent Act – none of these was really enough to pull the planks out from under the Conservatives. The Conservative Government still, by and large, delivered the goods – or at any rate appeared to be doing so. The 1955 Party Conference had proposed that a new statement of policy be developed over the next three years, which would restate socialism in contemporary terms attractive to the nation and the Party. The old type capitalism, to which nineteenth- and early twentieth-century socialism had been a response, had really disappeared now. Clause 4 (nationalization) appeared to many as a very doubtful vote-getter. The idea of indirect State control, by expanding State ownership of shares in private industry, was now explored. But it was not a winner either, and was left out of the 1958 pre-Election programme. So the Labour Party was reduced to developing policies designed to attract votes from particular groups, as old age pensioners, farmers, etc.[1] There were other difficulties. The retirement of elder statesmen like Attlee, Dalton and Morrison left Gaitskell a little exposed in the House. He had few experienced supporters to back him. Nor had he, after the honeymoon period was over, the support of outstanding union leaders able to deliver block votes at conferences. No trade union leaders of the standing of Bevin or Deaking surfaced to help him; and the constituency parties, further now from the realities of power, were for the most part supporters of Bevan and the extremists. Perhaps Gaitskell was not really a leader of men. He did not seem to inspire great admiration in these years. Perhaps his was a difficult background for a Labour Leader. Anyway, he seemed not very good at sensing the mood of his followers. He never, for instance, grasped the quasi-theological importance to his Party of Clause 4 (nationalization). He was an entirely honest and straightforward man. But these qualities are not enough for a political leader. He was also a man of considerable ability. He used his ability to fight for what he believed to be right, rather than for what he sensed to be politically expedient. He was intellectually honest to the point of obstinacy; and was apt to attribute disloyalty to those who disagreed with him. There have been many other men like him in British politics, and it can be argued that they have been, for generations, the backbone of Parliamentary institutions. But it is at least arguable that none of our

[1] Loewenburg, 'The Transformation of British Labour Party Policy since 1945', *Journal of Politics*, 1959.

top-flight leaders have been cast in quite this mould. Some other, less easily definable, quality is needed too. Whatever this was, Gaitskell did not seem to have it.[1] But possibly, whatever the quality of the Labour Leadership, and whatever the programme of the Labour Party, there would have been little real chance for a break-through until the economic prosperity of Britain began to crack.[2] When the team in, and batting, began to falter, then was the chance. But that was still in the future. As it was, from 1955 to 1959, the alternative team was insufficiently attractive. It was still deeply divided. The new leaders were not backed by experienced parliamentarians; nor by a responsible trade union vote. They had no new policies to offer, and the old ones became less attractive to the new middle class.

[1] Mackenzie, *British Political Parties* (2nd edn.), pp. 594–605. See also W. T. Rodgers, *Hugh Gaitskell, 1906–1963*.

[2] See Beer, op. cit.

CHAPTER THREE

The Conservative Government from October 1959 to October 1964

SUMMARY	page
1 The General Election of 8 October 1959	106
2 The Conservative Team	108
a The Prime Ministership of Mr. Harold Macmillan	108
b The Prime Ministership of Sir Alec Douglas-Home	117
3 Constitutional and Administrative Issues	118
a The Cabinet and the Prime Minister	118
b The House of Lords	119
4 Economic Issues	120
a General survey	120
b Summary of economic developments 1959–1964	121
c The Common Market	123
5 Domestic Affairs	125
a The Commonwealth Immigration Act	126
b The abolition of retail price maintenance 1964	128
c The National Health Service	128
d Hospitals	129
e Housing	129
f Education	129
(i) The Robbins Report on Higher Education	130
(ii) The Newsom Report	130
g The Police	131
h Aviation	131
i Railways	131
6 Defence Policy	132
7 Foreign Policy	135
a General	135
b The Anglo-American relationship	135
c The Communist world	136
d Europe	137
8 The Commonwealth	138
a General	138
b The Central African Federation	140
c Kenya	141
d Nigeria	142
e Tanganyika	142

            f Uganda   142
            g Malaysia   143
            h Aden and the South Arabia Federation   143
            i Cyprus   144
            j South Africa   144
         9 The Opposition   146
            a The Labour Party   146
            b The Liberals   151

1 THE GENERAL ELECTION OF 8 OCTOBER 1959[1]
Each General Election has, at any rate, in retrospect, its own flavour. The 1959 Election is one which almost at once made the moralists feel very prim indeed. The 1951 and 1955 Elections were each seen to have been fought over general-principle issues, so the argument went. In 1959 it was just material betterment. This charge was especially laid at the door of the Conservatives, who used slogans like 'You've never had it so good'; 'Life is better with the Conservatives – Don't let Labour ruin it'; and so on. Idealism of any kind was conspicuous by its absence.

The Conservatives none the less won a resounding victory, increasing their overall majority in the House from 59 to 100 M.P.s. This was their third consecutive victory; and the second at which they had increased the number of seats they held. They had thus well and truly defied the traditional 'swing of the pendulum' theory, and despite Suez. Indeed, their continued success made some of their Labour opponents wonder gloomily whether a Party in power could now ever be defeated. Modern governments were seen as having so many weapons at their disposal. It was going to be difficult, if not impossible, for the Party in opposition ever to wrest the initiative from the 'in' team.

The results were as follows: 78.8 per cent of the electorate went to the polls. The number of votes cast for the three main Parties was as follows:

	Votes	Percentage of votes	Seats obtained
Conservative	13,749,830	49.4	365
Labour	12,215,538	43.8	258
Liberal	1,638,571	5.9	6

The Conservatives, in spite of their large majority in the House, gained not quite 50 per cent of the votes cast, and support for the two major Parties in the country was still quite evenly balanced, although this was not reflected in the House, because of the Labour tendency to pile up

[1] See Nuffield Election Studies, D. E. Butler and R. Rose, *The British General Election of 1959*.

votes in safe seats. The Liberal Party, which polled double the number of votes it had in 1955, and had 216 candidates standing, had still the same number of seats.

What factors contributed to this third Tory victory? The by-election results from 1955 to 1959 had not pointed to a great increase in the Government's popularity.[1] Mr. Gaitskell had apparently expected a Labour victory. And even Mr. Butler had forecast a very narrow win for his Party.

Probably the expensive and sophisticated Conservative public relations campaign, instituted in 1957 by Lords Hailsham and Poole with a view to improving the general 'image' of the Party after Suez, paid considerable dividends. Half a million pounds had been spent on it. And the end result seems to have been to identify the Conservatives, in the public mind, with prosperity. This was the keynote of the Conservative campaign. Their Manifesto was entitled 'The Next Five Years' and they looked forward very hopefully. They could, they said, double the standard of living of the British people within a generation.[2]

By contrast the Labour Manifesto was not inspiring. It was entitled 'Britain Belongs to You'. But how the man in the street was going to benefit from this ownership was not made clear. The specific promises made were uninspiring. The abolition of the 11-plus examination, which Labour now sponsored, had not yet become a national issue. And municipalization of rented houses; expansion in hospital building; subsidies for recreation and the arts and for depressed areas; higher pension rates; and so on, all looked rather dubious after Mr. Gaitskell's promise made at Newcastle on September 28th not to increase income tax,[3] which was followed, on October 1st, with his promise to remove purchase tax from a range of essential goods. Mr. Macmillan pounced on this as 'the biggest budget leak in history'. And Mr. Butler remarked that the Labour motto appeared to be 'a bribe a day keeps the Tories away'.

The opinion polls suggest that, for the first ten days of the campaign, the advantage lay with Labour; and it may be that it was the rash Gaitskell speeches which swung the advantage to the Tories in the last ten days.

Certainly 1959 was a much more lively General Election than 1955. The opinion polls were in full swing and these heightened tension and excitement about the outcome. For the first time very full use was made of television so that the political battles really were brought into the homes of the people.

Issues of foreign policy were conspicuous by their absence. The

[1] Nuffield Election Studies, Butler and Rose, op. cit., p. 282.
[2] Kilmuir, op. cit., pp. 310–11.
[3] 'There will be no increase in the standard or other rates of income tax so long as normal peace time conditions continue.' Nuffield Election Studies, Butler and Rose, op. cit., p. 59.

Conservatives had learnt that these were not of great interest to the electorate. And, although their immediate record in this regard was quite good, they were anxious not to revive memories of Suez. The Labour Party was divided on a whole range of foreign policy issues, and did not want to advertise this fact.

In the end, the swing away from Labour seems to have come from the younger, better-paid, better-housed wage earners in the twenty-one to twenty-nine age group. These young workers probably now regarded themselves as 'middle class', and saw their future prosperity as being better protected and fostered by the Tory team, than by the now rather old-fashioned traditional Labour politicians.

Mr. Macmillan was undoubtedly a much better leader than Mr. Gaitskell. He was at his peak as a politician. Unflappable' Supermac' came over to his audiences very well indeed. He was amusing in a kindly way, powerful, and competent. He seemed to have a very able team lined up beside him, all ready to contribute, in their different ways, to an ever more affluent society in Britain. Most important of all, the economic cracks in the Tory edifice had not yet appeared. And Labour still looked an improbable and not very attractive alternative.[1]

2 THE CONSERVATIVE TEAM[2]

a *The Prime Ministership of Mr. Harold Macmillan, 8 October 1959 to 18 October 1963*

The first two years, from October 1959 until July 1961, saw Mr. Macmillan at the top of his form. He was popular, confident, relaxed, and very much in control. 'Supermac' or 'Macwonder' as he was dubbed, was at this time a first-class asset to his Party. He had saved the Conservatives from the catastrophe which had at first seemed likely after the Suez crisis. He had won the General Election in 1959 with a very comfortable margin. He knew that he could not rest for long on these achievements, and that storms were brewing on all sides. But he was ready to meet them. This urbane patrician, born in the nineteenth century, was, *au fond*, a reformer and an innovator, in domestic and in foreign affairs. Two or three threads seemed to run through his political life providing continuity, from his early years as an M.P. at Stockton in the thirties until his resignation in October 1963. One was a deep consciousness of the evils stemming from unemployment. Another was

---

[1] See H. Durrant, 'Voting Behaviours in Britain, 1945–1964', in *Studies in British Politics*, edited R. Rose, 2nd edn., 1969.

[2] See Butler and Freeman, op. cit., pp. 40–5, for a complete record of the membership of the Conservative Government between 1957 and 1964.

belief in material betterment. His efforts to improve the standard and quality of living of ordinary men and women were unceasing. He was not among those who equated material betterment with 'materialism'. He thought it of first-class importance, and made no bones about this. Another permanent strand in his thinking was a deep abhorrence of war. Hence his desire for 'summitry', which perhaps in the end came to seem somewhat naïve. He believed that Britain was in a uniquely advantageous position to negotiate for peace, poised as she was, between East and West, with the far-flung links provided by her Commonwealth. And, in the cause of peace, he believed that Britain should retain an independent nuclear deterrent, since without this she could not effectively make her views felt in Washington and Moscow.

Mr. Macmillan had a surprising ability to respond to changing circumstances and, though his roots may have been in the previous century, his interests were in the future. The most striking instance of this was, perhaps, the famous 'Wind of Change' speech, made to the South African Parliament at Cape Town, on 3 February 1960.[1] He understood, before most other politicians, the need for swift and radical change in Africa. He understood, too, the need for a change in Britain's policy towards Europe. And, in the summer of 1961, he said that he thought that Britain ought to take the plunge, and join the E.E.C. In this he was thwarted by President de Gaulle's *Non* in January 1963. Many of his colleagues in and outside the House may then have been secretly relieved. But most of his successors, both Labour and Conservative, came, a few years later, to agree with his judgement.

No student of this administration can fail to be impressed by the great array of Royal Commissions and inquiries of all kinds, set in motion in these years. The foundations of Mr. Wilson's much vaunted technological age were well and truly laid by this Conservative Government. Indicative planning of the economy; social problems; education; industrial reorganization – all these came under its review. And many of the inquiries became the basis of the new policies developed by the two Labour Governments from 1964 to 1970. In a very real sense, Mr. Wilson was quite often only jumping on to the band waggon.

In July 1960 some Cabinet changes were made, two of which were perhaps more important in retrospect than they seemed at the time. Mr. Selwyn Lloyd became Chancellor of the Exchequer in place of Mr. Heathcoat Amory who then resigned. And the Earl of Home moved to the Foreign Office in place of Mr. Selwyn Lloyd. Mr. Selwyn Lloyd

[1] 'The most striking of all the impressions I have formed since I left London a month ago, is of the strength of . . . African consciousness. In different places it may take different forms, but it is happening everywhere. The wind of change is blowing through the continent. Whether we like it or not, this growth of national consciousness is a political fact.'

was a Chancellor whose abilities have probably been underestimated. A barrister by profession, he had had nine years of experience in the Foreign Office.[1] Moreover he had been Minister of Supply from 1954 to 1955 and Minister of Defence in 1955. He had therefore had no previous Ministerial experience on the domestic side, and so he lacked some of the economic expertise required for his new post. However, he moved nearer to an incomes policy than had any of his predecessors and some of his ideas were subsequently adopted by Mr. Wilson. In July 1962 Mr. Macmillan replaced him by Mr. Maudling.

The appointment of the Earl of Home as Foreign Secretary in July 1960 was immediately seized on by the Opposition as unsuitable. The Foreign Secretary ought to be available, it was argued, to answer in person to the Commons. Mr. Macmillan's reply was that Mr. Heath, now Lord Privy Seal, was the new Deputy Foreign Secretary, and a member of the Cabinet, and would be continually available in the House, leaving his chief free to travel, which was now, Mr. Macmillan said, more necessary than ever before. But there was a lurking suspicion, perhaps unjustified, that Mr. Macmillan, as other Prime Ministers before him, thought it best to be his own Foreign Secretary.[2]

As time went on it became possible to surmise that Mr. Macmillan was developing a rather different view from most of his predecessors of the proper relationship between a Prime Minister and his colleagues. A Somewhat 'presidential' flavour seemed to be about. This suspicion was heightened by the 'purge' of July 1962. By this time things were beginning to go seriously wrong for the Government. The sterling crisis of July 1961 had not been successfully countered by a very unpopular, although probably necessary, 'pay pause'. In March 1962 Mr. Eric Lubbock won Orpington, hitherto a safe Conservative seat, for the Liberals. This was regarded as the worst Government defeat at a by-election since the war.[3] On 6 June 1962 the Conservatives lost Middlesbrough West to Labour. On 12 July 1962 the Conservative candidate in a by-election at north-east Leicester was beaten into a bad third place by the Liberal.[4] Indeed, between then and the General Election of 15 October 1964 the Con-

[1] As Minister of State, from 1951 to 1954; and as Foreign Secretary from 1955 to 1960.

[2] It is noteworthy that Lord Kilmuir, writing at a time when he was no great admirer of Mr. Macmillan, thought this a good appointment. 'The Foreign Office, which had been virtually under the personal direction of the Prime Minister since 1955, once again began to function as it should do.' Kilmuir, op. cit., p. 313.

[3] The Conservative majority of 14,760 was converted into a Liberal majority of 7,855.

[4] *Annual Register, 1962*, pp. 27-8. The Tory share of the poll fell by 23.9 per cent.

servatives lost a further five seats to Labour. They won no single by-election.[1]

It was against this background of failure that on 13 July 1962 Mr. Macmillan carried out a sweeping reconstruction of his Cabinet. Seven of his twenty-one colleagues were dismissed, most of them being given only a few hours' notice.

The Cabinet Ministers dismissed were:
(1) Mr. Selwyn Lloyd, Chancellor of the Exchequer. Letters between him and Mr. Macmillan were exchanged first, as was customary. None the less, a storm of protest arose, and seventy back-benchers held an angry meeting;[2]
(2) Lord Kilmuir, the Lord Chancellor;
(3) Sir David Eccles, Minister for Education;
(4) Mr. Hill, Minister for Housing;
(5) Mr. Maclay, Scotland;
(6) Sir Percy Mills, Minister without Portfolio;
(7) Mr. Watkinson, Defence.

Three days later, nine non-Cabinet Ministers were dismissed from the Government.

The new Cabinet Ministers were:
Mr. Maudling, Chancellor of the Exchequer;
Lord Dilhorne, Lord Chancellor;
Mr. Henry Brooke, Home Secretary;
Sir Edward Boyle, Education;
Sir Keith Joseph, Housing;
Mr. Noble, Scotland;
Mr. Thorneycroft, Defence.

There has been much speculation as to the motives behind these changes. Some argue that Mr. Macmillan sought to save the Party by introducing a younger, more vigorous element into the Government. Sir Edward Boyle, for instance, was only thirty-eight; Sir Keith Joseph was forty-four. Most of the new appointments seemed to suggest that the clever young were being brought in to replace the failing elderly. Perhaps this was the Macmillan counterpart to the Kennedy emphasis on youth. Macmillan and Kennedy were close friends. Macmillan greatly admired Kennedy, and he was impressed by the new style in American politics, with its emphasis on youth. Then, it was thought that Macmillan may have wanted to indicate not merely his readiness to take on the young, but also his wish to find new approaches. There ought to be growth and expansion and experiment, now that the years of restraint could be regarded as past. One of the grouses about his old friend Selwyn Lloyd was that the July sterling crisis appeared to have been handled in

[1] Nuffield Election Studies, Butler and Freeman, op. cit., p. 154.
[2] G. W. Jones, 'The Prime Minister's Powers', *Parliamentary Affairs*, 1964–5.

the same old way. Mr. Reginald Maudling, young, bouncing and clever, would surely be able to think up better ways of handling troubles of this kind.

Another explanation for this 'Night of the Long Knives', as it came to be called, was that by July 1962 Mr. Macmillan was beginning to be uneasy about his own position, and was ready to sacrifice his loyal supporters in order to re-establish himself by giving his Government a new and better image.[1] He did not try to get rid of his principal rivals – the Earl of Home, Lord Hailsham, Mr. Macleod and Mr. Butler.[2] This would have been too dangerous as they might then have led a revolt against him. But the lesser men were dispensed with in order to bring in some new and younger Conservative politicians.[3]

Whatever the motives for this massive reshuffle, it probably misfired. The new young men could not reverse the adverse economic trends. And the loyalty of the Conservative Party was shaken and undermined to an extent that Mr. Macmillan had not foreseen.

The winter of 1962–3 was difficult in every way. There was unusually bad weather, and a high level of unemployment. And, beginning in the autumn of 1962, there was a run of trouble on security issues.

For instance in October 1962 an Admiralty clerk, William Vassall, was sentenced to eighteen years for spying for the Soviet Union. His excuse was that the Russians had blackmailed him into giving information because they had evidence of his homosexual practices a few years earlier in Moscow. Rumours began to connect Vassall with Mr. Thomas Galbraith, a former Civil Lord of the Admiralty, and now Under-Secretary of State for Scotland. Mr. Galbraith resigned. The Prime Minister set up a judicial tribunal under Lord Radcliffe which, when it reported in April 1963, cleared Mr. Galbraith completely.[4] A great part of the trouble seemed to have come from unsubstantiated press rumours. But all this was hardly over before the Profumo case, also involving security, broke in June 1963. This turned out to be a much less important affair, as far as the nation's security went, than the Vassall case. But it was more spicy; and the press went to town on it. Rumours had been rife about Mr. John Profumo, Secretary of State for War, from January

---

[1] See Kilmuir, op. cit., p. 324. 'I got the impression that he was extremely alarmed about his own position, and was determined to eliminate any risk for himself by a massive change of government.'

[2] Mr. Butler became First Secretary of State, and, in effect, Deputy Prime Minister. He had, however, no departmental duties.

[3] See Kilmuir, op. cit., p. 324 and R. Bevins, *The Greasy Pole*.

[4] Cmnd 2009. Mr. Macmillan restored Mr. Galbraith to the Government, as Joint Parliamentary Secretary to the Minister of Transport. See Rebecca West, *The Vassall Affair* and *Hansard*, Series 5, vol. 677, cols 240–372, for the Vassall debate.

1963 onwards. Everyone, it seemed, had heard them, except the Prime Minister. Mr. Profumo shared a mistress, Miss Christine Keeler – with a Russian diplomat, Captain Ivanov, a former Russian travel attaché. This was certainly an unwise relationship for a Cabinet Minister.[1] On March 22nd in the House of Commons Mr. Profumo formally denied any impropriety in his relations with a Miss Christine Keeler. In June he resigned, after admitting that he had lied to the House. In retrospect, it all seems to have been a storm in a teacup and the Denning Report[2] on all this, published in September 1963, cleared Mr. Profumo of any breach of security. But the Prime Minister was blamed because he had not known about the whole affair sooner and nipped it in the bud. The issue found the British press and public at its most sanctimonious. *The Times* saw in this case evidence of a general decline in moral standards, which it rather curiously, at this stage, attributed to Tory affluence. The self-rightous press hounded one Dr. Ward who was arrested on the grounds that he had provided Miss Keeler with her flat, and was living on immoral earnings and procuring. In the end Dr. Ward committed suicide. The lives of other people peripherally concerned, such as Lord and Lady Astor, were made unpleasant, and indeed virtually intolerable. Many other people than Mr. Profumo had reason to feel ashamed of themselves before it was all over. But perhaps the real decline was not in morals, but in the credibility of the Government. And it was not because of Tory affluence, but because of the rising tide of unemployment, and the stop-go economy, which now seemed much more prone to stop than go. In politics, as in everything else, nothing succeeds like success. As Mr. Macmillan was to find, the reverse of this maxim is also apt to be true. Mr. Macmillan was increasingly coming to be associated with failure.

At the local government elections in May 1963 the Conservatives lost 525 seats. And, as the summer of 1963 wore on, increasing efforts were made by Tory back-benchers to persuade Mr. Macmillan to resign. There were by now several credible alternative Conservative leaders. It seems that during the summer of 1963 Mr. Maudling was the favourite. However, Mr. Macmillan reiterated, on various occasions, his determination to lead the Party at the next General Election, which clearly could not be very far away. Perhaps Mr. Wilson did not want Mr. Macmillan to resign, fearing the emergence of a more dangerous rival.[3] Be that as it may, the constant attacks from the Opposition made it very difficult for Conservatives to evolve an alternative Leader at all, as this would have looked like capitulation.

[1] H.C. Deb., Fifth Series, Vol. 679, cols. 34–175, 17 June 1963. Profumo debate. See also Clive Irving, *Scandal '63*.
[2] *Denning Report*, September 1963. Cmnd 2152.
[3] A. Howard and R. West, *The Making of the Prime Minister*, Ch. 3.

However, on 8 October 1963 Mr. Macmillan's sudden illness, on the eve of the annual Party Conference, brought an unanticipated end to the rumbling discontents. It seems that he thought, at the time, that his illness was more serious than in fact it turned out to be. So on October 10th he sent a message to the Party Conference indicating his intention to resign as soon as a new Leader could be found. Subsequent developments in the struggle for the Conservative Leadership are still far from clear, and different people involved have put very different interpretations on the succeeding events.

There were three main contenders:

(1) Lord Hailsham. He was, it later transpired, Mr. Macmillan's first choice. He was supported by right wing enthusiasts in the constituencies and by members of the Macmillan family. He at once indicated his availability by announcing, during the Party Conference, that he intended to renounce his peerage. This was now possible, under the 1963 Peerage Act. He was a good, if emotional, orator.

(2) Mr. Butler. As First Secretary of State, he was in effect the Deputy Prime Minister. He had been a close runner-up in 1957 and was now, in the view of many, the obvious choice. It was alleged that he had the support of at least half of the Cabinet, and of most left of centre Conservative M.P.s. But he was not, it seems, popular with the regional chairmen.[1] And Mr. Macmillan's manoeuvres suggest that he felt about Mr. Butler rather as Attlee had felt about Morrison. The reasons for this are not, and probably never will be, wholly clear. Perhaps he felt that Mr. Butler was not the man to unite the Party, which was now beginning to look a little fragmented; and that he had not enough fire and dynamism to provide the Leadership required.[2]

(3) Mr. Maudling. He seems to have been highly regarded by younger M.P.s earlier in 1963, about the time of the Profumo scandal. But at Blackpool he had few definite supporters. The serious contenders then were Lord Hailsham and Mr. Butler, and it seemed that Mr. Butler was away out ahead.

The time-honoured Conservative process of evolving a Leader took place, in part, in public at the Blackpool Party Conference, instead of behind the scenes. And the Conference, some thought, became rather like an American nominating convention. With the wisdom of hindsight, a good many people soon began to think that it would have been better if Mr. Macmillan had waited until the Conference was over before announcing his intention to retire. The Conservative Party Conference

---

[1] 'Donnish, dignified and dull' was, for instance, the verdict of Sir Gerald Nabarro, summing up the characteristics of the Party Leaders in a speech at Bolton Town Hall on 9 October 1963.

[2] See Ralph Harris, *Politics without Prejudice*, 1965, for Mr. Butler's earlier years; and Sparrow, op. cit.

has never been a policy-making, much less a Leader-selecting body; and it not surprisingly proved a quite unsuitable forum for this purpose.

Soon the scene shifted back to London, where Mr. Macmillan, from his hospital bed, decided to have 'soundings' made. On Tuesday October 15th the Cabinet approved Mr. Macmillan's plans, viz.
(1) The Lord Chancellor (Lord Dilhorne) should collect the views of the Cabinet.
(2) The Chief Whip in the Commons (Mr. Redmayne) should collect the views of Conservative M.P.s; and the Chief Whip in the Lords (Lord St. Aldwyn) those of the politically active Tory peers.
(3) Lord Poole, as Party Chairman, should make a report on the views of the Conservative Party in the constituencies.

Mr. Redmayne subsequently explained that his 'soundings' had not been conducted on a one man vote basis. Intensity of feeling had had to be taken into account. He was also, so he said, concerned to know which candidate had the fewest opponents.

By Thursday October 17th all the reports called for had been submitted to Mr. Macmillan. He decided upon Lord Home, a candidate nobody had hitherto thought of, as likely to be most generally acceptable to all concerned. On Thursday evening, a 'Stop Home' movement developed, and two of the other three contenders, Lord Hailsham and Mr. Maudling, agreed to serve under Mr. Butler. Mr. Macmillan apparently knew about this. But it is not clear who else knew what at this stage. In any event, Mr. Macmillan, having made up his own mind, thought it best to go ahead swiftly. On Friday October 18th he sent his letter of resignation to the Queen. When she came to see him at the hospital to ask for his advice on a successor, he advised Lord Home. So she sent for Lord Home and asked him to try to form a government. On Saturday October 19th Mr. Butler agreed to serve under Lord Home, as being the only way of preserving Party unity. Mr. Maudling and Lord Hailsham then followed suit. If Mr. Butler had refused to serve, perhaps they would have refused too. Mr. Macleod resigned.

It seems unlikely that Lord Home could have formed a government at all without the support of these three. He had no significant following in Parliament, or in the country, outside his Border constituency. Indeed, he was at that time virtually unknown as a public figure outside Foreign Office circles.

On October 23rd he renounced his peerage, becoming Sir Alec Douglas-Home. At the Kinross by-election he won a safe Tory seat, thus becoming a member of the House of Commons. On November 11th he was elected as the new Party Leader.

Why did Mr. Macmillan choose the Earl of Home? He had the same great disability that Sir Anthony Eden had suffered from – a total lack of experience of home affairs. He had no strong supporters, though he had done well at the Foreign Office. The other candidates – Lord Hailsham, Mr. Maudling and Mr. Butler – were all much more experienced, and had strong supporters.

It is hard to resist the Macleod explanation put forward in a long article in the *Spectator*,[1] namely that Mr. Macmillan at first preferred Lord Hailsham, but when he saw that Lord Hailsham, for all his oratorical skills and his popularity in the constituencies, could not unite the Party and was, indeed, rejected by the Cabinet, he chose Lord Home to keep Mr. Butler out. So the end of it all was that another Foreign Secretary, and this time a prominent member of the aristocracy, became Prime Minister. An alternative explanation is that offered by Lord Randolph Churchill.[2] According to this account, Mr. Macmillan simply thought that Lord Home was the best candidate available, and that was all there was to it.

Perhaps one lesson to be drawn from this episode is that when a sitting Prime Minister is being edged out of power, it is not desirable that he should be the controlling influence in the choice of his successor, any more than it was desirable that the Crown should be asked to play a leading part, as in 1957.

After this rather strange episode, certain consequential moves were made. Iain Mcleod and Lord Poole had been joint chairmen of the Conservative Party Organization. As one had supported Mr. Butler and the other Lord Hailsham, it was hardly possible for them to continue to act in this capacity. Mr. John Hare, who became Viscount Blakenham, was made the sole chairman of the Party Organization and Chancellor of the Duchy of Lancaster. He thus acquired a paid Cabinet post, as well as the chairmanship of the Party, following, in this respect, in Lord Woolton's footsteps.[3]

There were many ironies in this whole situation. Nor the least was that, as Professor Daalder has pointed out, whereas in 1923 Mr. Baldwin, an inexperienced commoner, was preferred to Lord Curzon, an experienced peer, in 1963 an experienced commoner was passed over in favour of an inexperienced peer.[4] And Lord Home, with no experience in domestic affairs, became Prime Minister at a time when Britain's domestic problems provided the main political issues, Mr. Butler, skilled in home affairs, being posted to the Foreign Office.

It is difficult to escape the conclusion that the end result was that the Conservatives acquired a Leader who was hardly anybody's first choice. But perhaps he did succeed, at that rather difficult time, in providing an umbrella under which all shades of Conservative opinion could find more

[1] Iain Macleod, 'The Tory Leadership', *Spectator*, 17 January 1964.
[2] Randolph Churchill, *The Fight for the Tory Leadership*.
[3] See Introduction, p. 18.
[4] See Daalder, op. cit., pp. 326–37.

or less adquate shelter. The Conservatives were not used to disunity, rebel groups, or rival ideologies. Although there have been plenty of examples of back-bench pressures and discontents over specific issues, there has been little division of the kind that the Labour Party has always had to accommodate. The possibilities of fissure in 1963 were novel and distasteful. Lord Home papered them over, anyway for the time being.[1]

b *The Prime Ministership of Sir Alec Douglas-Home, 18 October 1963 to 16 October 1964*
Sir Alec Douglas-Home was sixty years of age when he 'emerged' as Prime Minister. He belonged to an old and wealthy Border family. He had been educated at Eton and Oxford. He had done well at Eton, but did not have a distinguished university record. He went down with a Third, and there seemed then no reason to suppose that he would ever be heard of again, politically speaking. However, he got into the House of Commons as M.P. for South Lanark in 1931, and remained in the House until 1945. He returned in 1950, but succeeded to his peerage in 1951, and so had to move to the House of Lords. During the years from 1931 till 1945 he held a variety of offices, linked with Scotland, the Foreign Office, or the Commonwealth Relations Office.[2] He was virtually unknown to the man in the street, at any rate in England, when he became Prime Minister. He was considered to be on the right wing of the Conservative Party, although his views on the issues with which he was familiar were not extreme. An article in the *Observer*, on 26 October 1963, described him as 'A Scottish Earl who looks like an important senior faun'. He had done well in his various Foreign Office assignments. The same *Observer* article noted that 'he had just that touch of ambiguity which is so useful'. This may sound disparaging, and may seem to make Mr. Macmillan's choice even more incomprehensible. The fact is, however, that there was quite a lot that could be said in Sir Alec's favour. He was quick-witted, and with a sense of humour. He spoke his mind with, sometimes, a refreshing indifference to the effect that this was likely to produce. He had few extreme views, although he was apt to state the views he did have more uncompromisingly than most politicians. His performance at the Foreign Office was perhaps better than his performance at the Commonwealth Relations Office. Having no chips on his own shoulders, he had found it rather difficult to understand and sympathize with the emerging

[1] See Berrington, 'The Conservative Party: Revolts and Pressures. 1955–1961', *Parliamentary Quarterly*, 1961.
[2] He was P.P.S. to Neville Chamberlain 1937–40; Joint Under-Secretary for Foreign Affairs 1945; Minister of State at the Scottish Office 1951–5; Secretary for Commonwealth Relations 1955–60; Deputy Leader of the Lords 1956–7; Leader of the Lords 1957–60; Foreign Secretary 1960–3.

African and Asian countries, whose politicians had so many. And he did not care for their emotional style in politics. It is just possible to understand why Mr. Macmillan preferred him to the other contenders in 1963. There was about him a gaiety, a quickness and a resilience that could in other circumstances have made him a popular leader. No doubt the calculation was that, although he had in fact quite liberal views on many subjects, he would be very acceptable to the right wing of the Party. And it was from the right wing that most of the trouble was to be expected, in these years.

None the less, there can be little doubt that Mr. Macmillan miscalculated. Sir Alec did not seem able to acquire any mastery over economic problems, or much interest in domestic affairs, during his year at Number 10. He attracted no real following south of the Border. He was also about the most ineffective foil to Harold Wilson who could have been chosen at that time. The Conservative Party did fall in behind him, but Mr. Macmillan had left them with no alternative.

3 CONSTITUTIONAL AND ADMINISTRATIVE ISSUES

a *The Cabinet and the Prime Minister*

The years from 1959 to 1963 were the years of so-called 'presidential' rule. Mr. Macmillan dominated his Cabinet. He could not, perhaps, dispense with the services of those who enjoyed very high esteem in the Party and the country. But he could, and did, make quite frequent changes in senior Cabinet posts.[1] And certainly nothing quite like the 1962 'purge' had hitherto happened in twentieth-century Britain. Till then, the theory had been that the country was governed by a team of equals, although some, of course, were always seen as more equal than others. No one would have dissented from the view that the Prime Minister was the pivot on which the Cabinet turned – the without-which-not for effective government. No one would have disputed the right of a Prime Minister to drop individual Ministers, or to reshuffle the team. However, to dismiss, without any previous warning, seven out of twenty-one Cabinet Ministers did seem to suggest that a new relationship between the Prime Minister and his colleagues now obtained. The Prime Minister seemed to regard them as mere advisers, dispensable at will. It was difficult to see how this new relationship could be combined with any previously held ideas about collective responsibility.

Mr. Macmillan's apparent urge to move his colleagues very rapidly from one department to another further weakened the already shaky doctrine of Ministerial responsibility. The great departments of state had become far too complex to be mastered by birds of passage. The

[1] See Butler and Freeman, op. cit., p. 40.

inevitable result was to strengthen the position of permanent officials. But the higher echelons of the Civil Service were not really geared to the discharge of such onerous burdens, as the Fulton Commission was later to show.[1] Power, removed from the Cabinet, thus escaped in various directions. And it must be surmised that backrooms became more important for the formulation and execution of policy than they had ever been before.

b *The House of Lords*
On 31 July 1963 the Royal Assent was given to the Peerage Bill. The main intention of this Bill was to enable peers to renounce their titles for life, and stand for election as members of the House of Commons. Such a renunciation did not affect the subsequent inheritance of the peerage in question. Existing peers were given six months to decide, from the date of the passing of the Act, whether or not they wanted to resign their peerages; or, if they were minors, six months from their twenty-first birthdays. Peers succeeding after the Act was passed were given one year from the date of their succession, or coming of age, in which to make the choice.[2]

This Act was passed mainly as a result of the efforts of Mr. Wedgwood Benn, whose father, a Labour M.P., had gone to the Lords as Lord Stansgate, in the days before the Life Peerages Act of 1958, to strengthen Labour ranks in the Upper House. Lord Stansgate had tried, in 1955, to get a Bill passed enabling his son to renounce his peerage in advance. This had failed, perhaps because it had been feared that the result might be a rush to renounce peerages, in which all the politically able young peers would take part, and that this would greatly damage the Lords.

In 1960 Lord Stansgate died, and, despite a petition to the Commons, Mr. Wedgwood Benn was not allowed to remain a member of the House, or to state his case in person. He decided to contest the by-election at Bristol S.E., his former constituency. On May 4th he won a resounding victory, and doubled his majority. However, the Speaker refused to allow him into the House, and his case was passed on to a court of two judges. On 28 July 1961 this tribunal declared his Conservative rival the duly elected member for Bristol S.E. However, in December 1962, the Committee on Reform of the House of Lords proposed that the successor to a peerage should be able to surrender it for life, and that the right should be extended, initially, to those peers who had already succeeded.

Fortunately for Mr. Wedgwood Benn, some prominent Conservatives were also anxious for the passage of this Bill. Lord Hailsham, for instance,

---
[1] See Chapter V.
[2] For other minor changes made at this time, see Butler and Freeman, op. cit., p. 139. There is also a summary of the main landmarks in reform of the Upper House since 1908.

had long wanted it, and was now able to renounce his peerage. He did so in November 1963 when he became, for a brief period, a candidate for the Prime Ministership. The measure also came in in the nick of time for Lord Home, who could hardly have moved into No. 10 Downing Street had it not been on the statute-book. In fact, only some half dozen peers did renounce their peerages.

4 ECONOMIC ISSUES

a *General survey*

Throughout the period from 1959 to 1964 the pattern of 'stop-go' continued, and it became ever less possible to attribute this to chance episodes like the Suez crisis. Informed opinion became increasingly concerned over continued inflation, and more so still by the poor performance of the British economy as compared with that of other European countries. More and more people came to think that something was radically wrong. The Tory response, given notably by Mr. Macmillan, was a cautious advance towards planning. He now developed some important new initiatives in economic affairs.

(1) In the first place he set up the National Economic Development Council (N.E.D.C.) in 1961. This Council was given three responsibilities:

(a) to chart the growth plans of different sectors of the economy;
(b) to ensure that these plans were consistent with one another;
(c) to seek agreement on ways of improving the plans.

N.E.D.C.'s task was confined to advising. It was made up of representatives of employers, trade unions, nationalized industries, and various outside authorities. It was presided over by the Chancellor of the Exchequer. N.E.D.C. had a staff of economic experts to assist it; and it was responsible to Parliament.

The T.U.C. was at first very suspicious of this Tory move into what they regarded as their territory. The fear was that this was just another attempt to sell a policy of wage restraint. They agreed to co-operate only after a good deal of hedging and reservations.

The first meeting of N.E.D.C. was called in May 1962, and the growth target set by the planners was 4 per cent per annum.

Probably N.E.D.C. ought to be viewed, at any rate at this stage, as a political move. Mr. Macmillan saw that the Government had to appear to be doing something new about economic problems which, clearly, were getting out of hand.

(2) In 1962 he set up the National Incomes Commission (N.I.C.). Its terms of reference were to inquire into wage claims in the light of the public interest, although N.I.C. had no power to set aside wage agree-

ments. The T.U.C. refused flatly to have anything to do with this.
(3) The third general move was one towards regional planning. There were still, as in the thirties, serious economic problems associated with particular areas. In January 1963 Lord Hailsham was given special responsibility for the North-East. His mission was to inquire into measures specially designed to regenerate economic activities in this area. In October 1963 Mr. Heath was made Secretary of State for Industry, Trade and Regional Development. He took over Lord Hailsham's duties in the north-east, and assumed general responsibility for all the problem areas.

In 1964, a South-Eastern Regional study was published, setting out the new towns likely to be required in this booming area in the near future. Growth areas, as well as depressed areas, needed planning, it was now recognized.

(4) The fourth economic initiative was Mr. Macmillan's decision, made in 1961, to try to enter the Common Market. This whole problem will be discussed later, but it cannot be omitted from any general economic survey of these years. It was an essential part of the Macmillan strategy, which was planning at home – though as yet without compulsion; and entry into Europe as its counterpart, with all that that could mean in larger markets, and more competitive and challenging economic opportunities leading to a new period of growth. President de Gaulle vetoed the British application in January 1963.

b *Summary of economic developments 1959–1964*[1]
Economic crises dogged Mr. Macmillan's Government from the very beginning. After the Election of 1959 it soon became apparent that curbs would be needed. In January 1960 the Bank Rate was raised to 5 per cent, and then was raised to 6 per cent on June 23rd of the same year.

By the time that the 1961 Budget was introduced Mr. Selwyn Lloyd had become Chancellor of the Exchequer. His mandate was to encourage initiative and enterprise. With this end in view, the starting point for surtax on earned income was raised from £2,000 to £4,000. Inflation was to be curbed by various indirect taxes. The Chancellor of the Exchequer was to be given power to increase various taxes by immediate executive action in between Budgets, if circumstances warranted. These were known as 'regulators'.

In the summer of 1961, a serious sterling crisis developed, similar to that of 1957, but more ominous in that this time, unlike 1957, it was associated with a balance of payments crisis. In July, severe measures had to be taken to stop the drain on sterling; and the Bank Rate was raised to 7 per cent. Big loans were negotiated from the I.M.F. and the Central Banks; import duties were increased; a 'pay pause' was announced,

[1] See Annual Register for details of budgets.

to be continued until productivity had, as it were, caught up. At this time this merely meant that the wages of those employed in the government sector of the economy were to be frozen; and that the Chancellor hoped that other employees would follow suit. This tended to hit those workers then least able or least willing to exert pressure on their employers, such as hospital workers and teachers, while the industrial workers, represented by strong unions, could and did negotiate their own terms.

However, the measures were temporarily effective. By autumn the drain on sterling had been stopped and it became possible to reduce the Bank Rate again.

In 1962, difficulties over the pay pause were very much in evidence. Mr. Selwyn Lloyd tried in vain to persuade the T.U.C. to agree to a $2\frac{1}{2}$ per cent guide-line for wage increases. Government employees began to protest sharply. In 1962, the Post Office workers began a work-to-rule protest. In the spring, the nurses were offered a $2\frac{1}{2}$ per cent rise; the railwayman 3 per cent. But the difficulty inherent in this kind of government-sector-only pay pause was highlighted when industry offered the dockers 9 per cent.

It was against this background that Mr. Macmillan announced, in July, the setting up of the N.I.C., to which reference has already been made.

The 1962 Budget kept on with the policy of deflation. The intention was to keep down wages and prices at home, in the hope of helping exports and thus righting balance of payment difficulties. But in 1962 production hardly moved. The chief feature of the Budget was the levy on speculative gains. This was applied to profits from the sale of stocks and shares, if these had been held for less than six months. It was generally recognized as a politically motivated tax, which was a gesture to the unions to encourage them to join whole-heartedly in N.E.C.D. It did not do so. And increasingly public opinion began to question the Government's belief that pressure of home demand was the sole, or even the main reason for balance of payments crises. The Treasury belief that Britain could deflate its way out of balance of payment difficulties looked less and less plausible.

Mr. Maudling succeeded Mr. Selwyn Lloyd as Chancellor of the Exchequer in July 1962. The Budget of 1963 pledged expansion, and various tax reliefs were allowed, mainly designed to assist areas where unemployment was heavy and those income tax payers at the bottom of the scale. Schedule A tax on house property was at this time abolished. However, Labour attacked this Budget as full of electioneering gimmicks.

In the summer the trade gap widened again, and industrial production remained stagnant. The third, and much the most serious, sterling crisis in nine years was allowed to develop, and no serious avoiding action was taken. This is never politically rewarding, anyway in the short run, and the General Election was now close at hand.

In retrospect, it can be seen that the Government's economic policy shifted, between 1963 and 1964, from a policy of deflation and great caution to one of expansion and qualified optimism. One of the main reasons for the change seems to have been the N.E.D.C. expectation of a high annual growth rate of 4 per cent. This, as it turned out was a far too optimistic view of British economic prospects.

c *The Common Market*

Britain's application to join the E.E.C. was so much part and parcel of Mr. Macmillan's economic policy that it seems impossible to detach it from any survey of Britain's economic problems in these years, even though it may be argued that the real reasons for trying to join the E.E.C. were political. To join forces with the Europeans was, in Mr. Macmillan's view, the real answer to Britain's economic difficulties. And part of the subsequent trouble was that when General de Gaulle slammed the door on him, Mr. Macmillan really had no alternative to fall back on.

Entry into the Common Market meant a sharp break with earlier Conservative policy – to say nothing of that of the Opposition. The Americans it is true, had always wanted Britain to lead the Europeans towards integration – certainly economic integration; possibly political also. Always Britain had refused. She had been lukewarm about the Council of Europe. She had opposed the Schuman Plan of 1950. She had opposed the European Defence Community. And she had refused to join the signatories of the Treaty of Rome in 1957. So Macmillan's policy involved a big switch in Conservative thinking. This switch was not, it seems, the result of a change in public opinion. There was no strong demand for entry into the E.E.C., the pros and cons of which were not as yet apparent to the public. Nor, apparently, did all Mr. Macmillan's Cabinet colleagues share his views. Some commentators, indeed, saw the July 1962 Cabinet purge as an attempt by Mr. Macmillan to get rid of the outstanding anti-marketeers. Most of the Tory Party still probably preferred a Commonwealth solution to Britain's economic and political malaise. Mr. Macmillan, however, seems to have listened to some of his senior civil servants, and it may have been they who persuaded him of the need to go into Europe.

The reasons, some people think, were primarily political. The fear was that the Europeans were going ahead so fast with their integration plans that soon there would be one huge political unit, commanding vast resources, dwarfing those of Great Britain. The Commonwealth, whatever the Tory constituency parties might think, was fast disintegrating. In these circumstances, Europe would certainly soon supplant Great Britain as the main partner of the United States. Britain's relationship with the

Six was seen by Mr. Macmillan as a key foreign policy question, and no longer primarily as a narrowly economic issue, Thus, while Mr. Maudling, entrusted with dealing with the EFTA negotiations from 1957 to 1959, had been based at the Board of Trade, Mr. Heath, the new negotiator, was based at the Foreign Office.

There were, of course, important economic arguments, too, and these centered around the impressive growth rates of the E.E.C. countries, as compared with Britain's own very poor performance in the post-war years. However, economists were divided. Entry would clearly hit the less efficient British industries hard. It would present very considerable difficulties in the agricultural sector; and it would weaken what was left of the Commonwealth economic link. But many economists felt that these disadvantages would be more than offset by the great advantage of belonging to a large domestic market. The resultant competition could be expected to stimulate British industry, to speed up the elimination of restrictive practices, and to concentrate effort on the growth industries. This would take care of Britain's real economic problems much more effectively than fiddling with the Bank Rate, hire-purchase controls, regulators, deflationary budgets and all the rest, which had led only to the endless stop-go-stop cycle of which everyone was now so heartily tired.

Then the Americans, who were Mr. Macmillan's chosen partners in all his policies, were so much in favour. On balance, there seemed very little doubt as to where British interests lay.

The attitude of the Labour Party was at that time distinctly hostile. It always had been. Labour did not wish to join forces with the strong capitalist right wing European boom societies. Such a move would be likely to curtail the planning powers of a future Labour government. Better no allies at all, than flourishing capitalist allies, some thought. Some Labour M.P.s, however, did favour entry into Europe, and among them Roy Jenkins was prominent. Douglas Jay strongly opposed it from the beginning. Hugh Gaitskell did not, at first, commit himself. But, by the autumn of 1962 he had come out against Europe, at any rate for the moment. The Labour Party argued that the Government had no mandate for such a major change in policy, and that a General Election should be held; that the economic arguments for and against entry were more or less evenly balanced; and that the effect on the Commonwealth would be disastrous. And one certain consequence would be a sharp rise in the cost of food.

The course of the negotiations was as follows. On 31 July 1961 the Prime Minister told the Commons that Britain intended to apply for membership, on three conditions:
(1) That satisfactory arrangements could be made to safeguard British interests in general;

(2) that Commonwealth interests, primarily New Zealand's, could be taken care of;
(3) that the interests of Britain's EFTA partners could be provided for. Mr. Macmillan said that Mr. Heath, at the Foreign Office, would be the full-time British negotiator, at Brussels.

On 10 August 1961, Britain put in her formal application to join.

On 10 October 1961 Mr. Heath began his work in Brussels. And, meantime, Mr. Macmillan backed him up with 'summitry', and, in particular, by efforts to persuade the West Germans to support the British application. It was a long, tricky road, if only because Mr. Heath had to speak with two different voices, one for British ears and one for European.

In January 1963, de Gaulle's famous press conference effectively ended Britain's chances of being accepted by the Europeans.

There were, from the European standpoint, two main objections to accepting Britain:
(1) Britain's economic structure and her economic problems were very different from those of the Six. It was not a case of like joining with like.
(2) British entry, so the Europeans feared, would mean that Europe would have a subordinate status in an Anglo-American dominated alliance. Britain, in fact, would be the Trojan horse of American influence in Europe, for Britain still enjoyed a 'special relationship' with America. So, of course, did Germany, although this special relationship was of a rather different kind. But America dominated both of them. Thus together, Germany and Britain could be expected to dominate over France.

5 DOMESTIC AFFAIRS

These years were the seminal years for the legislation of the later sixties. A series of inquiries was launched between 1960 and 1961, all designed to facilitate the modernization of Britain. Some of these reported before Mr. Wilson came to power in 1964 and were used as the basis for subsequent Labour policies. For instance: 1960 the Guillebaud Committee Report on the Railways; 1963 the Newsom Report on Secondary Education; 1963 the Robbins Report on Higher Education, 1963 the Beeching Report on the Railways; 1963 the Buchanan Report on Town Planning.

The more closely one studies the Macmillan years, the more apparent it becomes that, old man though he was, and lacking though he was in the more highly regarded tools of the contemporary politician, he was none the less a planner at heart. He knew that change was needed, and he did his best to prepare the way for change.

Two major legislative Acts were put on the statute-book by this Government. Both were highly controversial. One was the Commonwealth Immigration Act of 1962. The other was the abolition of resale price maintenance in 1964.

a *The Commonwealth Immigration Act*
This Act was one of the major bones of contention, both between and within the Labour and Conservative Parties.

There had always, of course, been some immigration from the Commonwealth. But after 1953 the influx of coloured Commonwealth citizens began to increase steeply. One can speculate, not very conclusively perhaps, about the reasons for this. Between the wars, Britain cannot have looked like a very attractive place to migrate to – certainly not in the thirties, with massive unemployment, a stagnating economy, and the threat of war looming closer and closer. Anyway, dependent peoples in Asia, Africa and elsewhere had not then acquired the habit of moving about in their own countries, much less from one continent to another. Horizons were much more limited, and the immemorial patterns of living did not greatly alter from one generation to another, except perhaps on the European continent. The Second World War altered all this. People, and indeed whole societies were then uprooted and thrown into the melting pot. And, after it was all over, vast numbers on all continents began to reach after goals hitherto undreamt of, and think in terms of material betterment on a scale never before conceived. They had fought, through the war years, side by side with men from much richer, more sophisticated, technologically advanced societies, and this experience had given them a quite new slant on their own future. The ideas generated by nationalism, democracy, and self-determination, which had brought about a new Europe after the 1918 war, now began to work on other continents too. By 1953, when wartime restrictions were just about over, Britain must have seemed a very good country in which to live, to very many Asians, Africans and West Indians who had British citizenship. And, as Mr. Butler put it, in the debate on the second reading of the Commonwealth Immigrants Bill, it so happened that about a quarter of the world's population was legally entitled to come and live in England. Such was the legacy of Empire.[1]

There were other factors too, which about this time caused a critical increase in the number of people seeking to come in, as immigrants, to the United Kingdom. For instance, for many generations West Indians lacking prospects at home had been accustomed to emigrate to the United States. But in 1952, Congress virtually excluded them when it passed the McCarran-Walter Immigration Act. And other countries on the American mainland followed suit with similar legislation. Only Britain still main-

[1] H.C. Deb. Fifth Series, Vol. 649, cols. 687–812, 16 November 1961.

tained an open door policy. The difficulty for Britain was in the numbers now involved. Thus, in 1959, immigrants from the West Indies, India and Pakistan had numbered 20,200; in 1960 the number had risen to 58,100; in 1961 it had reached 115,150 per annum. In certain sectors the immigrants had proved a valuable addition to the British labour force. But they were concentrated in particular areas of London and some of the big industrial Midlands towns, and this concentration inevitably imposed severe strains on local services. It became increasingly obvious that Britain could not continue to absorb, indefinitely, unskilled immigrant labourers on this scale. The Commonwealth Immigration Act controlled entry by a labour permit system and very drastically reduced the net rate.[1]

If the labour force at home had to be planned to maintain full employment; if the cost of social services in the new Welfare State had to be calculated in matters like housing, education, and so on, how could this be done against a background of uncontrolled, and it seemed steadily increasing, immigration?

This was the general thinking behind the Bill of 1962.

Other happenings pointed in this direction too. Of these the most important were the race disturbances in 1958, in Nottingham and the Notting Hill area of London. In themselves these were tiny. No lives were lost. Little property was damaged. But these kinds of happenings were new to Britain. And, perhaps rightly, they were regarded as a straw in the wind. Increasingly, local authorities voiced their anxieties about the impact of unplanned and seemingly quite large-scale immigration on local services they were expected to provide.

So, in July 1962, the Immigration Bill became law. Its provisions were to run for a five-year trial period, and, very briefly, they were as follows:

Apart from those immigrants able to support themselves by their private means, Commonwealth citizens could apply for vouchers from the Ministry of Labour, if one of three conditions were met:

(1) if they had a job to come to;
(2) if they possessed skills or educational qualifications likely to be useful in the United Kingdom;
(3) they could come in on a quota whereby the Ministry would allow a certain number of applicants subject to any limit the Government chose to impose at any time.

The reactions to this Bill are of great interest. The argument was not along Party lines. If lines can be distinguished at all, they were those of class. The working people, whether Tory or Labour, were generally for the Bill. The Labour Leadership was against it. And the Tory Leadership was divided.

The Opposition attacked the Bill on the grounds that it introduced a

[1] Butler and Freeman, op. cit., p. 194.

colour bar into British legislation, since the number of white Commonwealth immigrants affected was negligible, and the southern Irish were excluded from it; they argued that the British economy needed immigrant labour anyhow. Later, however, Labour leaders were embarrassed, because when they came to power they did not wish to repeal the Act, since to do so would have brought them massive unpopularity from their own rank and file. Public opinion polls showed that there was general approval of the restriction of immigration.

b *The abolition of resale price maintenance 1964*
Mr. Heath was anxious to get a major innovation on to the statute-book, which he hoped would contribute to the battle against rising prices. He persuaded the Cabinet of the need to end the practice of resale price maintenance. That is, the agreement that goods bought wholesale should not be resold in shops at less than an agreed minimum price. This restrictive practice inhibited new trading techniques. Its abolition could expected to bring in some competition, which might well reduce prices and thus benefit the consumer. Mr. Heath had an uphill struggle, but he showed himself as alert, receptive and courageous. There was a great deal of Tory opposition from small shopkeepers, and from those who supported them. On the second reading, twenty-one Tories voted against the Bill, twelve abstained, and twenty-three were absent from the House. But the Bill was passed.

c *The National Health Service*
On 1 February 1961 an increase in N.H.S. charges was announced. The cost of the N.H.S. was rising steadily, and it was estimated that the increase would be of the order of 11 per cent for 1961-2. The easiest and most popular way of dealing with this would, of course, have been to leave it to the Chancellor of the Exchequer for inclusion in the next Budget. By this means the whole population would have paid in increased taxes of one sort or another. Instead, the Minister of Health, then Mr. Enoch Powell, decided to cover almost all of the 11 per cent by an increase in service charges. Thus, prescription charges were to be doubled; dentures became more expensive; and weekly contributions were increased. The Opposition decided to make an issue of this policy, for three reasons:

(1) Direct taxes were paid mainly by the relatively wealthy, whereas these charges were a flat rate, which bore most heavily on the poor.
(2) It seemed wrong that people should be obliged to pay at the time of illness, when they were least able to do so.
(3) Arrangements for the chronic sick were far from adequate.

Rowdy debates followed the Labour vote of censure moved on February

8th and the Bill did not get through the Commons until the middle of March 1961.[1]

d *Hospitals*
On 23 January 1962 Mr. Powell announced a large increase in spending on hospitals. Ninety new ones were to be built or begun, in the next decade at the cost of £500m. The final target was 200 new hospitals; and the replacement of half the existing ones. There was now a growing and uneasy awareness of the inadequacy and unsuitability of very many of the existing hospitals, especially those for mental patients.[2]

e *Housing*
A scandal which came to be known as 'Rachmanism' was one of the side issues brought to light as a result of the Profumo affair. Mr. Ben Parkin, Labour M.P. for North Paddington, had long been campaigning against rapacious landlords in his constituency, without, however, making much headway. His chief target had been one Peter Rachman, a Polish property dealer. It now appeared that Miss Keeler and another of Dr. Ward's 'girls' had at one time lived with him. Rachmanism meant sub-letting at extortionate rents; terrorizing of tenants; and exploitation of West Indians and Asians in particular. Labour tabled a motion of censure, putting all this down to the 1957 Rent Act, and the consequent de-control of rents. They promised to repeal the Rent Act when returned to power. The Conservatives argued that it was precisely the rigidity occasioned by rent control before 1957 that had given rise to most of the difficulties: and further, that the troubles in Paddington were part of a localized London housing problem which should not be blown up into a national issue.
    In any event, a Government inquiry into housing was set up.[3]

f *Education*
The years from 1959 to 1964 were the seminal years as far as educational reform went. In 1959, the Crowther Report on the education of fifteen- to eighteen-year-olds was published. This Report was the fruit of three years of investigation. It was pointed out in the Report that the numbers in this age group would drop, between 1965 and 1970, because the post-war population bulge would then be past. These were the years, therefore, when the school leaving age ought to be raised, at last, from fifteen to sixteen.[4] In January 1964 it was duly announced that the school leaving age would be raised to sixteen in 1970-1.

[1] H.C. Deb., Fifth Series, Vol. 634, cols. 406-590, 8 February 1961.
[2] *Annual Register, 1962.*   [3] *Annual Register, 1963*, pp. 34-5.
[4] *Annual Register, 1959.*

Two other educational reports of great interest were published, in 1963:
(i) *The Robbins Report on Higher Education* It was recommended in this Report that there should be a massive increase in higher education. The target was 390,000 full-time places by 1973-4, as against the existing 110,000 places. The Robbins Report advised:
(a) the foundation of six new universities;
(b) that the six new universities should be founded in or near big urban areas, and not, as heretofore, around old cathedral towns;
(c) that colleges of advanced technology (CATS) should be given university status;
(d) that new institutions of scientific and technological education and research should be developed;
(e) that there should be a closer association between teacher-training colleges and neighbouring universities.

It also proposed a new Ministry of Arts and Sciences with responsibility for the whole field of higher education.

The Robbins Report was hailed by the Government and by the country as a major break-through, and probably the most important State paper on social affairs since the Beveridge Report. Already, in May 1961, the Government had announced the establishment of four new universities, at Canterbury, Colchester, Coventry and Lancaster, in addition to those already in incubation at Brighton, Norwich and York. Much argument was now engendered on the question as to whether existing standards could or should be maintained, if this enormous increase in numbers took place.

The Prime Minister promised to find the necessary finance. Extra post-graduate places would be provided, from which the staff for the expansion could be recruited.

The recommendation for a separate Ministry for Arts and Sciences was not accepted, for the time being. The wisdom of such a division of the educational 'establishment' was widely questioned, both by Tory and by Labour M.P.s.

(ii) *The Newsom Report* on the education of average and below-average children, also published in 1963, repeated the Crowther recommendation to raise the school leaving age. This report, however, drew attention to the fact that educational programmes would have to be recast before the extra year could be added. There were great problems to be faced if another year at school was to become compulsory for all children. It was no use, said the Commissioners acidly, 'extending the period of boredom'. The Report recommended:
(a) a special study of teaching techniques for environmentally and linguistically handicapped children;
(b) syllabuses more closely related to everyday life;
(c) special provisions for slum areas;

(d) an extension of the Outward Bound type of adventure training;
(e) better sex education in schools.

g *The Police*
In May 1962, the Royal Commission on the Police published its Report. The problem here was the great multiplicity of local police forces, under the control of local government authorities. Many disadvantages ensued from this arrangement, the chief of which was, probably, the effect on recruiting. The absence of any credible carrer structure, unless perhaps in the Metropolitan Police Force, meant that there was little incentive for the better educated to enter the police service at all. A minority of the Commission favoured a national police force under central control. A majority considered that so drastic a change was not at present desirable, and instead proposed a reduction by amalgamation in the number of existing forces.

h *Aviation*
In 1963 a new chairman and managing director of B.O.A.C. was appointed, with a mandate to make B.O.A.C. pay and to end the big losses of recent years. One of the major problems at issue was whether B.O.A.C. ought to buy British aircraft, even if American ones were more economic.

The other big issue was the development of the Concorde, a supersonic airliner which it was hoped to build in conjunction with the French. In November 1962 the Government signed an agreement with France, providing for joint construction. In the summer of 1964 the Government had to admit that the estimated cost of the Concorde project had doubled. They were, however, willing to go ahead and develop it. The aircraft industry was thought to be of crucial importance to the British economy.

i *Railways*
In March 1960 the Guillebaud Report on railwaymen's wages recommended a series of increases, ranging from 8 to 18 per cent. The Government accepted these recommendations, but said that in return the railways would have to be radically reorganized, in order not to burden the economy too heavily.

In 1963 the Beeching Report made far-reaching suggestions on how to cut the railway's deficit. The main recommendations were:
(1) that half the existing railway stations should be closed; and that one-third of the tracks should be abandoned;
(2) goods traffic should be concentrated at 100 depots;
(3) a new fleet of 'liner trains' should be built, carrying containers that could be rapidly transferred from rail to road.

Lord Beeching acknowledged that this would involve capital expenditure of £250m. He calculated, however, that if his plans were accepted the railway deficit would have disappeared by 1970.

Surveying the long list of Royal Commissions and other Reports, it is impossible not to be impressed by the amount of re-thinking and planning going ahead in the years from 1959 to 1964. The information was to hand; the expertise was available. The desire to plan, transform and lead Britain into a new age – all were present. The Tory leaders concerned were, for the most part, able, and forward-looking men. The Prime Minister was himself still an enthusiastic planner as he had been long ago, in the thirties. The two major Parties, in spite of bickering, were in substantial agreement. Why, then, did it all amount to so little? Probably because the necessary economic strength to carry Britain through into the new technological age; to make her, again, prosperous, competitive, and able to play her full part in world affairs, as well as put her own house in order, was simply not there. Britain knew what was needed. What still eluded her leaders was how to plan and develop the economy, so that the capital resources for all these projects were available. Because they were not, the Conservatives lost the 1964 Election. And because of this too, British defence and foreign policy generally came to look ever less credible to the rest of the world, and, in the end, even to the British themselves.

6 DEFENCE POLICY

The background to all the arguments about defence in this period is that, despite the falling apart of the Empire, and despite Britain's economic weakness, the demands on her were still very great. In part, it was a matter of helping to defend the free world against Communism. Britain had commitments of this kind to the post-war regional pacts, NATO, SEATO, and CENTO (Baghdad Pact), which she had herself helped to negotiate. Under the NATO pact, for instance, she had the quite new commitment to station troops in peacetime in Europe. Britain had many other kinds of commitments up and down the world. And her chain of bases was intended to enable her to take appropriate action in emergencies of all kinds. On top of this was the new commitment involved in becoming, or remaining, in the nuclear power group of Great Powers. In the years from 1948 to 1953, this burden had seemed inescapable because war with Russia had then looked so likely. After Stalin's death in 1953 and the beginning of a period of relative *détente*, it began to look more questionable. And many thought that the 1957 decision to concentrate on nuclear, at the expense of conventional, weapons accorded ill with the kind of responsibilities which Britain still had to shoulder.

The 1957 decision to concentrate on nuclear weapons became in fact much more difficult to stick to in the life of this Government. Britain could not keep up, because she had simply not got the economic strength.

In April 1960 the Government announced the abandonment of the development of the British Blue Streak fixed-site missiles. It had become clear that fixed sites were too vulnerable and that Russian technological developments in this field had overtaken the British. There had to be much greater mobility. It had also become clear that the policy of an independent nuclear weapon development programme was beyond the resources of the British economy. The United Kingdom would, it was now decided, continue to possess nuclear weapons, but it would no longer attempt to develop its own. The 1960 decision meant the end of the British claim to be regarded as an independent nuclear power. Henceforth, Britain would be dependent on whatever nuclear weapons the United States chose to provide her with.

It was not, however, seen in this light by the Government. And in June 1960 it was announced, after the Camp David meeting between Eisenhower and Macmillan, that Great Britain would buy American Skybolt air-to-ground missiles when these had been developed. Apparently the Government had, at this time, the option between purchasing the Polaris submarine-based missiles and the Skybolt aircraft-delivered variety. The Government chose Skybolt because it did not then have the nuclear-powered submarines necessary to deliver Polaris, whereas it did have the V bombers capable of launching Skybolt. The *quid pro quo* for Skybolt was that Great Britain would allow the United States to have a floating base for their Polaris submarines at Holy Loch. Holy Loch and Skybolt were, of course, separate agreements. But the Government was convinced that the Holy Loch agreement would in fact oblige the United States to provide Britain with some nuclear weapons even when Skybolt became obsolete.[1]

At the end of 1962 the United States decided to cancel the Skybolt missile programme, on which the future British nuclear defence programme now depended. The American Government said that the reasons were technical. Skybolt was not developing well. And in any case, America needed to cut back on its research programme in order to finance its conventional forces. In British Government circles, however, the suspicion was that America was trying to end Britain's position as an independent nuclear power altogether.

Mr. Macmillan brought great influence to bear on President Kennedy, and, at the Nassau Conference in December 1962 the United States agreed to provide Britain with Polaris missiles to be fired from nuclear submarines now to be built by Great Britain. The proviso was that these submarines and their missiles should be handed over to NATO and used as part of a multilateral force, a scheme much favoured at that time by

[1] A. Schlesinger, *A Thousand Days*, pp. 856–62.

American planners. However, in a major emergency affecting Great Britain alone, the British submarines could act under orders from London. Mr. Macmillan insisted that Britain's nuclear independence was preserved because of this clause, and that there was much to be said for the Polaris submarines. They were less vulnerable than other vehicles of nuclear power; and they would not necessarily attract a nuclear retaliatory strike, since they need not be based on the United Kingdom. The V bombers delivering Skybolt would in any case have been obsolete by the early 1970s. However, when the United States made a similar offer to the French it was refused on the grounds that France did not wish to be dependent on America.

The significance of the Nassau Agreement was that the 'special relationship' so long existing between Britain and America was prolonged, despite the desire of many people in America to end it, and to end Britain's quasi-independence as a nuclear power by *not* offering her a substitute for Skybolt, thus forcing her into Europe and into participation in a NATO multilateral force.

It may be conjectured that the Nassau Agreement almost certainly played a part in influencing General de Gaulle in his refusal to admit Britain into the Common Market. It made it plausible for the General to argue that since this 'special relationship' still evidently existed, British entry would mean, ultimately, American dominance in Europe. His idea, so he said, had been that France and Britain should provide a genuinely independent European nuclear force. Now, the British/American agreement at Nassau had ruled that out. But most observers think that the General would have vetoed British entry anyway, using some other pretext if necessary.

In a way, the Nassau Agreement was a triumph for Mr. Macmillan, and for Britain. The Americans had not wanted or intended to make such an arrangement; Macmillan had persuaded them. But the writing was on the wall, and it was clearly doubtful whether Great Britain would again get such generous terms from the United States when Polaris, in its turn, became obsolete.

The British press outcry against the Nassau Agreement was perhaps rather surprising. A certain amount of it may be put down to Service rivalry. Just as the abandonment of Blue Streak for Skybolt had signified the passing of power from the Army to the Air Force, so now the abandonment of Skybolt for Polaris signified the passing of power from the Air Force to the Navy. So Service sensibilities were ruffled. Then, it was felt that the new planning involved a dangerous time gap. The V bombers without Skybolt would be obsolete by 1966. Polaris could not be ready until 1968. Would the U.S.S.R. be ready to take advantage of this two-year time gap? The many sectors of opinion now seriously committed to the E.E.C. plan felt that Nassau would constitute a formidable handicap.

7 FOREIGN POLICY

a *General*

The assumption still held during the life of this Government that Britain must maintain her Great Power status. It was this assumption that lay behind the desperate effort to remain in the nuclear club, even though it was becoming ever more clear that the British economy could not sustain such a role, and even though it put many of Britain's conventional commitments at risk. To achieve this end Mr. Macmillan saw his rôle, in the first instance, as in cementing the 'special relationship' with the United States. His friendship with, and admiration for the young President Kennedy gave almost the only substance that there was to this claim.

Mr. Macmillan also saw his rôle as that of a mediator between East and West. His first efforts were for a summit conference. But this came to nothing in 1960 when an American U2 reconnaissance plane was shot down over Soviet territory, just before the Great Powers were due to meet. But Mr. Macmillan's efforts continued, and the signing of the Test Ban Treaty in 1963 probably was, at any rate in part, due to his steady pressure on Mr. Kennedy to negotiate.

Mr. Macmillan's decision to apply to enter the Common Market was no doubt motivated by a variety of considerations. He wanted to keep the special relationship with the United States. But the United States very much wanted to see Britain in Europe. Perhaps both would be possible. The Commonwealth was, he saw, fast breaking up, and nothing could or should be done to stop this, or even to retard it. When General de Gaulle said Non, Mr. Macmillan was left high and dry. There was a disintegrating Commonwealth; an increasingly unreal and strained 'special relationship' with the United States; a make-believe nuclear status; and a Europe from which Britain was excluded. After January 1963, Mr. Macmillan was a highly vulnerable politician.

b *The Anglo-American relationship*

In some ways, this was closer than it had been in the life of the 1955-9 Government. Then, the relationship had been complicated by the rivalry and dislike between Eden and Dulles, which had culminated at Suez in 1956. Macmillan had been able to repair the breach with President Eisenhower, an old wartime friend. But the real realignment did not come until the start of the Kennedy administration in 1960. Macmillan and Kennedy were close friends, each greatly respecting the other. In June 1961 President Kennedy visited Mr. Macmillan in London for an informal talk, which was to mark the beginning of what became Kennedy's closest link with any foreign leader, and this despite the great difference in age! The American Government listened to the British

Government and took account of its views, not because Britain was in any sense the equal of the United States, but because the President and the Prime Minister were close friends. Each, it may be surmised, had something to give the other, in encouragement and friendship. In December 1961 came the Bermuda meeting, when the main topic was whether or not the United States should resume atmospheric nuclear tests because the Russians had done so. Mr. Macmillan urged, over and over again, that there ought first to be an attempt at disarmament. A summit discussion might persuade the Russians to yield in view of the massive cost of nuclear research. Mr. Schlesinger records: 'The nightmare of nuclear holocaust stirred more than ever under Macmillan's Edwardian flippancies.'[1] In February 1962 President Kennedy decided to resume tests, but declared his willingness to call them off, if a comprehensive Test Ban Treaty were signed. This Krushchev refused. So the American tests began, on April 25th. But the Test Ban Treaty was finally signed in 1963 and it owed very much to Macmillan's continuing pressure on Kennedy. However, the influence of the British Government was, in retrospect, probably not very great generally. In October 1962, for instance, at the time of the Cuba crisis, the Americans acted alone, consulting neither their allies nor the U.N. Security Council. Mr. Macmillan gave loyal support to the President. But the British press was, at the time, distinctly hostile. Why should the Americans be allowed to act alone in this way? Britain had sought to tackle a wrong-doer at Suez, by prompt action, and had been rapped over the knuckles and told to deal through the U.N. However, the American intervention was decisive and successful, as the British intervention had not been. And in the end the free world came to see that it owed much to President Kennedy's nerve, skill and firmness.

c *The Communist world*
On 20 May 1960 Mr. Macmillan reported to the Commons: 'We must face the fact that the period ahead may be one of retrogression instead of progress.'

On 27 June 1960 the Russian delegates walked out of the Disarmament Conference at Geneva, although deadlock was by no means imminent.

However, in September 1960 Krushchev visited the U.N. headquarters in New York. Macmillan went too. And the atmosphere got friendlier. But in 1961 the Berlin crisis ended in the building of the wall dividing East from West Berlin. The Russians chose to put pressure on the Allies in Berlin, because here the Allied position was least tenable, and they could perhaps be forced to accept Russian policies. After Cuba in 1962, however, when America and the U.S.S.R. had come right up to the brink of nuclear war, the relations between the two super powers improved

[1] Schlesinger, op. cit.

again and the improvement culminated in the Nuclear Test Ban Treaty of 1963. Macmillan's role in all this was to urge over and over again, the need both to negotiate and to halt the nuclear arms race.

d *Europe*

Britain's policies *vis-à-vis* Europe were difficult, not only because these were the years when France was blocking her desire to enter Europe, but also because British policies towards Europe were not really in line with those of America, her chosen partner.

America in these years wished most strongly to discourage the spread of nuclear weapons, as being likely enormously to increase the risk of nuclear war. Kennedy's strategy of the Grand Alliance was that the European states, including Britain, should be closely linked together; and together be able to repel any attack with conventional forces from the East, with their own conventional forces. The European alliance would be provided by the United States with a nuclear shield, in one form or another. Each of the European countries would have a finger, as it were, on the nuclear trigger, and so would have no incentive to go to the vast expense of developing their own nuclear weapons. The Europeans would not, however, be able to start a nuclear war on their own. America would still be the ultimate arbiter, and the spread of nuclear weapons throughout the world would thus be contained.

This solution was wholly unsatisfactory to the French, who had already started to manufacture nuclear weapons, and whose settled determination it was to be independent of American aid. It was not really satisfactory to the British, who saw themselves as an old-established nuclear power, and who wished to maintain independent nuclear status through their special relationship with the United States.

It was reasonably satisfactory to the Germans, who were precluded by the terms of the 1954 Treaty establishing the F.D.R. from developing or acquiring nuclear weapons at all. It thus represented a slight advance for them.

It was regarded with the deepest suspicion by the Russians, who, far from seeing the policy as a method of preventing Germany from acquiring nuclear status, felt that, on the contrary, it was actually giving her nuclear status. Germany would, if the Grand Alliance plan came off, actually have a finger on the trigger. Russian fear of West Germany was probably increasing steadily, and it was a factor that the West greatly underestimated. Mr. Macmillan seems to have been one of the few statesmen who did not.

The British, as well as the Europeans, were fearful of the change in American strategic thinking. America seemed to be saying that nuclear war was out of the question. If this was so, the nuclear deterrent, on which Western security had hitherto rested, could not deter. But, if security had to depend not on nuclear but on conventional weapons, the Western European Allies were hopelessly outclassed by the Soviet Union. The suspicion grew that America would not use nuclear weapons simply because European security was at stake because she would fear massive retaliation on the United States. She might well prefer in future to withdraw from Europe and keep out of its squabbles. If this was to be the case, a European nuclear deterrent, independent of the United States, was required. This was probably, *au fond*, the British position.

8 THE COMMONWEALTH

a *General*
In the first half of the sixties twelve Commonwealth countries surfaced and became independent:

Nigeria	1960	It became a republic in 1963.
Cyprus	1961	
Sierra Leone	1961	
Tanganyika	1961	It became a Republic in 1962. In 1965, it merged with Zanzibar and became known as Tanzania.
Jamaica	1962	
Trinidad	1962	
Uganda	1962	It became a republic in 1963.
Zanzibar	1963–4	
Kenya	1963	
Zambia	1964	
Malawi	1964	
Malta	1964	

The majority of these new independent states[1] were African. And it was throughout the African continent that advance towards self-government was most marked.[2] At the beginning of this surge forward in January 1960, Mr. Macmillan set off on an African tour to see for himself the problems of the African continent. He saw Africans struggling to be free, and in many of these countries white settlers clinging to their privileges. He remarked, before his take-off: 'We must not take ... too gloomy a view; these are exciting days for Africa.' In Cape Town on February 3rd he made his famous 'Wind of Change' speech to the South African Parliament.

[1] Butler and Freeman, op. cit., 2nd edn., p. 261.
[2] W. P. Kirkman, *Unscrambling an Empire. A Critique of British Colonial Policy 1956–1966*.

The most striking of all the impressions I have formed since I left London a month ago is of the strength of this African national consciousness. In different places it may take different forms, but it is happening everywhere. The wind of change is blowing through the Continent. Whether we like it or not, this growth of national consciousness is a political fact . . . our national policies must take account of it.

Though there were to be tremendous struggles in the next few years in individual countries, involving agonizing conflicts of loyalties, none the less, the Conservative Party followed Macmillan, despite its long attachment to empire. Only a little band of right wingers – the League of Empire Loyalists – organized some opposition.

Of course, it was not the case that British statesmen had suddenly and, as it were, overnight, tumbled to this problem in 1960, and that till then nothing had been happening. But hitherto the lack of African administrators and technically and professionally qualified people had seemed to make a more speedy advance impossible. The training of Africans to take over the machinery of government had only just started. In 1960, some effort was made to provide a Commonwealth technical and advisory service which would be available to newly independent states; but this kind of provision seems all to have been too little and too late. And now the pace of African advance became much faster.

The British Government was still, in these years, convinced of the value of federal solutions to awkward colonial problems. Thus, in spite of the failure of the Central African Federation, which was fully apparent by 1960 and formally recognized in 1963, and the disintegration of the West Indies Federation, which ended in May 1962, the British Government built up two new federations in this period – Malaysia and Southern Arabia. Both were to prove short-lived and abortive.

One of the difficulties now, for the British, was that the aspiring new states were vociferously supported at the United Nations and elsewhere by the already independent Asian states. Another difficulty was that the United Kingdom was no longer able to provide all the aid required in the difficult years leading up to independence. This meant that aspiring new states looked to the United States and to other donors, playing off one against the other. Then there were the problems associated with the now redundant colonial civil servants, some of them still required on short term contracts in the new states. Either their new salary levels had to be supplemented by the United Kingdom Government, since the new states were poor states, or they had to be found other employment. In fact, the problems associated with disengaging from the Empire were many faceted and nearly overwhelming. And most of them came to a climax in the life of this Government.

Different people have, of course, given different reasons for the accelerating rate of change. Why did the wind suddenly begin to blow with such immense force? The Hola Camp tragedy, said Mr. Macleod, who was as much responsible as anyone for the accelerated pace of British withdrawal. This triggered off all that followed.[1] But that seems not wholly plausible. There had been Hola Camp type tragedies before. The example of President Nkrumah, of Ghana and his All African People's Conference in Accra, says Dame Margery Perham. He showed potential leaders in the rest of Africa how to employ the force of the colour argument to arouse resistance in their own states, and especially in those states where the boundaries did not correspond to tribal boundaries. Only colour could overcome the weakness caused by disunity.[2] It seems certain that President Nkrumah did much to break the spell of African acquiescence in Britain's leisurely constitutional march towards self-government. He understood, and made others understand, how to appeal to the masses, and bypass the educated minority. Be this as it may, the fact was that Britain's power in Africa rested, and had always rested, on consent. It could never have been otherwise. Once the consent was gone there was only one possible end. And after 1945 it was going or gone. The mistake, perhaps, was not to have seen, after 1945, how fast the change was coming. If Britain had seen, she could perhaps have used the last few years more effectively in a crash programme of preparation for African administrators. But in the early and middle fifties, most people thought they had twenty years before them.

b *The Central African Federation*
The Monckton Commission, appointed in July 1959 to review the constitution of the Central African Federation, reported in 1960.[3] Its findings were that, in the two northern territories, Northern Rhodesia and Nyasaland, a majority of the Africans were opposed to the Federation, whereas the Europeans favoured it. In Southern Rhodesia the Africans favoured it, as the Federation's African policy was more liberal than that of Southern Rhodesia. But most of the Europeans did not. The dislike of the Africans in Northern Rhodesia and Nyasaland was, the Monckton Commission found, assuming almost pathological proportions, and it was associated everywhere with a picture of Southern Rhodesia as a white man's country, with racial policies very similar to those of South Africa. Expectations that the opposition would decline as the economic advantages of the Federation became apparent had not materialized. The fear was that the C.A.F. would be granted independence before African self-government was assured, and that the African Affairs Board was an insufficient and unreliable safeguard. The Monckton

[1] *Weekend Telegraph*, 12 March 1965. [2] *Listener*, 27 May 1965.
[3] Mannsergh, op. cit., pp. 141–52.

Commission therefore recommended the continuation of a federal association, but with the right to secede accepted. The federalists, led at that time by Sir Roy Welensky, fought these proposals tooth and nail. Secession was out of the question, they thought.

However, in December 1962 the Government accepted Nyasaland's right to secede from the Federation, and in March 1963 that of Northern Rhodesia. On 31 December 1963 the Federation was formally dissolved. In July 1964 Nyasaland became an independent state, known as Malawi; and Northern Rhodesia became independent as Zambia. Independence was not granted to Southern Rhodesia, much the most advanced of the three territories, because here the white settlers and the African views on their future seemed to differ too greatly to permit of this.

Mr. Butler, although at the Home Office until July 1962, had already in March taken on responsibility for Central African affairs. It was under his auspices that the Federation came to an end. He remarks, sadly:

> Politics is the art of the possible, and what I found it possible to achieve was an orderly dissolution of the Federation, the establishment of two new states in Zambia and Malawi, and the chance given to Southern Rhodesia to have a strong army and air force, with the opportunity for its ruling clique to open their doors to Africans if they paid any heed to world opinion. The present outcome of a white minority drawing up a republican Constitution and excluding Africans does not surprise me, but it does deeply offend me as a negation of human liberty and dignity.[1]

c *Kenya*
On 10 November 1959 Mr. Macleod announced the end of the Mau Mau emergency. In January 1960 a conference on Kenya was held at the Colonial Office, led by Mr. Macleod. The Conference recommended a compromise constitution, within a multi-racial framework. Another constitutional conference was held in 1962, and in 1963 independence was granted. The Europeans, and also if necessary the Asians, were to be phased out while Kenya became an independent African state. Kenya Asians were given the option of United Kingdom citizenship and promised in this case the right of entry to the United Kingdom.

The Europeans, whose farming skill had made the so-called White Highlands among the most prosperous parts of Africa, were bitter. They had been encouraged, even as late as the fifties, to believe that Kenya would remain in white hands indefinitely. They had endured the Mau Mau years with fortitude. The change in attitude now seemed to them a betrayal. Mr. Blundell, one of the leading moderates among the white settlers, said bitterly that the British Government was so preoccupied

[1] Butler, op. cit., p. 230.

with an affluent Welfare State at home that it wished to be disassociated from awkward issues further afield.

d *Nigeria*

In October 1960 Nigeria was given her independence, on a federal basis. This was the culminating point of a long series of developments, which had started in 1946. In that year a Legislative Council had been set up for the whole of Nigeria, with regional assemblies for the North, South and East. In 1951 this central body was made substantially elective. The 1954 constitution had finally set up Nigeria as a Federation. In 1957 Eastern and Western Nigeria had been granted internal self-government. In 1959 Northern Nigeria, the largest but also the most backward of the regions, was given internal self-government. Then in October 1960 came formal independence.

It did seem as though, in this case, there had been no mad rush but a deliberate and carefully thought-out progress towards independence, going back over fifteen years. But no sooner had independence been granted than troubles came thick and fast. Here the difficulty was not a white settler population, which did not exist, but the great disparity in racial, social and economic background as between all three regions, and, more particularly, between the north and the other two.

e *Tanganyika*

This, like Nigeria, was another African country virtually untroubled by a white settler problem. There were some German settlers, and a few British. But the white group was less cohesive than the all-British Kenyan whites, as well as being fewer in number. It was granted its independence in 1961; and became a republic under President Nyerere in December 1962.

f *Uganda*

In Uganda, there were serious problems of tribalism; and also problems arising out of the presence of Indians. The chief difficulty was in the relationship between the people of Buganda, ruled by the Kabaka in the centre of the country, with the rest, particularly the Bunyoro. The Buganda were the largest of the thirteen tribes. Buganda had enjoyed a considerable measure of self-government for many years and now wished to secede. But this would have left the rest of the country high and dry, an assortment of small tribal groups, quite unable to sustain a separate life. In 1955, the Hancock Commission had recommended that Buganda should not be permitted to secede, and that the powers of the Kabaka be reduced. But by the end of 1960, Buganda was again demanding independence. Mr. Macleod therefore appointed another commission, under Lord Munster, which reported in June 1961, again strongly recommending that Buganda should not be allowed to secede. In 1961 it was agreed at a constitutional conference that Buganda should have a federal relationship with the rest of the country. But the dispute between Buganda and the Bunyoro people, which went back to the war between them in 1893, was not really settled when the British left the country to its first African Prime Minister, Dr. Milton Obote.[1]

g *Malaysia*
Malaysia at the other side of the world, was another of the unsuccessful federal projects of these years. Here, the idea came from the Prime Minister of Malaysia in November, 1961, with the proposal that the Malay States should join with Singapore, North Borneo, Sarawak, and Brunei. Great Britain had two concerns:
(1) her defence commitments in the Far East, for which the Singapore base was thought to be essential, and
(2) her responsibility for the constitutional development of the backward and primitive peoples of North Borneo and Sarawak.
One should perhaps add a third:
(3) her concern in the Far East with problems associated with the spread of Communism.
    By 1963, this somewhat ill-assorted federation was launched. But immediately formidable difficulties emerged:
(1) the age-old antagonism between the Chinese and the Malays, in Malaya and Singapore;
(2) the resentment of the Borneo territories at political domination by the Malays;
(3) the fact that the Sultan of Brunei would not join;
(4) the fact that the whole Malaysian Federation came under attack from Indonesia, because it embodied the principle of the continued military presence of the former colonial power.
    In August 1965 the Malaysian Federation was dismantled.

h *Aden and the South Arabia Federation*
In 1961 the British Government decided that there ought to be a closer link between Aden and the Federation of Southern Arabia, which was a British protectorate. Here, the trouble was that Aden was progressive, reasonably prosperous and with nationalist aspirations, whereas the Protectorate states were backward, feudal in structure and controlled by autocratic rulers.
    In Aden itself the Arab nationalist wanted more self-government. But the moderate business community did not.
    In July and August of 1962, a constitutional conference was held, and

[1] Kirkman, op. cit., Ch. 6, and Kirkwood, op. cit.

agreement was reached on proposals by which Aden would enter a federation in which her special position would be safeguarded. Great Britain's sovereignty over Aden and the bases there would not be affected. But, increasingly, popular feeling indicated a wish not to merge with the autocratic and backward protectorate states, but with the revolutionary movement in the Yemen. This, however, would have been unacceptable to the British on strategic grounds. So it was decided to force the merger through. It was agreed that independence should be granted in 1968.

i *Cyprus*
Here, yet another type of difficulty was encountered. The Greek majority in the island faced the implacably hostile Turkish minority. However, in March 1961 Cyprus was admitted, as an independent state, to the Commonwealth. On 28 December 1963, British troops went back to Cyprus, at the request of Archbishop Makarios, to keep the peace between the Greeks and the Turks. On 15 February 1964 Britain requested help from the United Nations, and by the end of March the U.N. command in Cyprus became operational.

j *South Africa*
In March 1961 South Africa withdrew from the British Commonwealth. It may be of interest to survey briefly the events leading up to this. In 1948, Dr. Malan and the Afrikaner Nationalists had defeated General Smuts.

Until well into the fifties, the British reaction to this was fairly complacent, although some of Dr. Malan's policies from 1948 to 1951 had aroused very strong opposition, for instance: his release of war criminals who had supported Nazi Germany; his emphasis on the need to foster the Afrikaans language and culture, and thus, by implication, to supersede the British; his policy of apartheid, with its consequential legislation, as, for instance, the law of 1950 prohibiting mixed marriages; the fact that South African universities were no longer, even in theory, open to men of all races – and so on.

Increasingly, the policy and political philosophy of the new government came to be regarded as offensive, not only to British South Africans, Cape Coloured and Africans, but also to other African states, to the Government of the United Kingdom and to the rest of the Commonwealth.

In March 1960 a campaign was organized in Britain by members of the Labour and Liberal Parties to boycott South African goods. The Prime Minister disassociated the Government from this, not wishing to alienate the South African Government, which it still hoped to be able to influence.

On 21 March 1960 the Sharpeville shootings occurred, when sixty-seven Africans were killed in clashes with the police in the campaign against pass laws.

In April 1960, the Labour M.P. Mr. Stonehouse, urged the Government to use the forthcoming Commonwealth Conference to impress on South Africa the strong feelings of the British Government about South African domestic policies.

On 3 May 1960 the Commonwealth Prime Ministers' Conference opened. There was a rule that at these conferences domestic affairs should not be discussed. But in this case there was general agreement that South Africa's domestic affairs were in a special category, and were of compelling concern to all Commonwealth members. Hostility to South Africa was almost universal.

On 5 October 1960 a referendum was held in South Africa on whether or not to become a republic. The all-white electorate voted for this by a small majority. The South African Parliament approved a republican constitution and this came into effect on 31 May 1961. There was no difficulty here. There were by now several other republics in the Commonwealth.

Meanwhile, in March 1961, a Commonwealth Conference had met to consider the problems of South Africa in the knowledge that South Africa, though a Republic, wished to remain a Commonwealth member. The British Government wanted South Africa to stay for many reasons – mainly perhaps because it was felt that, while within the Commonwealth, it was still possible for Britain to exert some influence, and to safeguard to some extent the interests of the white British South Africans as well as the coloured and the Africans. Mr. Macmillan said in the House of Commons:

> I was not satisfied that the exclusion of South Africa from the
> Commonwealth would best help all those European people who
> do not accept the doctrine of apartheid . . ., nor would it help the
> millions of Africans.[1]

However, after three days of discussion, Mr. Verwoerd withdrew South Africa's application for membership. Most of the other Commonwealth leaders appear to have been relieved by this decision. South Africa retained her Commonwealth trade preferences.

The problems of disengagement from empire were many sided and immensely complicated. The acquisition of an empire had been a relatively simple matter. The dismantling required a much higher order of skill. It is worth noting that it took place in these years without bloodshed, and on the whole, in an atmosphere of mutual goodwill.

It remains to draw attention, again, to the impact on the Commonwealth of Britain's attempt to join the Common Market; and on the

[1] H.C. Deb., Fifth Series, Vol. 637, cols. 441–9, 22 March 1961.

enactment of the Commonwealth Immigration Act of 1962. Both are to be viewed as a direct consequence of the dismantling of empire, and as an attempt by Britain to build a new society, orientated in other directions, and with other concerns than with the well-being of peoples who had now opted out of the British relationship.

9 THE OPPOSITION

a *The Labour Party*
The Labour Party was defeated at the polls for the third time running in October 1959, each defeat being more decisive than the last. The Party Leadership did not initiate any official inquiry into the reason why. Possibly it was felt that an official inquiry would be abortive, since such diametrically opposed 'reasons' were being bandied about unofficially. The battle was, as usual, between the 'revisionists' led by Mr. Gaitskell, now the Party Leader, and the 'fundamentalists', led by Mr. Crossman, Mrs. Castle, Mr. Mikardo and some of the new left wing trade union leaders such as Mr. Cousins.

The revisionists thought that the Labour creed had begun to look rather old-fashioned. Clause 4 of the 1918 Party Constitution (nationalization) had now become something of a non-issue and might even have been a positive disadvantage, electorally speaking, they considered. The left wingers on the other hand thought that Clause 4 should be retained and indeed re-emphasized. According to this view, the Labour creed had become too diluted; too devoid of socialist content; too like the Conservative creed. And its appeal to the workers was in consequence negligible. The argument was that a 'Me Too' approach in politics was never a success. The left wingers, whose real strength at this time was in the Labour movement outside Parliament, were also insistent in their claim that Party Conference decisions should be regarded as binding on the Leader and the P.L.P.

Mr. Gaitskell thus faced some difficult and delicate issues. He did not, initially, show much adroitness in his approach to them. At Blackpool in 1959, after the third General Election defeat, and again in a speech at Nottingham in February 1960, he made a frontal attack on Clause 4, demanding its repeal, without prior warning or consultation with other Party leaders. The nationalized industries, he argued, by which the left wingers set so much store, were not seen by the average Party member as bastions of democracy. Those who worked in them were no better and no worse off than workers in any other industry. Anyway, nationalization was now viewed by economists as an outmoded way of securing control over the economy.[1] Apart from the issue of nationalization, there was

[1] Mr. Bevan, winding up the debate, urged the case for keeping public

need to alter the image of Labour as an exclusively working-class movement. Labour must now seek to represent also the new middle class, and must concentrate on issues more relevant to the electorate in the sixties than Clause 4, as, for instance, equal educational opportunities; urban planning; and world disarmament and control of nuclear weapons.[1] And socialists should, in particular, beware of lecturing on the evils of material wealth.

Early in 1960 M. Abrams and R. Rose conducted a survey in fifty parliamentary constituencies, the conclusions of which were particularly depressing for the leftists, and seemed to give considerable support to the revisionist thesis.

> The image of the Labour Party, held by both its supporters and its non-supporters, is one which is increasingly obsolete in terms of contemporary Britain. Both groups see Labour as identified with the working-class – especially the poor and labouring working class; and at the same time many workers, irrespective of their politics, no longer regard themselves as working class.[2]

In the nineteen to twenty-four age group, for the first time since the war, potential Tory voters outnumbered potential Labour voters. It was this age group which was most likely to see itself as a new middle class.

It was easy to understand the line of reasoning which caused Mr. Gaitskell and his friends to wish to jettison Clause 4. But the fundamentalists argued that left wing Parties could only retain their strength through long periods of Opposition provided that they remain committed to radical change. A left wing Opposition Party must consistently put forward radical policies, even when a right wing government in power seems popular.[3] People like Mr. Crossman agreed, however, that the type of nationalization undertaken by the Attlee Government might have to be re-examined. Socialist principles, he thought, had been compromised by the civil servants who set up centralized boards, independent of Parliament and not really subject to full public control.[4] However, the moral protest against the inequalities of capitalism, the need to warn of the coming crisis in capitalist economies and the desire to transform society must be kept in the forefront.

It was not only the left wingers in the Labour Party who felt strongly

---

ownership in the Labour programme. Shortly afterwards he died, thereby depriving the economists of one of their major supporters.

[1] C. A. R. Crosland, 'Can Labour Win?' 1960 and 'The Future of the Left' *Encounter*, March 1960.
[2] M. Abrams and R. Rose, *Must Labour Lose?*
[3] R. Crossman, 'Labour in the Affluent Society', Fabian Tract 325 (1960).
[4] Crossman, 'The Spectre of Revisionism', *Encounter*, April 1960.

about Clause 4. Mr. Morrison, a veteran of the right, felt that it should not be discarded if only because it was desirable to keep a clear-cut issue going, between the Parties. For old times' sake, this had better be Clause 4.[1] Mr. Roy Jenkins, who certainly could not be described as a left winger, thought that the Party constitution had better be left alone, but that Labour should, in effect, forget nationalization, and concentrate on issues more relevant to a modern electorate.[2] But the angry and disgruntled extremists felt that this was not enough. What was required was a more positive return to first principles. And this meant a re-emphasis of the Party's belief in Clause 4.

In the end, the Clause 4 debate stirred up such a hornet's nest in Labour ranks that in March 1960 the N.E.C., after a long debate, announced its decision to retain the whole of the 1918 constitution, thus leaving Clause 4 intact; and the matter was not raised at the Party Conference in the autumn. No more was heard of any further nationalization plans.

Possibly the tactical retreat was made by the Party Leadership because a more important issue was coming to the fore, viz. unilateral nuclear disarmament. On this, Mr. Gaitskell and his friends felt very strongly indeed. Unilateral nuclear disarmament would, they thought, be disastrous and would necessitate not only the ending of the Anglo-American special relationship, but also withdrawal from NATO. Britain would be left friendless, and without defences. The consequences for world peace and for Britain's future would be bleak indeed. Mr. Gaitskell was supported in these views by the majority of the P.L.P.; the majority of the N.E.C.; and, curiously enough, by a majority of the constituency parties.[3] Some of his most powerful opponents, as on so many issues in these years, were trade union based. Unfortunately for him they were able to exert very great influence, and at the Blackpool Party Conference in 1960, the vote for unilateral nuclear disarmament won the day. This issue was not wholly unrelated to the Clause 4 issue. Support for Clause 4 and C.N.D., for instance, seemed to go together; just as support for Mr. Crosland's revisionist ideas seemed to go with support for NATO.[4] But in 1960 at the Scarborough Conference, when the official defence policy of support for NATO, put forward by the N.E.C., was defeated, it seemed that most of the unilateralist opposition came from three large and several small unions, which thus ranged themselves against a large majority of the constituency parties, the P.L.P. and the N.E.C.,[5] and the structure of the Labour movement is such that a moderate Party Leadership is

---

[1] Morrison, op. cit.

[2] Roy Jenkins, 'British Labour Divided', *Foreign Affairs*, April 1960.

[3] K. Hindell and P. Williams, 'Scarborough and Blackpool', *Parliamentary Quarterly*, 1962.

[4] Beer, op. cit., pp. 224–7.   [5] Hindell and Williams, op. cit.

much more at risk when it clashes with trade union militants than when it clashes with constituency parties, who provide only 13 per cent of votes at conferences.[1]

The dispute about unilateral nuclear disarmament and the defeat of the Party Leadership on this issue at Scarborough posed yet another delicate and perhaps even more important issue. Where, in the Labour movement did the final responsibility for policy-making lie? Did the last word rest with the Party Conference, that unwieldy federation of groups of divergent size and interests, which met together annually at Blackpool or Scarborough or some other watering place? Or did responsibility for policy lie with the parliamentary Party? And, within the parliamentary Party, was it vested in the Leader, who was at liberty to choose his team as he pleased, from the ranks of the parliamentary Party: or did he have to accept the team selected for him by the P.L.P.?

These were by no means simple questions. While the conventions of parliamentary and Cabinet government required that final authority should rest with elected M.P.s, in Parliament, it was an inescapable fact that the Labour Party had never been and still was not quite like the other Parties in this regard. It had originated as an offshoot of the Labour movement outside Parliament, and had, for long years, been almost wholly financed by contributions from extra-parliamentary groups, as the trade unions and the co-operative societies. He who pays the piper must in some sense have the right to call the tune. And, even in the sixties, the piper was still being paid, to a very large extent, by the trade unions, without whose financial backing the Labour Party could hardly have hoped to fight a General Election. And many Labour M.P.s were still partly financed by the unions.

There had not, in the past, been very much difficulty over this issue. Trade unionists had not been greatly interested in politics, and had been willing enough to leave the politicians of the movement to get on with it. But it had always been recognized that troubles might arise. Now they did. Mr. Gaitskell, leader of the Parliamentary Party, had very different views on what ought to be Labour policy from Mr. Cousins and other leading trade unionists, who now seemed determined to lead the parliamentary Party from outside Parliament. The background reasons for this sudden assertion of authority on the part of the trade unions are not hard to see. Once government aspired to manage the economy, determine the tolerable level of unemployment and exert influence over prices and wages, the trade union leaders in the Labour movement were bound to become more interested in politics. And it was only too likely that their views would, on occasions, not coincide with the views of the P.L.P.

Between 1960 and 1961 Mr. Gaitskell, working through the 'Campaign

[1] See L. D. Epstein, 'Who makes Party Policy: British Labour 1960–1', *Midwest Journal of Political Science*, 1962.

for Democratic Socialism', worked hard to get a majority for his views. It was the first time that right wing groups within the Party had organized. Hitherto all the organizing had been done by groups on the left. Mr. Gaitskell's efforts were rewarded, for, at the Blackpool Conference in 1961, five of the six big unions voted for his policy. He made it very plain that he would not regard himself as being in any way bound by decisions on policy taken at the Party Conference. But the fact that he went to great pains to persuade the 1961 Scarborough Conference to reverse the 1960 Blackpool decision, and succeeded in doing so, suggests that he did feel that it was at the very least desirable that the P.L.P. and the Conference should be in agreement over major issues of policy. And certainly events in Parliament between the Scarborough and the Blackpool Conferences suggested that this was so. Unilateralist M.P.s, for instance, claimed Conference authority for refusing to vote with the Leadership for any motion implying support for a nuclear deterrent policy. Thus, on 13 December 1960, seventy-two Labour M.P.s abstained from the official Labour motion. And of course the dissident M.P.s claimed that it was Gaitskell and his followers who ought to be disciplined since it was they who were flouting Conference policy. Gaitskell's victory at Blackpool in 1961 was not 100 per cent, since the Conference refused to agree either to the training of German troops in Britain, or to the establishment of an American Polaris base.

In the autumn of 1960 there was a contested election to the Leadership,[1] and Mr. Wilson stood against Mr. Gaitskell. Those who supported Mr. Wilson, who included the unilateralists, as well as the Crossman group, hoped that he would be more aggressive towards the Tory Government, and less aggressive in his treatment of his own Party. But Mr. Gaitskell remained at the top of the poll; and Mr. Brown defeated a left wing candidate for the Deputy Leadership. At the Shadow Cabinet elections, Mr. Wilson dropped from the first to the ninth place; and Mr. Callaghan, then a strong Gaitskellite, came top.[2]

It may be that Mr. Gaitskell was seen as the most likely candidate to win the next General Election for Labour.

Mr. Gaitskell's opposition to the Government's Common Market policy was, in a way, very surprising, if only because most of his closest supporters on the right of the Party supported Britain's entry. Some commentators see, in his anti-Common Market stand, an element of political calculation. Was this an effort, on his part, to win over the left, alienated now, by his policy on Clause 4, and on defence, and, perhaps, on the role of the Party Conference?

In January 1963 Mr. Gaitskell died suddenly. Mr. Wilson was elected as Leader in his place, in a three-cornered contest in which he defeated

[1] This was the first time that a Leader had been challenged for re-election.
[2] *Annual Register, 1960.*

both Mr. Brown, Deputy Leader since 1960, and Mr. Callaghan.[1] Mr. Wilson had, apparently, at that time little support in the Shadow Cabinet, or among those who mattered in the Party hierarchy. The Gaitskellites, it is said, disliked him. Mr. Brown had the support of the right, and much union support too. Why did Wilson win?

Perhaps his debating skill was noted. Certainly it was greatly respected by Labour back-benchers. And of course he had already had some experience of office, as President of the Board of Trade.

Mr. Brown's excitable personality told against him. It seems to have been felt that his 'style' was now not quite right. He had entered politics via the T.G.W.U., and had there acquired the habit of calling everyone 'brother'. However, he remained as Deputy Leader. None of Mr. Wilson's other rivals looked really credible.

In a way, Mr. Wilson seemed to bridge neatly the dangerous gulf between right and left wingers. He had the support of the left, but was not himself a doctrinaire left winger. He had, for instance, never been a unilateralist.

In Parliament, from 1963 to 1964, Mr. Wilson played his cards well, and there was little criticism of him. At last, the Party in Opposition seemed united, and confident. After the Party Conference in October 1963 he received a long ovation following his speech on the importance of science in a new technological age. The new theme of a scientific revolution, and the related themes of planning, economic growth, and, more cautiously, an incomes policy, seemed to be lifting Labour at last out of its rut.

The other, and more important, reason for the rapid recovery of the Labour Party after its 1959–61 troubles was, of course, the difficulties into which the Conservative Government was now running, from at any rate 1962 on.

b *The Liberals*

It remains to comment briefly on the course of the Liberal revival during these years. They did well in by-elections and in local elections. And in March 1962 a Liberal, Mr. Eric Lubbock, won a hitherto safe Tory seat in a residential suburb, Orpington. After this, however, the Liberal vote in local elections and by-elections fell off.

At the time of Orpington, political commentators forecast significant Liberal gains at the next General Election. But, in retrospect, it seems that the Liberal vote was really a minor protest vote, against the Government. Liberal policies were vague. Their attraction was for some sectors

---

[1] On the first ballot the votes were as follows: Mr. Wilson 115; Mr. Brown 88; Mr. Callaghan 41. On the second ballot, Mr. Wilson 144; Mr. Brown 103. George-Brown, op. cit., pp. 83–4.

of the now increasing disgruntled middle class, disappointed in the stop-go economics of conservatism, but unwilling to go the whole way and move over to Labour. This was much too narrow a base for a political party seriously contending for power.

CHAPTER FOUR

The Labour Government from October 1964 to March 1966

SUMMARY	page
1 The General Election of 15 October 1964	153
2 The Labour Team	157
3 Constitutional and Administrative Issues	159
4 Economic Issues	160
5 Domestic Affairs	162
a The proposed re-nationalization of steel	163
b Education	163
c Housing	163
d Industrial legislation	164
1 Trade Disputes Act	164
2 Redundancy Payments Act	164
e The death penalty	164
f Race Relations	164
g The National Health Service	165
6 Defence Policy	165
7 Foreign Policy	167
a General	167
b The Anglo-American Relationship	168
c The Communist world	169
d Europe	169
8 The Commonwealth	169
a Southern Rhodesia	171
b Gibraltar	172
9 The Opposition	173
a The Conservative Party	173
b The Liberal Party	177

1 THE GENERAL ELECTION OF 15 OCTOBER 1964[1]
The General Election of 15 October 1964 looked like being rather dull, but in fact turned out to be very interesting at any rate as far as the results went. It took place a month before the end of the Conservatives' statutory period of office. Why did the Conservatives leave it till almost

[1] See Nuffield Election Studies, D. E. Butler and A. King, *The British General Election of 1964*.

the last minute, instead of having a General Election in the spring of 1964 as many Conservatives had wanted? Various reasons were put forward. There had been a change of leadership in October 1963 when Sir Alec Douglas-Home had taken over from Mr. Macmillan, and it was thought that time was needed to establish the new Prime Minister before embarking on all the hazards of an Election campaign. Also, and more importantly, the Tories thought that time was on their side. From 1961 on their opinion poll ratings had been low. But by the summer of 1964 the pollsters showed that the gap between Conservative and Labour was narrowing. It seemed worth holding on. And, at the end of September, the Gallup poll showed the Tories as 15 per cent ahead. It thus looked as though the Parties were then running neck and neck, with the Conservatives likely to pull out ahead in the near future. However, the danger of an imminent balance of payments crisis perhaps persuaded the Conservative Party leaders to hold the Election in October rather than wait until November.

The Labour Manifesto was entitled 'The New Britain'. It concentrated on the economy and on domestic affairs. Growth and technological advance were the keynotes. Labour would set up four new Ministries: economic planning; technology; overseas development; and Wales. The steel industry would be re-nationalized. The 1957 Rent Act would be repealed. A Parliamentary Commissioner, or Ombudsman, would be appointed to deal with complaints from the public against Government departments. Regional planning boards would be set up. Tax changes, which would stimulate enterprise, would be introduced. Employees would get a charter of rights. Secondary education would be re-organized on comprehensive lines. It was a quite good manifesto from the vote-catching angle, with something for everyone. The right and left wings of the Labour Party were both discreetly catered for. There was response to the mood of the early sixties; the wish for a break-through on the economic front; the attempt to give a new impetus to regional policies, and so on. Wisely, the Labour Party was silent on issues of foreign and defence policy. They were divided on these issues; and the electorate was not greatly interested in them anyway.

The Conservative Manifesto was entitled 'Prosperity with a Purpose'. It stressed the importance of a British nuclear deterrent.[1] It promised action on monopolies and mergers; an inquiry into the structure and functioning of trade unions; a review of the social services; rating reform; and 400,000 new houses a year.[2]

The campaign did not go well for the Conservatives. Sir Alec concentrated on the British deterrent and foreign policy generally. This was his field, and he was at his best on these subjects. But the electorate was,

[1] L. D. Epstein, 'The Nuclear Deterrent and the British Election of 1964', *Journal of British Studies 1965–1967*. [2] *Annual Register 1964*, p. 39.

The General Election of 15 October 1964

predictably, not very interested. It was bad luck for the Tories that the news of Krushchev's fall, and the first Chinese atom bomb did not come until October 15th and 16th. If these two happenings had occurred a little earlier Sir Alec might have found his audiences a little more receptive. He was not good, in general, with hecklers. And his performance on television was generally regarded as poor. This was serious, as the campaign was very much a television contest. No doubt wisely, Sir Alec declined Mr. Wilson's challenge to meet him in a TV debate. Although the Conservatives attacked Labour social policies as 'a menu without prices' Mr. Maudling did his sums on the cost in taxes of the policies set out in the Labour manifesto (£966m.–£1,200m. per annum) too late for their significance to be brought home to the electorate. They were not available until October 13th.

Labour M.P.s attacked the Conservatives' record as 'thirteen wasted years'. They laid very great stress on the weakness of the British economy, and on the troubles which lay ahead. The publication of a set of bad trade figures for the second quarter of 1964 provided the necessary background for this argument, which probably gained them some electoral advantage, although it certainly increased their subsequent difficulties since it not only undermined the confidence of wavering Tory supporters, but also the confidence of the international community in Britain's economic stability.

Mr. Wilson dominated the campaign, on the Labour side, fully demonstrating, perhaps for the first time, his immense skill and agility as a political leader. This led to some criticism of Labour as a 'one-man band', and of Mr. Wilson as conducting a presidential style campaign. But there was little doubt that the Labour movement needed a powerful leader at that time, strong enough to pull the Party together and erase earlier impressions of deep fissures. Mr. Wilson did this admirably.

The result of the General Election was surprisingly close, when it is remembered that for over two years a massive Labour victory had been expected. It was as follows.[1] 77.1 per cent of the electorate voted:

	Votes	Percentage of votes	Seats obtained
Labour	12,205,814	44.1	317
Conservative	12,001,396	43.4	304
Liberal	3,092,878	11.2	9

The Labour Party's overall majority was 4. This was the closest election result since 1847, although in 1951 the Labour majority had only been 6. The average swing to Labour was 3.5 per cent.

It was probably an Election that the Conservatives lost rather than one which Labour won. In fact, Labour polled 10,000 fewer votes than in

[1] See Butler and Freeman, op. cit., p. 144.

1959, and the Labour vote was the lowest at any General Election since the war. Labour won, it seemed, because of the massive abstention of Conservative voters amounting to one and three-quarter million.

One interesting feature of this General Election was the unevenness of the swing to Labour. Thus, the Midlands and South-East England stayed Tory; and in seven Midland seats there was a swing to the Conservatives. In London, however, there was a 4 per cent swing to Labour.

A portent of things to come was the defeat of Mr. Patrick Gordon Walker, the Labour Foreign Secretary designate, at Smethwick, a Labour seat which he had held for nineteen years. His Conservative opponent, Mr. Peter Griffiths, made capital out of the presence of a big Pakistani community, and waged what the Labour Party described as a 'racialist' campaign. Mr. Gordon Walker had already become unpopular in his constituency after his speeches in the House of Commons in 1962, attacking the Commonwealth Immigration Bill. The electors of Smethwick had a very positive wish to check further immigration of coloured people and so were in favour of this measure.

The Liberals achieved their target of over three million votes, their record poll since 1929. They got double the number of votes cast for them in 1959; but they had a net gain of only two seats. All but one of their nine seats were in the Celtic fringe. However, the Liberal vote did increase all over Britain. The big Liberal policy line was regionalism. Mr. Grimond, the Liberal Leader, said that this was the great issue of the sixties, just as unemployment had been in the thirties.

Outside the Celtic fringe areas Liberal tactics were to fight in the safe, rural Tory seats, where not too much effort was being expended by the other two Parties, and where they therefore hoped to make most impact.[1]

It seems that Labour suffered more from Liberal candidates than the Conservatives did. The Conservatives retained their marginal seats more easily when a Liberal was standing as a third candidate.[2]

One of the interesting questions is why Labour did not do better. The result was almost a dead-heat. In part, of course, this reflected the swing back to the Government during the Election campaign, which had occurred at every General Election in the past twenty years. In part, the relatively poor Labour showing may have been because the Conservatives spent three times as much money as Labour, on pre-election advertising; and business organizations spent lavishly on anti-nationalization campaigns.[3]

[1] J. D. Lees, 'Aspects of Third Party Campaigning in the 1964 General Election', *Parliamentary Affairs 1965–1967*.
[2] See Nuffield Election Studies, Butler and King, op. cit. See also Rasmusen, *The Liberal Party*.
[3] R. Mackenzie, 'Between Two Elections', *Encounter*, January and February, 1966.

2 THE LABOUR TEAM

The Labour team was dominated by its Leader. It is difficult to recapture, even a short time later, the excitement and hope which swept the country after the 1964 Election. Disappointment, distaste and unease had been increasing over the past few years as the electorate surveyed the goings on of the Conservative Leadership. The whole style of public life seemed to have slipped disastrously. The Profumo case; the various security leaks; the failure of the Government's bid to enter the Common Market; and, most of all, the evidently deteriorating economic situation, made very many people predisposed to think that the time was ripe for some kind of new deal. And Mr. Wilson and his government seemed to offer just this. The Labour Party had been out of office since 1951; and its behaviour during the years of opposition had certainly not been such as to inspire great public confidence. However, the Attlee years from 1945 to 1951 had been creditable enough, and certainly not alarmingly 'left'. Mr. Wilson himself had reached the top only after Gaitskell's death in 1963. He had played a part in the Opposition years, but it had been a relatively minor part. Now, therefore, he was able to make his début as Leader, virtually unhampered by earlier mistakes, commitments, broken promises and so on.

Mr. Wilson at once provided the electorate with high hopes, and inspired considerable confidence. He showed himself as a politician of the first rank. He was extremely good on television; splendid in the House; and soon became a father-figure almost akin to Mr. Baldwin. His new deal was not too new and not too left wing. What was needed, he said, was an advance into the new technological age. The increasing wealth created by Government-sponsored technological changes should feed back into an ever advancing Welfare State. Individual citizens, hampered for so long by Tory mismanagement of the economy could look forward confidently, under the guidance of a professional economist, to a much more prosperous future, when once the follies of Tory mismanagement were dealt with.

At first, the fear was that this splendid future might be put in jeopardy by the smallness of Mr. Wilson's majority in the House. But Mr. Wilson quickly showed that he could use this seemingly hampering circumstance to his own and his Party's advantage. It was a siege situation, and it could not of course go on for too long. But while it lasted it did at least serve to draw the P.L.P. together. Division spelt defeat, and a possible return to Conservative rule. So, under the Prime Minister's leadership, the P.L.P. learnt to unite, and to await the day when their Leader would think it safe to go to the electorate and ask for a fuller mandate. Things were going their way and it was just a matter of hanging on till the right moment. Their Leader would know when the time was ripe. Meantime, as Mr. Wilson so often told them, they had to stand close together.

Mr. Wilson's Cabinet was a large one by the standards of previous years. There were twenty-three members; and their average age was fifty-six.[1] Mr. Wilson himself was the second youngest member. Altogether, one-third of the Parliamentary Labour Party held Government appointments, and it was necessary to amend an eighteenth-century law limiting the number of Ministers in the Commons. Very little was known by the general public about most of the new men, and, partly because of this, the Tories were able to criticize the Cabinet as a one-man band. In a way Mr. Wilson as a politician did seem to tower above his colleagues at this time, but in fact his Cabinet was not a weak one.

Mr. Callaghan was Chancellor of the Exchequer. Mr. George Brown was Minister for Economic Affairs, and as head of the new Department of Economic Affairs had responsibility for the development of this new Ministry. Mr. Patrick Gordon Walker was Foreign Secretary. He had been defeated at Smethwick in the General Election, but the intention was to find him another safe Labour seat as soon as possible. Three leading left wingers were given Cabinet posts: Mr. Frank Cousins as Minister of Technology; Mrs. Barbara Castle as Minister for Overseas Development and Mr. Anthony Greenwood as Colonial Secretary. Mr. Wilson thus built up his Cabinet from both the left and the right wingers of the Party. And it is noteworthy that before the 1966 Election, no Cabinet Minister resigned.

The immediate problem was, of course, how to govern at all with this tiny majority of four. One possibility was a coalition with the Liberals. This would have given Mr. Wilson a little bit more room for manoeuvre. Mr. Grimond, the Liberal Leader, apparently made overtures to him during the summer of 1965[2] but Mr. Wilson chose not to respond. There were, he found, some compensations in the tiny majority. Party unity, so recently and precariously achieved, was easier to hold on to when it was apparent that the price of revolt would be the fall of the Government.

The second problem was to plan for another General Election as soon as it became evident that Labour would be in a position to win it. Some Labour M.P.s thought that the summer of 1965 would be the most advantageous time. Sir Alec Douglas-Home's popularity was thought to be low, and it might be best to strike before the Conservative Party found a new and perhaps more popular leader. But the Prime Minister's instinct was to wait. He had expected a massive Labour victory in 1964 and had not got it. Now he was disposed to caution. The portents for

[1] Apart from the Prime Minister, only two of the twenty-three members had sat in a Cabinet before. Harold Wilson, *The Labour Government, 1964–1970, A Personal Record*.

[2] Nuffield Election Studies, D. E. Butler and A. King, *The British General Election of 1966*, pp. 76–80.

Labour in the spring of 1965 had not been all that favourable. County Council elections in March had shown a swing to the Tories. And in May the borough elections brought large scale Tory gains, indicating a 7 per cent swing back to them since October 1964. It would be better, Mr. Wilson thought, to hold on, and demonstrate that with courage and skill and very hard work, a Labour Government could govern, even in present very unfavourable circumstances.

Just how unfavourable the circumstances were was probably not appreciated at the time. One of the great difficulties for the Government was not in its work in Parliament, but in the widening gulf between the Government and the extra-Parliamentary Party, where there was, of course, not the same incentive to support the Government as there was within the P.L.P. The grounds for quarrelling were various. For instance, in February 1965 the Government announced the setting up of a Royal Commission on the trade unions, under the chairmanship of Lord Justice Donovan, a former Labour M.P. This looked like the beginning of an attempt by the Government to discipline the T.U.C. The Government's proposals for a compulsory early-warning system for wage claims were bitterly opposed. So was the Prices and Incomes Board which was set up in the spring of 1965. Then, at the Blackpool Party Conference in September 1965, the Government's support for American policy in Vietnam came in for fierce criticism from left wingers. The immigration issue began to look like a divisive and difficult one. Mr. Wilson was in some measure protected by the composition of his Cabinet. The potential leaders of a revolt against him were his own Cabinet colleagues who were thus more or less precluded from action.

In general, Mr. Wilson's response to a very difficult situation was to stick to tried and orthodox policies. This was true in matters of defence, foreign policy, the Commonwealth, and domestic and economic issues. In these years Mr. Wilson showed himself as a very conservative Labour Prime Minister.

3 CONSTITUTIONAL AND ADMINISTRATIVE ISSUES

This short-lived administration lacked the time required to deal with far-reaching constitutional reforms. However, four new Ministries were set up as an earnest of things to come: the D.E.A. (Department of Economic Affairs); the Ministry of Technology; the Ministry of Overseas Development; and the Welsh Office. These had all been promised in the Labour Election Manifesto. The main institutional changes were on the economic side, and will be dealt with under that heading.

The case of Mr. Gordon Walker, the Labour Foreign Secretary designate and his search for a constituency, is perhaps worthy of special note. After his defeat at Smethwick at the General Election he continued at the Foreign Office and stood for Leyton, a safe Labour seat, in January 1965.[1] He was, again, defeated by an 8.7 per cent swing to the Conservatives. It seems that the electors of Leyton very much resented the action of Transport House in foisting a candidate on them who was not of their own choosing. After this second defeat Mr. Gordon Walker resigned as Foreign Secretary and his place was taken by Mr. Michael Stewart.

4 ECONOMIC ISSUES

One of the Labour Party's main themes at the General Election had been the need to put the economy in order, and to modernize Britain by re-structuring industry. Labour would lead her into a new and even more prosperous technological age. 'You've never had it so good' seemed now to give way to 'You could have it better'. The electorate, disillusioned by Tory stop-go policy on the economic front, was ready to let Mr. Wilson have a try at this. Britain had never before had a professional economist as a Prime Minister, and it seemed a reasonable hope that he might provide some of the economic expertise which recent Prime Ministers had so evidently lacked.

But the crisis economic conditions which confronted Mr. Wilson in the autumn of 1964 proved very hard to handle. It seemed that several of the leading economic advisers to the Government advocated devaluation at once, on the grounds that there was a fundamental disequilibrium in the balance of payments which could not be put right by any other means. The decision not to devalue was probably taken by Mr. Wilson on political rather than on economic grounds. Labour Governments had devalued in 1931 and in 1949. If yet a third, and even more precariously based Labour Government devalued in 1964, there would probably be a political crisis of confidence which might well unseat the Government altogether. If there had to be devaluation, this should be deferred till after another General Election, when a new Labour Government might hope to have a larger parliamentary majority than four. Meantime, other new measures could be tried out, such as a more fully developed policy for economic growth;[2] a prices and incomes policy; changes in the tax structure; and, rather vaguely, a technological revolution, which might conceivably do the trick without devaluation.

In October 1964 an import surcharge of 15 per cent was introduced, with a view to discouraging imports and thus easing the balance of payments crisis. This, of course, upset Britain's EFTA partners as it

[1] Leyton was a lower-middle-class constituency in East London. It had returned a Labour M.P. with a majority of 7,926 in October 1964.

[2] In September 1965 the National Economic Plan was published.

virtually eliminated EFTA's advantage in the British market. In the spring of 1965 the surcharge had to be reduced to 10 per cent.[1]

In November 1964 there was a special autumn Budget, which seemed, quixotically, to give with one hand, and take away with the other. Pensions were increased,[2] and prescription charges were abolished. The latter was an unfortunate move in that foreign confidence was shaken. It seemed, to many Europeans, that there was a lack of sound financial management. But the tax on petrol was increased by 6*d* a gallon. National insurance contributions went up by 2*s* a week for employees, and by 3*s* 3*d* a week for employers, and warning was given of a rise in income tax in the spring of 1965, and the adoption of a capital gains tax and a corporation tax. M.P.s' pay was raised from £1,750 to £3,250, and there were also increases in Ministerial salaries. The pound continued to weaken, and, in November 1964, Bank Rate was raised to 7 per cent. Eventually, the International Monetary Fund gave Britain $3000m. emergency credit to save the pound.

In December 1964 the Declaration of Intent on Productivity, Prices and Incomes was signed by representatives of the Government, employers and the trade unions. This was a move in the right direction, and it was taken on Mr. Brown's initiative. The Government announced its intention of setting up machinery to review the movement of prices and incomes, and employers and the unions agreed to co-operate in general terms although the unions undoubtedly disliked this plan from the beginning. In March 1965 the Prices and Incomes Board was set up, headed by Mr. Aubrey Jones, a Tory M.P. It had, however, no statutory authority.

In March 1965 a White Paper was published on prices and incomes. The White Paper stated that average annual increases in money incomes should not exceed 3–3½ per cent. But there was no wish, it was said, to resort to compulsion. In fact, during 1965 the norm of 3–3½ per cent was ignored, and wage rates rose on average by 9 per cent.

The Budget of April 1965 was mildly deflationary: 6*d* was put on to income tax; and taxes were levied on consumption, e.g. cigarettes and alcohol.[3] Two new taxes were at this time devised, allegedly by Professor Kaldor: the capital gains tax and the corporation tax.

Mr. Heath organized a team of young financial experts to attack the whole Finance Bill and especially the corporation tax. He emerged with

[1] It had to be abolished altogether in November 1966.

[2] Pensions increased by 12*s* 6*d* a week for a single person; by 21*s* for a married couple; and by 20*s* for a widow. The increases were to take effect in the spring.

[3] 6*d* was put on to the price of a packet of cigarettes; 4*s* on a bottle of whisky or gin; 1*d* a pint on beer. Extra duties were imposed on wine. The motor vehicle licence went up by £2 10*s* a year. Some attempt was made to curtail entertaining on expense accounts.

an enhanced reputation, which probably played some part in his election to the Tory Leadership in July 1965.

In July 1965 the third Budget in six months was introduced, providing for further deflationary measures. Public investment was cut. So was the defence programme. It was hoped that these measures would reassure foreign holders of sterling and thus enable the Government to get more credit to stave off devaluation. Public investment in the social sector was deferred. The building of houses, schools and hospitals had to be kept within the existing programme. And other non-industrial projects like roads had to be delayed for six months. Some attempt was made to curtail local government expenditure. Defence expenditure was cut by £100m. Restrictions on hire purchase were tightened up.

In September 1965 the first big fight with the T.U.C. on all this occurred at the meeting of the T.U.C. General Council. Mr. Brown's attempt to persuade the T.U.C. to accept a compulsory early warning system for wage claims and price increases was voted down, in favour of a voluntary system.

In September 1965, the Government published the D.E.A.'s 'National Plan', which set the target of a 3.8 per cent average annual growth. The Government had high hopes of the National Plan. But in fact it turned out to be largely an academic exercise.

Throughout the life of this Government, Mr. Brown remained at the D.E.A., as First Secretary of State, and Secretary for Economic Affairs. The intention – or at any rate Mr. Brown's intention – was that this new Ministry should exercise overall control over economic affairs, and should not be dependent on the narrower Treasury orthodoxy. Unfortunately there was, from the beginning, friction between Mr. Brown at the D.E.A. and Mr. Callaghan at the Treasury. There was a third power centre at No. 10 itself, in the person of Professor Balogh, the Prime Minister's personal economic adviser, though his influence was probably not very great after the first six months. As Mr. Brown remarked sadly, 'There were too many of us, advising and counter-advising one another.'[1] And the advice bandied about was contradictory. Thus, it seemed that while the D.E.A. was always keen to start things up, the Treasury was anxious to damp things down.

5 DOMESTIC AFFAIRS

This Government was severely hampered by the continuing background of economic crisis in carrying out its election pledges, and some legislation had in the end to be tailored to meet rising costs. However, a good start was made.

[1] George-Brown, op. cit., p. 100.

Domestic Affairs

a *The proposed re-nationalization of steel*

The steel industry had been nationalized initially by the second Labour Government in 1951. It had been de-nationalized by the subsequent Conservative administration. Its re-nationalization by Labour had been in Labour's 1964 Manifesto. But public opinion polls showed that, as in 1951, so in 1964, this was a non-issue for most of the electorate which could quite quickly become counter-productive for Labour. It was an issue dear only to left wing zealots. The Liberals were now pledged to vote against it; and two right wing Labour M.P.s – Messrs. Donnelly and Wyatt – had indicated that they too would oppose it. But among the reasons which prompted the Government to take some action was the fact that Labour had done particularly well in 1964 in the steel areas of South Wales, South Yorkshire and Teesside when they had campaigned on this issue. And such a measure would, it was hoped, placate the left, now deeply disquieted over the Labour Government's support for American policy in Vietnam.

On 30 April 1965 a White Paper was published by the Ministry of Power which proposed the nationalization of fourteen of the biggest companies, producing 90 per cent of the industry's iron and steel. The grounds for nationalization were presented as the inefficiency of private industry; its uncompetitive prices by international standards; inadequate research; and too many interlocking directorships. Compensation for shareholders was provided for. In the debate on the White Paper Mr. Brown said that he would listen to proposals from the steel industry. He did not, in any case, intend that there should be 100 per cent State ownership.

In the end, legislation was postponed because of the pressure of business at the end of the session. Steel re-nationalization was not included in the 1965 Queen's speech.

b *Education*

Comprehensive schools In 1965, the Department of Education and Science asked local authorities to submit plans for reorganizing secondary education on comprehensive lines, with a view to ending selection at 11-plus. This was to be the opening skirmish in a long campaign. It did seem, however, that the comprehensive principle had now been accepted by both parties, and that the argument had moved from 'whether' to 'how' and 'when' and 'how much'. But in 1965 it was not an issue which excited great interest in the electorate.

c *Housing*

In 1965 the Government passed a new Rent Act, which was intended to reverse the hated 1957 Rent Act, which was regarded as a landlord's act.

The intention was to fix fair rents for private tenants, and to provide greater security of tenure. Probably the only real remedy to the housing problem was to build a great many new houses. But for this Mr. Crossman lacked the resources. And the difficulties which surrounded the whole housing problem in the congested areas – and especially in the Greater London area – were formidable indeed.

d *Industrial legislation*

1 *Trade Disputes Act* In 1965 a Trade Disputes Act was passed, giving union officials full legal protection against actions which arose because there had been a threat to break the contract of employment.

In 1965 the Government set up a Royal Commission on trade unions, led by a Labour peer, Lord Donovan. The Commission reported in 1968.

2 *Redundancy Payments Act* This provided, at the expense of employers and the Government, for workers made redundant through no fault of their own. It was hoped that greater mobility of labour would ensue.

e *The death penalty*

The death penalty was at last abolished under the Murder Act of 1965 and life imprisonment was substituted. However, this Act was passed for a trial period only. It was to expire in 1970 unless previously prolonged by a resolution of both Houses.

f *Race Relations*

The Race Relations Act of 1965 was intended to prohibit racial discrimination in public places, and to make incitement to race hatred a criminal offence. The Conservatives were opposed to this latter on technical grounds, and in the end it was made unlawful but not criminal.

A Race Relations Board was set up, to organize local conciliation committees and to settle cases out of court wherever possible.

The Labour Government seemed willing to accept previous Conservative policy on the control of immigration. And the Front Bench, supported by a majority of Labour M.P.s, and under pressure from the constituencies, deserted the Gaitskellite line of wholesale opposition to the 1962 Commonwealth Immigration Act. Both the major Parties were anxious to take the race issue out of politics. Both were determined to treat coloured people already in Britain as first-class citizens on a level with everyone else. They seemed, however, to be outdoing each other in their attempt to restrict further immigration.

In August 1965 the Government brought out a White Paper on immigration policy, based on an inquiry which had been undertaken by Lord

Mountbatten. Entry from the Commonwealth should be restricted, it was said, to 7,500 permits a year for professional and skilled workers only. In addition 1,000 per annum should be allowed in from Malta, because of Malta's special economic difficulties.

g *The National Health Service*
Prescription charges were abolished – a move which earned the Government the hostility of the medical profession, and laid it open to the charge of currying favour with the public at the expense not only of taxpayers, but of the over-worked and under-paid doctors.

6 DEFENCE POLICY

It might have been expected that a Labour Government would look at defence commitments from a very different angle from the previous Conservative administration. This turned out not to be the case. From the first, Labour in office developed defence and foreign policies little if at all different from those of its Conservative predecessors.

Early in December 1964 Mr. Wilson, Mr. Gordon Walker (still Foreign Secretary, although without a seat in the Commons) and Mr. Healey (Defence Secretary) visited Washington, and reaffirmed support for existing British and American commitments in the Far East. This meant, on the British side, moral support for American policy in Vietnam and South East Asia generally; and on the American side support for British policy in Malaysia.

Mr. Wilson in his speech in the Commons on 16 December 1964, dwelt on the fact that Britain had now to maintain three rôles: the strategic nuclear rôle; the conventional rôle in NATO, in defence of Europe; and a world rôle, because of Britain's commitments throughout the Commonwealth. He admitted that the cost of all this was too high. He said:

> The plain fact is that we have been trying to do too much. The result has been gravely to weaken our economic strength and independence, without producing viable defences.[1]

He did not, at that time, see salvation in a withdrawal from east of Suez, but rather from cuts in British spending on European defence. His argument was that there was no need to go on trying to provide NATO with expensive and sophisticated conventional weapons, capable of penetrating Soviet defences. In Europe the two nuclear Great Powers, the United States and the U.S.S.R., confronted each other. And their nuclear stalemate made Europe safe. It was, however, desirable, he thought, to

[1] H.C. Deb., Fifth Series, Vol. 704, cols. 415–43, 16 December 1964.

recast some of the existing nuclear arrangements. He did not, for instance, wish to give West Germany even a finger on the nuclear trigger, and hoped for the development of some kind of Atlantic nuclear force.

In the same House of Commons debate, in December 1964, Mr. Wilson made it clear that he took Britain's east of Suez obligations very seriously: 'we cannot afford to relinquish our world role ... sometimes called our "East of Suez" role.'[1] Commonwealth commitments, Britain's economic interests, and strategic considerations, all required this, he said. There were three areas to be considered:

(1) the Persian Gulf. Here Britain had large oil interests at stake. These were protected by treaty commitments of very long standing;

(2) the African Commonwealth. Britain had made herself responsible for the general well-being of the new East African states;[2]

(3) Malaysia and Singapore. Here, however, both Australia and the United States could be expected to provide some of the support needed, to help Malaysia in her confrontation with Indonesia.

In all three cases it seemed likely that British obligations could be tapered off within the next decade.[3]

It is certain that at this time, the United States was most anxious that Britain should keep up her 'east of Suez' role. The Indian Ocean was one of the few areas in the world where America did not have an alliance system, or military bases. For this reason, Britain must, the Americans thought, be encouraged to stay on. But British and American interests in the area were probably not the same. The Americans viewed Indian Ocean defence as part of the general policy of containing Communism, and in particular Chinese Communism. Britain was not disposed to worry too much over this, apart from her general obligations as a signatory of the SEATO Pact.

There was some discussion, at this time, of the possibility of moving from existing land bases to island bases like the Seychelles; or even of developing a great new military base in Australia. But was it worth while? What threat could be credibly foreseen in the Indian Ocean?

In December 1965 the Defence White Paper proposed a reduction of 70,000 men in the Territorial Army. The thought was that large ground forces would not be necessary in Europe, where there was a nuclear shield, albeit this was now mainly an American shield.

In February 1966 the Defence White Paper announced that no more aircraft carriers would be built for the Navy. But, by this time, the rifts

[1] H.C. Deb., Fifth Series, Vol. 704, cols. 415-43, 16 December 1964.

[2] Britain did in fact go to their rescue in 1964 and 1965, when troubles beyond the control of local forces broke out.

[3] See Alastair Buchan, 'Britain in the Indian Ocean', *International Affairs*, 1966, and Michael Howard, 'Britain's Strategic Problem East of Suez', *International Affairs*, 1966, No. 2.

in Labour defence thinking were opening up and the Navy Minister, Mr. Christopher Mayhew, at this point resigned.[1] He argued that the decision to build no more aircraft carriers was incompatible with sustaining a major military role east of Suez. Such a rôle was, in his view, an anachronism. But, if Britain wanted to play it, the £200m. per annum suggested was much too small. On the other hand, if the British rôle was to be tapered off, it was too large. The effect of the Government's policy would be, he argued, to make the British auxiliaries rather than the allies of the United States in the Far East. The White Paper called for shore-based aircraft, as cheaper than carriers; and the purchase of F111As from the United States for this purpose. Aden would be abandoned shortly when necessary arrangements for her future could be completed. But British commitments to NATO, SEATO, CENTO, the Persian Gulf, Gibraltar, Malta, Hong Kong, Cyprus and Singapore would continue to be honoured. West Germany would be pressed to meet the foreign currency cost of maintaining British forces on the Rhine. And a fresh drive would be launched to increase the export of British arms.

7 FOREIGN POLICY

a *General*
As with defence policy, so Labour foreign policy from 1964 to 1966 differed very little from the foreign policy of the Conservative Government of 1959–64. It was shaped by events beyond Britain's control and Mr. Wilson's room for manoeuvre was almost non-existent. There were now three Great Powers – the United States of America, the U.S.S.R., and, since 1962, Communist China. Their relations with one another, in all the crisis areas of the world, determined the course of events. Russia and China were now mutually hostile powers; and if only for this reason there can be little doubt that Russia wished for a *détente* with the West perhaps as much as the West wished for one with Russia. Unfortunately, the growing involvement of American armed forces in Vietnam made this harder to achieve; and, on this issue, Russia and China joined in their condemnation of American policy. The fear grew that this conflict might lead to a third World War; and persistent efforts were made from many quarters to bring it to an end. But by 1965 the United States seemed to be more committed than ever to the survival of South Vietnam as an independent state; and more convinced than ever that for America to withdraw and leave South Vietnam to the Vietcong and to North Vietnam could encourage Chinese expansionist ambitions, and convince other South East Asian allies that American protection could not be relied on. The United States therefore decided to hold on and pour in

[1] H.C. Deb., Fifth Series, Vol. 725, cols. 254–65, 22 February 1966.

more troops. Australia, New Zealand and South Korea also sent small contingents of troops. In February 1965 the United States began air raids on military targets in North Vietnam, ostensibly as a reprisal for Vietcong attacks on American troops in South Vietnam, but probably really in an attempt to demonstrate what America could do if the U.S.S.R. and North Vietnam were thinking of intensifying the war. The air raids led to further fears of escalation. On 23 March 1965 the U.S.S.R. threatened that they might send 'volunteers' to North Vietnam. And China warned the world at large that she would not stand idly by if there were further American attacks on North Vietnam. Further appeals came from all over the world for an end to the fighting. India, for instance, called for an international conference.

It is against this background, and against this major crisis, that British foreign policy in these two years must be viewed.

b *The Anglo-American relationship*
The Anglo-American alliance was without any question the cornerstone of the Labour Government's foreign policy. This meant that the, Labour Government had to give at least moral support to American policy in Vietnam, despite the bitter anger of its own left wingers. On 4 March 1965 over fifty Labour M.P.s, headed by Sidney Silverman, signed a motion calling on the Government to declare 'publicly and unequivocally' that it could not support the United States in a war against Vietnam. But Mr. Wilson, in the Commons, repeatedly made it clear that he could. The left wingers felt it particularly inappropriate that Great Britain should take sides in this way, since, as co-chairman with the U.S.S.R. of the 1954 Geneva Conference guaranteeing the independence of Vietnam, she had a special international role as a mediator. But the U.S.S.R. and China, the other two Great Powers, were hardly possible as alternative allies and since the Europeans had rejected Britain no other option seemed open. A country the size of Britain could not stand alone. And anyway, the weakness of sterling made American financial support of crucial importance.

Mr. Wilson did manage not to send even a token British force to Vietnam. And he, personally, made great efforts to achieve peace. In June 1965, for instance, at the Commonwealth Prime Ministers' Conference, he proposed a Commonwealth Peace Mission to Vietnam. But this came to nothing and Mr. Chou En-lai pronounced the whole idea a hoax. On July 8th Wilson sent Mr. Harold Davies, Joint Parliamentary Secretary to the Ministry of Pensions, to Hanoi. Mr. Davies was a very junior figure but he had strong left wing views, and he went with the approval of North Vietnamese contacts in London. However, his reception in Hanoi was on a very low level, and he was not able to see any North Vietnamese Ministers. It did seem that the Vietcong wished to continue with the war, in spite of the arrival of large American reinforcements. In February 1966, Mr. Wilson visited Moscow, as co-chairman of the Geneva Conference of 1954, to try to get some kind of joint Anglo-Soviet action on Vietnam. This again was of no avail.

c *The Communist world*
British efforts at a *détente* were overshadowed by the many problems associated with Vietnam. The Russians made it clear that British support for American bombing in North Vietnam was a virtually insuperable obstacle to any co-operation with her.

The talk of a German finger on the nuclear trigger was another difficulty. Britain had all kinds of reasons for feeling that this would be an unwise development. But most of all, perhaps, was her conviction that this would be bound to provoke extremely sharp reactions from the U.S.S.R., whose almost pathological fears of West Germany were a continuing factor in Russian diplomatic relations with the West.

The British Government's efforts to get the U.S.S.R. to agree to a nuclear non-proliferation treaty similarly came to nothing. The mere discussion of a NATO nuclear scheme suggested to the Russians that the West was not serious about non-proliferation.

d *Europe*
Britain was full of fears: fear of General de Gaulle, and his adventures, which might perhaps include nuclear foreign policy over which Britain could have no control; fear of a possible Franco-German line-up from which Britain would, of course, be excluded; and fear of a United States-German association which might involve some German nuclear control. This Mr. Wilson feared most of all.

There was little interest, at this time, in Britain joining the Common Market. This had never been a favourite Labour policy. And anyway, the General had said *Non* in January 1963.

8 THE COMMONWEALTH[1]

These two years, from 1964 to 1966, saw great changes in the structure of the Commonwealth and the Labour Government had to respond, as best it could, to crises which arose all over the Commonwealth. The crises were not of its making and few options were open. However, as an earnest of good intentions the Government created a new Ministry of Overseas Development, headed by a Minister of Cabinet rank. Its terms of reference were to channel economic aid to parts of the Commonwealth where it was most required. And in 1965 the Commonwealth Secretariat was set up in an effort to provide a common service useful

[1] *Annual Register*, 1964, 1965, and 1966. Kirkman, op. cit.

to all members. There was no denying, though, that in recent years the Commonwealth, whatever that term still meant, had taken some rather severe knocks, for instance:

(1) The racialist policies in South Africa, which had culminated in the withdrawal of South Africa from the Commonwealth in 1961.
(2) Mr. Macmillan's attempt to enter the Common Market at the end of 1962 – with all the implications that that move had for Commonwealth countries.
(3) The United Kingdom Commonwealth Immigrants Act of 1962, restricting the right of entry into the United Kingdom.

The late forties and fifties had seen Britain divesting herself of her responsibilities to the great Asian dominions, and to the larger, and, hopefully, more or less economically viable African states. In the sixties Britain was confronted with the much more intractable problems of the tiny dependencies, now also putting forward their claims to 'independence'. Mr. Anthony Greenwood, the then Colonial Secretary, made great efforts to achieve some new thinking on the status of these tiny dependencies – the smaller Caribbean islands, for instance, left high and dry after the break-up of the West Indian Federation; land-locked African dependencies like Bechuanaland, Swaziland, and Basutoland, unfortunately located in the middle of South African territory. Of course not all of these tiny dependencies aspired to independence. The British Virgin Islands, for instance, a little group of islands with a population of about 7,000 were very fearful that 'independence' would mean a take-over by the much richer American Virgin Islands just next door. They wanted, merely, an advance towards some kind of self-government under the British umbrella. Some dependencies, for instance those in and around the Indian Ocean, Britain wanted to retain, if at all possible, for strategic reasons.

In February 1965, Britain took the plunge into the mini-state era by granting 'independence' to the Gambia – 300 miles long, and, at its widest, 30 miles wide – a strip of territory along the banks of the Gambia river, entirely surrounded, except for its tiny little bit of coast, by Senegal. Senegal was very French and Gambia was very English. Efforts made to promote association between Senegal and Gambia came to nothing. So Gambia was launched – an economically unviable independent state, subsidized by Britain.

The Commonwealth came under very severe strains of another kind in these two years. In September 1965 war broke out between two Commonwealth members, India and Pakistan, over the vexed question of Kashmir. Nothing quite so serious as this had ever happened before within the ranks of the Commonwealth. Britain's inability to deal with it greatly. damaged her standing in the eyes of the rest of the Commonwealth and indeed in the world at large. In the end, in January 1966 it was Mr.

Kosygin of the U.S.S.R. who persuaded both India and Pakistan to come to the conference table, at Tashkent. And Russia succeeded where Britain and the Commonwealth had failed.

a *Southern Rhodesia*
Southern Rhodesia was a very much more serious, and very much more intractable problem. The attitude of the white Rhodesians was becoming desperate. There had been rumours of a unilateral declaration of independence since 1963. Talks started by the Conservative Government in 1964 continued into 1965, but with no real progress being made.

In January 1965 Mr. Smith had a meeting in London with the Prime Minister and the Lord Chancellor. In February the Lord Chancellor and the then Commonwealth Secretary, Mr. Bottomley, visited Rhodesia. But in April, a Rhodesian Government White Paper concluded that Rhodesia had little to lose and much to gain by becoming independent. However, at that time Rhodesian business interests had grave misgivings about the probable economic consequences of such a step.

At the May elections in Rhodesia in 1965 Mr. Smith's Rhodesian Front got a landslide victory. It was apparent that the European electorate was overwhelmingly behind him in his wish to achieve independence on the basis of the 1961 Constitution. But the Labour Government stood firm on the so-called 'five principles' first put forward by Sir Alec Douglas-Home in 1964. These were:

(1) An amended constitution guaranteeing unimpeded progress towards majority rule.
(2) Guarantees against retrogressive amendments to that constitution.
(3) Immediate improvement in the political status of the African majority,
(4) A firm intention to end racial discrimination.
(5) Some assurance that the new constitution would be acceptable to the Rhodesian people as a whole – whether black or white.

Finally, on 11 November 1965, Mr. Smith declared in a broadcast, the independence of Rhodesia. 'We have,' he said,

> ... struck a blow for the preservation of justice, civilization and Christianity; and in the spirit of this belief we have this day assumed our sovereign independence.

Rhodesia would, however, remain loyal to the Queen, so Mr. Smith said.
Meantime, Sir Humphrey Gibbs, the Governor of Rhodesia, told Mr. Smith that he and his Ministers were dismissed. They were now, Sir Humphrey said, private persons, who could exercise no legal authority in Rhodesia. Sir Humphrey refused to leave Government House. Sir Hugh Beadle, the Chief Justice, joined him there.

Economic sanctions were imposed on Rhodesia. The Labour left wing called for the use of force. So did African states, ever more vociferously, at the U.N. Mr. Wilson was, or professed to be, optimistic about the efficacy of economic sanctions. It could only be a matter of a few weeks, he said, before the illegal Government of Mr. Smith in Rhodesia was brought down. Rhodesia would find no markets for her tobacco. And oil sanctions would quickly bring the whole economy to a halt. But South Africa and Portugal gave discreet assistance to Rhodesia over oil. And Rhodesian tobacco did find its way, by devious routes, on to the world markets. Rhodesia showed no signs at all of imminent collapse.

Why did Mr. Wilson reject the idea of using force? He feared, one may suppose, that this might trigger off a general, bloody, war that might spread far and wide over the African continent. The economic cost would anyway have been, probably, prohibitive. Behind all this there was 'the Suez reflex'. If Britain had learnt anything from Suez, it was that force could provide no answers. Then, the example of the Congo must have been very much in the minds of those in authority. Deliberately to tear down and destroy the authority of an existing and functioning government was to invite disaster of a kind which no responsible person could lightly contemplate. Britain could advise from the sidelines. But to use white troops against white settlers might lead to mutiny. And in any event, Britain could not make herself directly responsible for setting up and running government and administration in a society wholly different from her own, and whose problems she barely began to understand. To accept that some moves, however desirable in themselves, are really beyond the reach of a country's resources is surely no small part of wisdom. It is difficult not to agree with Mr. Wilson's refusal to use force. His real mistake was, perhaps, in the massive miscalculation about the effect of economic sanctions. This did indeed detract from his credibility both as an economist, and as a Prime Minister.

b *Gibraltar*

Trouble of a different kind blew up over Gibraltar. Here, the rather disconcerting story was that Gibraltar steadily and embarrassingly refused to leave Britain, and Britain was pilloried by Spain and the U.N. for aiding and abetting her in her wish to stay on as a British dependency.

Gibraltar was two and a quarter square miles in size. Its population was between 24,000 and 25,000 people, of mixed Genoese, Portuguese, Spanish and British descent. There were also some 10,000 workers, who travelled in daily from Spain. Spain revived her ancient claim to Gibraltar after the end of the Second World War, in general terms – and more precisely after 1954. In that year, the Spanish Government began to impose restrictions on the movement of goods and people across the border. In 1963, the U.N. began to show interest. And in April 1965 the

British Government published a White Paper setting out the British, the Spanish, and the Gibraltarian standpoint as they saw it. The Government announced an increase in British aid to Gibraltar, designed to help in adjusting the economy to the new circumstances, and to ease housing and labour problems.

The Spanish 'case', put to the U.N. Committee in 1963-4, was that the British Colony of Gibraltar was an intolerable relic of colonialism in Europe. Gibraltar was Spanish territory, which had been yielded to Britain on various conditions, including the understanding that if Britain ever relinquished her sovereignty Spain would be the first legatee. Now Britain seemed to be proposing something akin to independence for Gibraltar, and this would certainly involve Britain relinquishing her sovereignty. Representative institutions had been introduced gradually from 1950 onwards; and these had culminated in the 1964 constitution, with a chief Minister, and a majority of elected members on the Legislative and Executive Councils. Spain refused to admit the existence of a bona fide local nationalism in Gibraltar, and asserted that Act 73 of the U.N. Charter, concerning the right of self-determination, could not apply to the people whom she termed pseudo-Gibraltarians.

9 THE OPPOSITION

a *The Conservative Party*

The results of the General Election of October 1964 had further demoralized and confused the Tory Party, already seriously shaken by the events of 1961-4. These years had seen the Profumo case; serious security leakages; General de Gaulle's *Non*; Mr. Macmillan's illness; Sir Alec's unhappy 'emergence'; squabbles among the Tories over resale price maintenance; and, most menacing of all, the steadily worsening economic situation. The Party was clearly in serious disarray – perhaps more serious even than the disarray of 1945. And this time Mr. Butler was too old to pull any clever ideas out of his hat to rescue them; and there was no equivalent to the smiling and benign Lord Woolton. Furthermore, 1964 was not, as 1945 had been, a dream untroubled of hope. The Conservatives could not relax and give themselves time to think up new programmes, and better ways of organizing themselves. The narrowness of Labour's victory meant that the prospect of another General Election in the near future could not be ruled out, and thus that it was necessary to begin, immediately, to prepare for this eventuality. The Tory Party was at this time inexperienced in Opposition; but there was an uneasy feeling that, as after the 1945 defeat, another reorganization was now needed – and would have to be carried out at top speed. They did their best. The Central Office was reorganized, and a new post of Deputy

Chairman was created. The Deputy Chairman was to be a liaison between the chairman and the various full-time party officials. A new, young chairman – Mr. Edward du Cann, aged forty – was selected. It was hoped to make the whole organization more political and less involved in social activities; and to introduce up-to-date business techniques into the finance and publicity departments of the Central Office. Higher salaries for agents in the constituencies were introduced, along with training schemes for agents. A system of subsidies was worked out for marginal constituencies to enable them to attract better agents from the safer seats. An effort was made to bring the Party in the constituencies into closer touch with the Leadership; and, cautiously, to reduce the proportion of peers, landowners, business men and service officers among the Party's candidates and leaders.

Mr. Heath was appointed as chairman of the Advisory Committee on Policy and he began his work without delay. Younger M.P.s were brought into the Shadow Cabinet and into the Party organization at all levels.

The first big issue to be tackled was the working out of a new procedure for the selection of the Party Leader because of the barrage of criticism which had met the 'emergence' of Sir Alec Douglas-Home in 1963. The new method of electing a Leader, agreed in February 1965, was as follows:

The Leader was to be elected by all the Tory M.P.s from among their number.

(1) At the first ballot each M.P. would have a single vote. If one candidate got an overall majority, and 15 per cent more of the votes cast than any other candidate, he would be elected. If not, there would be a second ballot.

(2) The first ballot nominations would be void unless candidates were renominated. New names could be introduced. Again, each M.P. would have one vote. This time, if any candidate got an overall majority of the votes cast, he would be elected. If not, there would be a third ballot.

(3) The three candidates who came highest on the second ballot would stand for this third ballot. Each M.P. would have two votes, to be cast in order of preference. The candidate with the lowest number of first preferences would be eliminated; and the votes given to him redistributed among the other two, according to the second preference of the voters. The candidate who then emerged with the most votes would be 'presented for election as Party Leader to the Party meeting,'

i.e. the Annual Conservative Conference would as in the past be invited to acclaim the Leader already chosen; but now to be chosen by the Tory M.P.s.

The Tories, having formerly left everything more or less to the old-boy network now went rather far in the other direction. The pretence that the constituencies and prospective parliamentary candidates were at least 'consulted' was now dropped. And it may be noted with interest that the single transferable vote system adopted for the third ballot was that which had long been advocated by the Liberal Party for national elections – though resisted by the Tory and Labour Parties, for reasons not hard to understand.

It is interesting to speculate on how, if at all, this change in the procedure for selecting a Leader may in future affect the Royal Prerogative. It had always been regarded as the Sovereign's right to take advice and to give advice on the selection of a Prime Minister, at any rate as far as Conservative Leaders went. The Labour Party had always elected its Leaders. No Sovereign will, in future, be able to question the choice of Leaders of either of the major Parties. There will be no room for manoeuvre, unless a situation arises comparable to that of 1931 when a National Government had to be formed, without a General Election. But it is, of course, not inconceivable that the Sovereign might have a role if an elected Leader, who was Prime Minister, got into serious difficulties within his own Party without actually losing his majority in the Commons. In any event, the value of the Sovereign is as a reserve power, to be used in case of emergency. It is in the nature of the case that emergencies cannot be foreseen.

After the new procedure had been agreed on, some Tories felt that Sir Alec should resign and submit himself at once to election. However, until Mr. Wilson said categorically, in June 1965, that there would be no dissolution that year, the possibility of a sudden Election made a change in the Leadership look too chancy. No Party would choose to fight an Election with a new and untried Leader.

Why, it may be asked, was there this surge of feeling against Sir Alec? After all, he had come very near to winning the October 1964 General Election for the Conservatives.

Opinion polls showed that he was less popular with the electorate than Mr. Wilson, then very popular indeed. The thought was that a new Leader with a new image might do better. Britain was much preoccupied, at this time, with the idea that Elections were fought and won by Leaders. It was fashionable to view British government as somewhat presidential in style. Then, Sir Alec was certainly no match for Mr. Wilson in parliamentary duels. Perhaps most important of all he had little knowledge of economics, now seen as the central issue of the parliamentary battle.

In the end, in July 1965, Sir Alec resigned, before he was forced to go. 'I took the decision, and the decision was mine,' he said firmly.

So, on 17 July 1965, the new procedure was used for the first time. There were two main contenders – Mr. Maudling and Mr. Heath; and support for them seems to have been quite evenly balanced. Mr. Enoch Powell was also a contender.

Mr. Maudling had been a serious contender for the Leadership in the summer of 1963. He had had a good deal of Ministerial experience. In 1959 he was President of the Board of Trade; in 1961 Colonial Secretary; and in 1962 Chancellor of the Exchequer. He was popular, though generally regarded as a rather lazy person.

Mr. Heath, a relatively unknown figure at the time of his election, had had in some ways a more impressive career. He had been to a grammar school and then to Oxford. From 1955 to 1959 he had been Chief Whip in the Conservative Party, and had, in 1957, played a not inconsiderable part in helping Mr. Macmillan to 'emerge'. He was Minister of Labour from 1959 to 1960; he was Lord Privy Seal from 1960 to 1963. (He was at that time in the Cabinet, and second in command at the Foreign Office.) From 1961 to 1963 he was in charge of the Brussels negotiations for entry into the E.E.C. In 1963-4 he was President of the Board of Trade, and responsible for the ending of resale price maintenance. In 1965 he was Shadow Cabinet spokesman on economic affairs. He led the opposition to the Finance Bill – and his good performance then probably tilted the ballot in his favour.

In the end, the complicated three ballot procedure for choosing the new Leader was not required. On the first ballot, the voting was as follows:

> Heath   150
> Maudling   133
> Enoch Powell   15

According to the rules, a second ballot would have been needed since Mr. Heath's majority was not large enough. But Mr. Maudling and Mr. Powell withdrew, and Mr. Heath was thus returned unopposed. He was forty-nine years old.

On August 5th he announced his Shadow Cabinet. Mr. Maudling was the Deputy Leader; Sir Alec remained in the Cabinet with overlordship of external affairs. Mr. Macleod took over economic and financial affairs.

In October 1965 the Conservatives published a document called 'Putting Britain Right Ahead' – a compendium of new Tory policies. The main proposals included entry into Europe – about which the Tories had been silent during the 1964 Election campaign; reduction of direct taxation; trade union reform; and the concentration of welfare provisions on those most in need.

In November 1965 the first major difficulty for Mr. Heath loomed up – Rhodesia. There had already been signs of trouble, at the Conservative Conference in October, when the strength of right wing feeling had become apparent. Lord Salisbury and his followers were determined that the Conservative Party should back the white Rhodesians. But when Mr. Smith declared U.D.I. Mr. Heath supported Mr. Wilson, and voted for sanctions. However, when it came to the vote on oil sanctions he felt, for a variety of reasons, less certain, and advised his followers to abstain. The Party was then seen to be split three ways, for fifty voted against the Government and thirty for it, and the rest, led by Mr. Heath, abstained.

By the end of 1965 Mr. Heath's position had considerably deteriorated. He had not come over strongly as the new Leader. Indeed, the polls showed him as even less popular than Sir Alec had been. The public at large seems to have sensed a coldness, and an inability to communicate with them. His failure to hold his team together over Rhodesia seemed ominous. And, although he was chosen largely because it was thought that he would be a match for Mr. Wilson in the Commons, it was soon apparent that he was nothing of the kind.

b *The Liberal Party*
The Labour victory at the General Election in October 1964 meant that Mr. Grimond's strategy had failed. He had hoped, it seemed, for a 'realignment of the left' following a Labour defeat, and the consequent disillusion and splits in the Labour camp. A new radical party of Liberals and moderate Labour people would then emerge, he hoped.

Mr. Wilson, in spite of his narrow Labour majority of four, made no overtures to the Liberals, who did not, after all, hold the balance – although it remained a possibility that they might, after a couple of marginal by-elections, and two or three dissentient Labour backbenchers. It was Mr. Grimond who made the first move, in June 1965, when he indicated that he would seriously consider a Labour offer of a coalition. He believed, at that time, that by the autumn the Liberals really would hold the balance and would be able, in effect, either to hold the Labour Government in office, or to precipitate a General Election. He wanted to negotiate a joint programme, which would incorporate some Liberal policies. Others in the Liberal Party looked on these plans with great suspicion, fearing that the Liberals would lose their separate identity, swallowed up in the much larger Labour mass.

But in fact Mr. Wilson never responded to Liberal advances. And the Liberals never did hold the balance. All that can be said is that, in the Queen's Speech in the autumn of 1965, Mr. Wilson, for whatever reasons, included several policies the Liberals approved of, e.g. the Parliamentary Commissioner; and omitted some which they did not approve of, e.g. the re-nationalization of steel.

So the Liberals had to decide each issue on its own merits. Mr. Grimond said that his followers should not embarrass the Government unless it introduced measures clearly contrary, in Liberal eyes, to the national interest. And in the end, the public in general, and Liberal voters in particular, seemed to have the impression that the Liberals were keeping Labour in power. Not, perhaps a fair impression since, by May 1965, the Liberals had voted with the Government forty times, and against it eighty-five times. They had abstained three times.

The Liberals were caught in a cleft stick. They were critical of Labour, but had no desire for a Conservative Government. They did not want to force a General Election, for fear they might either give Labour a larger majority, or else bring back the Conservatives.

On the whole, by-elections and opinion polls showed a steady decline in the Liberal vote. The one exception was Roxburgh, where, in March 1965, Mr. David Steel won a Tory seat.

CHAPTER FIVE

The Labour Government from March 1966 to June 1970

	page
SUMMARY	
1 The General Election of 31 March 1966	180
2 The Labour Team	182
a Cabinet Changes	182
b Decline in support for the Government	185
c By-elections; local government elections; opinion polls	189
3 Constitutional and Administrative Issues	189
a The Parliamentary Commissioner	190
b Parliamentary Committees in the House of Commons	190
c The House of Lords	191
d The Parliamentary Committee of the Cabinet	193
e Age of Majority	193
f The Fulton Report on the Civil Service	193
4 Economic Issues	194
5 Domestic Affairs	205
a The Commonwealth Immigration Act 1968	205
b The Race Relations Act	206
6 Defence Policy	207
7 Foreign Policy	208
a General	208
b The Anglo-American relationship	208
c The Communist world	209
d Europe	210
(i) NATO	210
(ii) The Common Market	210
e The Middle East	214
8 The Commonwealth	214
a Membership	214
b Rhodesia	216
c The Nigerian Civil War	217
d The West Indies	217
9 The Opposition	218
a The Conservatives	218
b The Liberals	220

1 THE GENERAL ELECTION OF 31 MARCH 1966
On February 28th it was announced that a General Election would be held on 31 March 1966. A variety of circumstances made the spring of 1966 look like a good time for increasing Labour's majority. In January 1965 there had been a swing of 4½ per cent to Labour at the North Hull by-election. And the polls from then on consistently gave Labour a big lead. But clouds were looming up. The state of the economy must have given rise to great anxiety for those in the know. It might be possible to keep going in the hope of growth and better times ahead for just a little longer, but a major storm might break at any time. By the autumn of 1966 it might no longer be possible to disguise the seriousness of the economic situation.

The Labour Manifesto was entitled 'Time for Decision'. Much was made of Labour's record in the past eighteen months; of the 'thirteen wasted years' of Tory misrule; and of the need for a long period of radical reconstruction. Much emphasis was laid on planning, not then, as it subsequently became, almost a joke word. 'Socialism' was hardly mentioned and only one 'socialist' measure, the re-nationalization of the steel industry, was proposed. The Labour Party was in something of a dilemma in approaching a General Election. Labour strategists did not really want too quiet a campaign – fearing, as always, apathy and abstention among Labour voters. But on the other hand, they did not want to raise too many new issues which might provide the Tories with targets. Mr. Wilson himself hoped to stand aloof from the campaign, and thus preserve his 'presidential' image. But in the end he had to take part.

The Conservative Manifesto, entitled 'Action Not Words' was launched by Mr. Heath on March 6th. Three principles were made explicit; and all three stemmed from Mr. Heath's personal political philosophy. Competition was to be encouraged, and state activity cut back. Social services were to be provided on a selective basis, rather than as a universal hand-out to which people were entitled irrespective of need; and there was categoric commitment to the policy of joining the Common Market. The Conservatives were in a difficult position as far as the state of the economy went. They were convinced that very serious economic troubles were just around the corner. But to say this, with the bankers of the world all ears, might make what they feared was anyway a bad situation worse. And then it would be argued afterwards that the troubles had in fact been caused by Tory rumour mongering.

The Liberals' Manifesto, 'For All the People', launched by Mr. Grimond on March 10th, claimed that the small group of Liberal M.P.s in the previous Parliament had been able to restrain some of Labour's wilder moves. The Liberals urged an end to Britain's nuclear role; a cut in conventional defence commitments; an end to 'east of Suez'; regional government; cuts in direct taxation; and entry into Europe. *The Times*, one of the few papers without a firm Party preference in 1966, stressed the desirability of a large Liberal vote. The *Guardian* supported Labour.

The Communist Party had fifty-seven candidates, and called their Manifesto 'New Britain – People's Britain'. They found half a dozen industries that they wished to nationalize.

The campaign was rather dull. Nobody dropped any notable bricks. The turn-out of voters was low – 75.8 per cent.[1] There was a 3.5 swing to Labour, and the results were as follows:

	Votes	Percentage of votes	Seats obtained
Labour	13,064,951	47.9	363
Conservative	11,418,433	41.9	253
Liberal	2,327,533	8.5	12
Communists	162,112	0.2	nil

The Labour Party now had an overall majority of 97, including the Speaker. Thus the 1966 Election left Labour in almost exactly the same position that the Tories had been in after the 1959 Election when they had gained 365 seats against Labour's 258. Some thought that the pattern of the fifties, when the Conservatives won three Elections running, might be becoming a general pattern. Perhaps the pendulum was going to take longer to swing because of the control of a government in power over the mass media; and because of the possibility of manipulating the economy, particularly before and during Election times.

In this General Election, unlike that of 1964, there was uniformity in the swing to Labour. Mr. Wilson had acquired a good public image. The voters still seemed disposed to believe that Tory mismanagement had, in large measure, been the cause of the economic difficulties in the early sixties. Mr. Heath had not yet made much impact. He did not, as the jargon had it, 'communicate' well.

The Conservatives failed to gain a single seat. And several former Tory Cabinet Ministers lost their seats, for example, Mr. Soames, Mr. Thorneycroft and Mr. Brooke. Many of the old right of centre Tory M.P.s did not seek re-election, and were replaced by younger and sometimes more radical men.

The Liberal share of the poll dropped, partly, no doubt, because there were fewer Liberal candidates in 1966. They made a net gain of two seats, but their moment had clearly passed. They had hoped to hold the balance in the 1964-6 Parliament and this had not happened.

Of the seventy-two new Labour M.P.s who entered Parliament between 1965 and 1966, 57 per cent had a professional background; and only

[1] This was the lowest poll since 1945.

14 per cent a working-class background. 68 per cent had had a university education.

2 THE LABOUR TEAM

a *Cabinet changes*

Although there were changes there was no major reshuffle of the Cabinet after the Election; nor did Mr. Wilson seek to make his large team any smaller. Perhaps its size suited his style of government. He had never been one for collective decision-taking, so the fact that there were too many Cabinet members to make this feasible may have seemed a positive advantage.

Although there was no major Cabinet reshuffle, there were twenty-five changes in the Government, two of which may be noted. Mr. Roy Jenkins came to the Home Office, succeeding Sir Frank Soskice who retired because of ill health. Mr. Richard Marsh, aged thirty-eight, became Minister of Power. He was an official of one of the white collar unions (The National Union of Public Employees).

In July 1966 Mr. Frank Cousins, Minister of Technology, resigned on the day before the publication of the Prices and Incomes Bill, and was succeeded by Mr. Wedgwood Benn. Mr. Cousins was General Secretary of the Transport and General Workers' Union, the largest of all the trade unions. Mr. Wilson had probably hoped that, by taking him into the Government, the hostility of the trade union left, which he represented, would be neutralized. But the Government Prices and Incomes Bill was more than Mr. Cousins as a good trade unionist, could stomach. His presence in the Cabinet for two years had greatly helped to maintain anyway the façade of unity in the Labour movement. His absence in the future was unfortunate. At the Labour Party Conference in October 1966 Mr. Cousins attacked the Government's prices and incomes policy, and, in particular, its decision to invoke Part IV of the Prices and Incomes Act to make a wages freeze compulsory. He described the Government's incomes policy as 'a contradiction of the philosophy upon which our Party is based.' And although the Conference in the end supported the Government, it was obvious that its economic policies were causing widespread and grave concern to the trade union wing of the Conference.

On 10 August 1966, Mr. Brown left the D.E.A. to become Foreign Secretary, thus changing places with Mr. Michael Stewart. From all accounts Mr. Brown had not been a success at the D.E.A. He did not work easily when in close relationship with the Prime Minister; and he did not get on well with the Treasury officials. He had already threatened resignation in June (resignation was a threat which Mr. Brown used fairly often) so his move in August did not come as a surprise. By June

1966 he had become convinced of the need for devaluation, and had put this to his Cabinet colleagues. But the Prime Minister, and the majority of the Cabinet were against it, preferring, as Mr. Brown sadly said, a policy of 'cuts, squeezes and freezes'. Mr. Brown, realizing that he would not be able to give any public explanation, at that time, for his resignation, stayed on to see the Prices and Incomes Bill through Parliament. When it passed its third reading on 10 August 1966, he left to take over at the Foreign Office, and thereafter the D.E.A. came effectively to an end as an independent Department.[1] On 26 July 1967 Miss Margaret Herbison, Minister of Social Security, resigned. No reasons were given, but it was assumed that she had wanted higher family allowances and higher benefits generally, and that the Cabinet had rejected her case.

A major reshuffle came on 28 August 1967. This was directly related to the deteriorating economic situation. The Prime Minister took over direct control of the economy, assuming personal responsibility for the D.E.A., although the Minister, Mr. Stewart, was nominally replaced by Mr. Peter Shore, a young newcomer to the Cabinet. Mr. Stewart remained in the Cabinet as First Secretary of State, with the task of supervising the Cabinet's social policies. Five Ministers left the Government, including Mr. Douglas Jay, who was a strong opponent of Britain's entry to the Common Market. Mr. Gordon Walker went to the Ministry of Education.

On 29 November 1967 Mr. Callaghan resigned as Chancellor of the Exchequer, following devaluation on November 18th. It would have been difficult for him to stay on as Chancellor, since on the one hand he bore much of the responsibility for the policies which had made devaluation necessary, and on the other hand, he had recently stated so categorically that there would be no devaluation. He did not, however, leave the Government, but became Home Secretary in place of Mr. Roy Jenkins, who moved to the Treasury. On 17 January 1968 the Earl of Longford, Lord Privy Seal and Leader of the Lords, resigned over the deferment of the raising of the school leaving age.

On 15 March 1968 Mr. Brown resigned as Foreign Secretary and Deputy Prime Minister. The immediate cause for his resignation seemed trivial. An important meeting of the Privy Council had been called and he was not informed in time to be present. But it was obvious that this was merely the last straw. In his letter of resignation Mr. Brown complained of the way the Government was run and the manner in which decisions were reached.[2] This complaint was probably echoed by a good

[1] George-Brown, op. cit., p. 117.

[2] 'I resigned on a matter of fundamental principle, because it seemed to me that the Prime Minister was not only introducing a "presidential" system into the running of the government that is wholly alien to the British constitutional system, but was so operating it that decisions were being taken over the heads and without the knowledge of Ministers, and far too often outsiders in his

many Ministers, who were now openly critical of the somewhat personal way in which Mr. Wilson ran the Government. Later, in an article published by the *Sunday Times* on 11 October 1970, Mr. Brown was considerably more explicit about the circumstances of his resignation. There had been, he said, a number of issues about which he had had trouble in the Cabinet in the months immediately preceding his resignation. One such had been the sale of arms to South Africa for the defence of trade routes, now so important to Britain because of the closing of the Suez Canal, and the growing Russian presence in the Indian Ocean. 'I did not see how the argument could be sustained that the sort of arms and equipment which the South African government was anxious to obtain from Britain could really be said so to jeopardize the position of black South Africans as to make it wrong for us to be willing to supply. There was also of course the little point that, if we didn't supply, France or someone else was waiting on the doorstep pressing the South Africans to let them do it at our expense.' Mr. Brown said that, with the knowledge of the Prime Minister, he had in 1967 sent a letter to Dr. Müller, the South African Foreign Minister, suggesting that the South Africans might find it worth their while to be patient, as this was an issue on which the Labour Party was at present deeply divided, and there were strong feelings. Mr. Healey was also of his opinion, said Mr. Brown, as were other Cabinet colleagues. But the Prime Minister had suddenly veered around and organized opinion in the P.L.P. against the sale. This kind of thing, said Mr. Brown, was always happening. No one could know when or why the Prime Minister would change course. Mr. Brown, although he left the Government, remained as Deputy Leader. He was not yet prepared to pull out of Labour Party politics altogether, and wished, in particular, to retain his seat on the N.E.C.

In April 1968 a further Cabinet reorganization took place. The luckless Mr. Gordon Walker, Minister of Education, was dismissed. He had now blundered over a range of educational issues and it seemed that this nice, reasonable and able man was so prone to brick dropping that he was too great a liability to be carried any longer. Mr. Edward Short, the Postmaster General, replaced him. The Prime Minister at this juncture promoted two of his own political friends, who were leading left wingers. Mrs. Barbara Castle, formerly Minister of Labour, became First Secretary of State for Employment and Productivity, with responsibility for the Government's incomes policy. It was apparently hoped that she would achieve what Mr. Peter Shore at the D.E.A. had failed to do. At the same time Mr. Crossman was given overall responsibility for the Social Services, and he was replaced as Leader of the House by Mr. Fred

---

entourage seemed to be almost the only effective Cabinet.' George-Brown, op. cit., p. 169.

Peart. There was thus, in the spring of 1968, a decided leftward shift in the Government. This was a period when the Government was in constant trouble, both with its own back-benchers, and with the T.U.C. over the Prices and Incomes Bill, which renewed and extended the 1967 Act. On its second reading in the House on May 21st the Government's usual majority of seventy became a mere thirty-five. The unions were now considerably less willing to help than they had been in 1966 and 1967. And in May the results of the local government elections seemed like a nation-wide rebuff to Labour. On 30 June 1968 Mr. Gunter, a bluff, sturdy, middle of the road trade unionist resigned somewhat abruptly from the Government.

On 5 October 1969 another reshuffle was announced, which involved not only shifts of individual Ministers, but also some important reallocation of their functions. Thus the D.E.A. and the Ministry of Power were abolished; and the old Board of Trade was swallowed up in the new Ministry of Technology, now to be headed by Mr. Anthony Wedgwood Benn. The former President of the Board of Trade, Mr. Anthony Crosland, became Secretary for Local Government and Regional Planning. Mr. Richard Marsh, the young Minister of Power, still only forty-one, was dropped. The average age of the outgoing junior Ministers was sixty years, of the newcomers thirty-eight.

b *Decline in support for the Government*
1964 to 1966 had been Labour's heroic years. And particularly they were the Wilson years. He seemed then to tower above all other men in public life. He achieved the high esteem, and even affection, that the British electorate sometimes accords to those who lead them, or appear to be leading them, out of particularly awkward and tricky situations. This towering above all other colleagues suited his own style well. He has recorded, in his memoirs, his own view of the functions of a Prime Minister. 'It was, and is, my strong view that in modern Britain, the Prime Minister's grip on every major subject, particularly finance and economic affairs, industrial policies and industrial relations, foreign and Commonwealth affairs ... should be such that he can dictate, without a departmental brief, the main text of any speech he has to make, in Parliament or in the country.'[1]

His memoirs are full of accounts of personal telephone calls to all parts of the world, on every conceivable topic. On one occasion at least he complained that while other Ministers seemed able to take holidays, he never could. And on another occasion he recalls that, while on a brief holiday in the Scillies, he took a walkie-talkie around with him, so that he could keep in touch from any point on the islands.[2] The twenty-one-

[1] Harold Wilson, op. cit., p. 45.   [2] Ibid., p. 274.

hour days; the take-over of problems, large or small, from other Ministers; the beer and sandwiches at Downing Street in the middle of the night to help settle crises – are all faithfully recorded. The wonder is that a man who pushed himself so hard for six long years survived to tell the tale.

But, perhaps because salvation cannot in reality come from any one man, and because the British electorate has sufficient sense to know this, the personal pre-eminence seldom lasts for long. Lloyd George enjoyed this kind of pre-eminence after 1916. So did Baldwin, for a period in the inter-war years. So did Churchill during the Second World War. So did Mr. Macmillan after 1957. But the British electorate does not subscribe to the *führer prinzip* for long. And as it had happened to other men before him, so now it began to happen to Mr. Harold Wilson in the years from 1966 to 1970. The British *au fond* preferring collective leadership, soon got to know and respect other members of the Wilson team. And soon also, they were disenchanted with Mr. Wilson even as the team leader. The years from 1966 to 1970 were distinctly stormy, and it took Mr. Wilson all his time to remain on top. There were times when *primus inter pares* would have seemed an overstatement.

Mr. Wilson had tried in 1966 to include all sectors of Labour opinion in his Cabinet, thus ensuring that back-bench opposition to his government would lack leadership. But it was not to be. Mr. Cousins defected on the left; and Mr. Brown and Mr. Douglas Jay defected on the right. Some valuable middle of the road supporters also dropped out such as Mr. Gunter, the trade unionist, Miss Herbison, the dedicated, loyal social worker and Lord Longford, a plain, honest Labour peer. The big people who stayed in the Government were, long before it ended, doubtfully loyal to the Prime Minister. Mr. Callaghan was certainly a threat. The new Chancellor of the Exchequer, Mr. Roy Jenkins, who took over after devaluation, was a threat in embryo. These were not men who could readily be manipulated and out-manoeuvred. They were possible alternative Party Leaders. The attempt to reassert the Wilson primacy in the 1970 Election campaign may well have been a powerful reason for Labour's defeat. The electorate did not warm to Mr. Heath, if any credence at all can be attached to opinion polls. But it is probable that they instinctively preferred his more restrained and collective style of leadership, and mistrusted Mr. Wilson's so-called 'presidential style'.

Mr. Wilson's dominance at Westminster had probably been a consequence of his electoral popularity, as shown in by-elections, local government elections and opinion polls. But in the life of this Government his popularity declined steadily and it is possible to trace this decline, step by step. Thus, as early as July 1966, probably most of the electorate agreed with Frank Cousins's verdict on the Prices and Incomes Bill as being 'a contradiction of the philosophy upon which our Party is based'.

Frozen wage packets were followed by mounting unemployment. The feeling grew, among Labour voters, that the Labour Government was trying to find a way out of its difficulties by attacking the standard of living of the very people who had put them in power. The Prime Minister was a professional economist, but faith in his capacity to solve the country's economic problem was waning. In the autumn of 1966 the Party Conference did still support the Government, but even as early as that, it was touch and go.

Already, in the first summer, the left wing of the Party began to make vociferous protest over the Government's foreign and defence policies. The level of defence expenditure; the continued British presence east of Suez, and, most of all, the support given to the United States Government over its Vietnam policy, all came under attack in July 1966, and in February 1967 at least forty-six Labour M.P.s abstained in a vote on the defence White Paper.

Then, in March 1967, the Prime Minister made his famous 'dog licence' speech, in which, attacking Labour left wing defence rebels, he hinted at harsher disciplines to come, and said flatly that the duty of Labour M.P.s was to maintain a Labour Government in power. Mr. Wilson said: 'Every dog is allowed one bite, but a different view is taken of a dog that goes on biting all the time. . . . He may not get his licence renewed when it falls due.' Fateful words from a British Prime Minister to his supporters in the House of Commons, where already there was a deep resentment at the way back-benchers and their views were now customarily disregarded. Many date the decline in his popularity to this unwise speech.

In May 1967 thirty-five Labour M.P.s voted against the Government's Common Market policy and forty more abstained. The Labour movement had always viewed any form of closer association with Europe with misgiving. European recovery after the war had been too closely associated with the triumph of free enterprise and conservative capitalism. The European leaders of this spectacular resurgence had been orthodox to their fingertips in all their politics. They were capitalists not socialists. In post-war Europe conservatism had been an embarrassingly spectacular success in just those ways in which the Labour Party had always forecast its failure. To join up with these Europeans might well put socialism, the Welfare State, and planning designed to achieve a more egalitarian society, at serious risk. Mr. Wilson had always said so in the past. Now, it seemed that he had changed his mind. But not all of his followers had changed theirs. At the Prime Minister's instigation, seven Parliamentary Private Secretaries were dismissed for failing to support the Government, and faith in the Prime Minister was not enhanced when the Europeans said No to him in 1968.

In November 1967, devaluation had temporarily closed the ranks, as it was felt that the Government had at last taken some positive action. But Mr. Wilson's comment that 'the pound in your pocket will still be worth the same' brought another bad mark, as all too soon the shoppers found that this was certainly not the case.

In the early summer of 1968 there was a press campaign to persuade Mr. Wilson to retire as Prime Minister. Mr. Cecil King mounted an attack in the *Daily Mirror*. 'Enough is enough', Mr. King said. He argued that the country faced the greatest financial crisis in its history, and called on the Parliamentary Labour Party to depose Mr. Wilson. Other more influential journals took up the *Daily Mirror*'s cry. And in June and July 1968 *The Times* too campaigned for the resignation of Mr. Wilson. Mr. Wilson's relations with the press, once so good, had now become very bad indeed. It soon became an article of faith with the Prime Minister that the mass media conspired against him. But, short of a General Election, there is no way of forcing an unpopular Prime Minister to stand down. And a General Election, when the opinion polls were showing a swing of around 18 per cent against Labour, would have have been unthinkable. Only a Labour group of 1931 proportions would have been returned to Parliament and the Labour M.P.s were well aware of this.

By the summer of 1968, political commentators felt that the worst was over, and the Prime Minister had weathered the storm. However, the state of the economy, and the weakness of sterling on the exchange markets continued to cause great anxiety. And on November 22nd Mr. Jenkins was obliged to introduce an autumn Budget designed to dampen down the high level of internal demand. The very large tax increases in the 1968 April Budget had not done the trick.

In early December 1968, a wave of rumours swept through the City and European financial centres that Mr. Wilson was about to resign, and that a Coalition Government would be formed. *The Times* called for this in a leading article on December 9th. But both the Government and the Opposition dismissed the idea briskly.

The spring of 1969 saw further very serious set-backs to the Labour Government. The Bill on the reform of the House of Lords had to be abandoned on April 17th in the face of serious obstruction from both back-benches. And the Government's Bill to reform the trade unions, based on the Royal Commission on trade unions, which reported in 1968,[1] and on the Government White Paper *In Place of Strife*[2] was the subject of fierce dispute in the Party. On 26 March 1969 the N.E.C., which represented both the unions and the Party organization, voted against the Government's policy by sixteen votes to five, thus formally opposing the Labour Government for the first time since 1964. And it

[1] Royal Commission on Trade Unions and Employers Associations (Cmnd 3623) under the chairmanship of Lord Donovan.   [2] Cmnd 3888.

was a noteworthy fact that Mr. Callaghan, the Home Secretary, who was on the N.E.C. as Party treasurer, voted against the Government of which he was a prominent member. Again, the threat to Mr. Wilson's Leadership seemed very real. But crisis was averted on June 19th by further retreats.

c *By-elections; local government elections; opinion polls*
The decline in the popularity of the Labour Government with the electorate through these years can best be charted by by-election and local government election results which showed, from May 1967, massive swings away from Labour. During these years Labour safe seats became marginals, and Conservative marginals became safe seats. There was a steady erosion of Labour's parliamentary majority, and each batch of defeats ate deeper into Labour Party morale. The one ray of hope for the Government seemed to be that by-election results did not show much increase in Conservative or other Party votes, but just massive Labour abstentions. The hope to cling to was that at the next General Election the abstainers might somehow be enticed to the polling booths.

The trend away from the Government first appeared in the borough elections of May 1967. After these Labour was left in control of only two of the twelve largest cities. There followed a series of by-election defeats, and further local government set-backs.

Throughout 1969, much the same patterns obtained, both at by-elections and in local government elections. But, by the summer of 1969 the Conservative lead in the opinion polls had dropped from a high of 23 per cent to 9 per cent, and it seemed not unreasonable to hope that the tide against Labour was slowly turning. Speculation about the date of the next General Election began to be rife. The Tories would need a swing of 4.3 per cent to gain overall control of the House of Commons. It would be necessary to go to the country at just the right moment, when the 9 per cent pro Tory swing dipped; and when Labour electors could be coaxed out to vote. The timing would be tricky. It would call for steady nerve, and a very accurate reading of the barometer of public opinion. Mr. Wilson could hardly be faulted on the first count, but he was gravely misled by the pollsters on the second.

3 CONSTITUTIONAL AND ADMINISTRATIVE ISSUES
Political institutions must be constantly adapted to the changing needs of society. And in these years society was changing very rapidly indeed. Just as Mr. Wilson enjoyed the manipulation of issues and individuals, so also he enjoyed rearranging, or attempting to rearrange, the patterns of the institutions within which he exercised power. To a large extent the changes which came about were necessitated by the great increase in the scope of government which was a result of Labour policies. Some,

however, had been considered before the Labour years, and were merely concluded under Mr. Wilson's auspices.

a *The Parliamentary Commissioner*

The idea of a Parliamentary Commissioner or 'Ombudsman' had been under consideration for some time. The necessary legislation was passed in the 1966–7 session, and the first Parliamentary Commissioner for Administration, Sir Edward Compton, took up his duties on 1 April 1967. His function, in which he was aided by a special Civil Service department, was to investigate complaints passed on to him by M.P.s, concerning the actions of any Government department or public body mentioned in the Act. There were some important exclusions from his investigatory powers – for instance, local government authorities, nationalized industries, the National Health Service and the police. However, with these exceptions, if the Parliamentary Commissioner thought that there had been an injustice caused by maladministration in any of the major Government departments, he could report it to Parliament. He had no power to order a remedy. The object of the operation was, really, to improve Parliament's control over the administration, rather than to put a new weapon into the hands of the citizen.

Over half the complaints received in the first nine months turned out to be outside the scope of the Parliamentary Commissioner's jurisdiction.

The *First Annual Report*, published in March 1968, found maladministration in only 19 out of the 188 cases investigated.

b *Parliamentary committees in the House of Commons*

For a long time discontent had existed in the House of Commons, and disquiet outside it, over the steadily increasing power of the Government. The thought had been that the introduction of some kind of committee system might restore control to the floor of the House, and thus make the lives of the back-benchers more meaningful. The American analogy was much used – though perhaps not by those who understood the American system best. Mr. Crossman was inclined – anyway at that time – to the belief that Ministers really ought to be more responsive to opinion in Parliament; although he also thought that parliamentary procedures ought to be streamlined, so that more business could be transacted. Perhaps these two aims were not compatible. However, in January 1967 two new committees were set up:
(1) Science and Technology;
(2) Agriculture, Fisheries and Food.
Each committee consisted of fourteen back-bench M.P.s. Each could summon witnesses, examine them, hear evidence in public, and ask for papers and records. Senior officials could be questioned on the activities of their departments. Reports could be made as required.

The Committee on Agriculture, Fisheries and Food decided to investigate the effects of possible entry into the E.E.C. The Foreign Office was not co-operative. It refused to provide documents, and objected to the Committee's proposed visit to Brussels, to check up on the accuracy of the information provided by the Minister of Agriculture. It was perhaps a pity that the Committee took on so controversial a subject for its first assignment.

Neither committee was a success, and both were subsequently abolished.

c *The House of Lords*

In November 1967, in the Queen's Speech, the Government announced the setting up of an all-Party committee to try to find a formula 'to reduce the powers of the House of Lords and to eliminate its present hereditary basis'.

By the spring of 1968 there were not unnaturally clear signs of rebellion from the House of Lords.

The crisis in the relationship between Lords and Commons came in June 1968 over the Rhodesia Sanctions Order. Statutory Orders, unlike Bills, cannot be amended, but must be accepted or rejected in their entirety. A Lords' veto on an Order is final. But a new version of the Order may be reintroduced by the Commons.

The Tory peers, who rejected the Order with the narrow majority of nine, made it clear that they did not wish to impose a permanent veto, but merely wished to give public opinion time to consider the matter.

The issue which produced the clash was not a clear-cut one. The Tory Party was united against any further stiffening of U.N. sanctions and had in any case always opposed taking this issue to the U.N. at all. The Party especially objected to the ambiguous invitation which seemed to be embodied in the U.N. resolution, to foment civil war in Rhodesia. Led by Lord Salisbury, the Conservatives in the House of Lords said No, by a narrow majority of nine.

The Labour Party feared that the veto would mean that other countries would be half-hearted about the application of sanctions if Britain was seen to hesitate.

The constitutional implications in this dispute were, of course, considerable. Here was the Lords, a predominantly hereditary body, once again rejecting the considered political decisions of an elected government, and, in effect, tampering with its foreign policy. There was much talk of peers versus people, and a return to the old 1910 crisis. The House of Lords might have fared worse if the electorate had been at all interested in the particular issue raised.

After the veto Mr. Wilson dissolved the all-Party committee on Lords reform, and said that the Government would in the near future bring in a bill to curtail the power of the House of Lords, and to alter its hereditary basis. He would not, however, wish to abolish the second chamber altogether, he said.

On 30 October 1968 it was announced in the Queen's Speech that 'Legislation will be introduced on the composition and powers of the House of Lords.' A White Paper (Cmnd. 3799) on Lords Reform was published on November 1st based, after all, on the recommendations of the all-Party committee. The existing composition of the House of Lords, whereby about half the members who put in an appearance attended by right of succession, and half were life peers, or peers of first creation, was to be altered. The hereditary basis for membership of the Lords was to end, although existing hereditary peers could continue to sit during their lifetime, but without the right to vote. About 230 life peers would be nominated by the political Parties, and their number would ensure the government of the day a small working majority. These peers would be paid, and would undertake to attend at least a third of the sittings in a session. The House of Lords so constituted would have a limited power to delay legislation, but it would no longer be able to veto orders made under existing Acts. A number of existing hereditary peers would be made life peers, to enable them to continue to take an active part in politics. The position of the Law Lords would remain unchanged. The bishops of the Church of England would be reduced in number from twenty-six to sixteen.

The new House of Lords would thus have been a nominated body and, for the most part, nominated by a small number of successive Prime Ministers. It would have ceased to be in any sense a regional House, for those who sat in it would have no territorial base; and men who attract the attention of Prime Ministers are, inescapably, for the most part likely to be those who make their homes and careers in London.

The reformed House of Lords would have had a two-tier structure, comprising about 250 peers with the right to speak and to vote, and non-voting peers, which would include all the existing hereditary peers who would be entitled to sit and to speak in the House, during their lifetime. After the reform had been passed, succession to a hereditary peerage would no longer carry the right to a seat in the House of Lords, although some peers by succession would be created life peers, and would thus become speaking and voting peers. Voting members in future would be exclusively 'created peers'. Peers who, at the time the Bill was passed, sat by right of succession, could withdraw from the House, while retaining their titles. Future and existing peers by succession who chose to renounce membership of the Lords, would be able to sit in the Commons if elected. All peers would be qualified to vote in parliamentary elections.

The reformed House would be able to delay an ordinary public Bill for six months.

These proposals were approved by the House of Lords on November

21st, after three days' debate, by a majority of 251 votes to 56. The House of Commons was much more critical, although in the end the Bill was passed by a majority of 111 on 3 February 1969. But back-bench M.P.s of both Parties were suspicious of a measure which would give more powers of patronage both to the Prime Minister and to the Leader of the Opposition of the day.

In the end, in April 1969, the Government abandoned the Bill, perhaps discouraged by the continuing opposition which made the committee stage of the Bill so long-drawn-out a battle.

d *The Parliamentary Committee of the Cabinet*
Mr. Wilson decided, in the spring of 1968, to reduce the number of meetings of the full Cabinet. A new Parliamentary Committee of the Cabinet was set up. It was to be composed of senior Cabinet Ministers, and was to meet twice a week. Issues would be discussed first in this committee, and then reported to the full Cabinet, which would only meet once a fortnight. From this important inner group the Home Secretary, Mr. Callaghan, was excluded!

e *Age of Majority*
On 10 April 1968 the Attorney General said that the Government would accept the recommendation of the Latey Committee that the age of majority should be reduced from twenty-one years to eighteen years. Those between eighteen and twenty-one would then be free to marry without parental consent; buy houses; take out mortgages, and make legal contracts. The question of the age of voting was then still under review by the Speaker's Conference on Electoral Law. Eventually, the right to vote at eighteen was passed into law in time to enable eighteen-year-olds to vote at the General Election of June 1970.

f *The Fulton Committee on the future of the Civil Service (Cmnd. 3638)*
This was the first comprehensive review of the Civil Service since the Northcote-Trevelyan reforms of 1854, so it is perhaps not surprising that some far-reaching changes were recommended.

The Report was critical of the Civil Service for what was described as its continued cult of the talented amateur. Scientists, engineers and other specialists did not get the responsibility and authority they deserved. And there were too few of them. Management expertise was largely disregarded. The division into three classes, administrative, executive and clerical, meant that some good people entering the clerical or executive grades did not reach the upper echelons of the service. And there was too little contact between the Civil Service and the rest of the community.

The Report suggested the following changes:
(1) A new Civil Service Department should be set up, to take over

responsibility for the Civil Service from the Treasury. It should be responsible for recruitment, training and career structure.
(2) A Civil Service College should be created, which would provide specialist training in administration and management.
(3) There should be a single grade structure.
(4) Temporary interchange of staff with industry, commerce, nationalized industries and local government should be encouraged.

The Prime Minister accepted (1), (2) and (3) at once; and indeed did not specifically reject any of the Fulton recommendations.

Most civil servants welcomed the new proposals, although there was some bitterness over the opening paragraphs of criticism, and the outdated and amateur image presented.

4 ECONOMIC ISSUES

Mr. Callaghan introduced the first Budget of the 1966–70 Government on 5 May 1966. Contrary to general expectation, there was no increase in income tax, surtax, spirit duties or car licences, any or all of which had been expected. M.P.s were just beginning to sigh with astonished relief when, at the end of the Budget speech, Mr. Callaghan announced the introduction of a major new tax, the Selective Employment Tax. This was a tax thought out, so it was rumoured, by Mr. Nicholas Kaldor, one of the academic economists brought in to advise the Government on tax reform. The hope was that it would prove to be a comparatively painless way of extracting a large sum of money from the taxpayer, almost unnoticed. It was to be levied on all employers for each male employee at 25s a week; for women, and boys under eighteen, at 12s 6d a week; and for girls under eighteen at 8s a week. The tax was to be collected by the simple device of an increase in the cost of the weekly National Insurance stamp which all employers had to purchase for their workers.

The purpose of this large new levy on the taxpayer was not only to raise revenue, withdraw money from circulation and thus, it was hoped dampen inflationary pressures. It was also intended to encourage redeployment of labour from the so-called service industries to the export industries, whose activities had to be stepped up if a favourable balance of payments was ever to be achieved. Thus, the tax was to be refunded to manufacturers, with a bonus; and to nationalized industries and agriculture, without a bonus. In short, the service industries were to be encouraged to shed some of their labour force. The net gain to the Treasury, after the refunds, was estimated at £241m. in a full year.

It was recognized that some of the cost to the service industries, in cases where the labour force could not be reduced, would probably be passed on to consumers in higher prices. But the Government hoped that S.E.T. would encourage the introduction of labour-saving devices, and thus more efficient use of labour; and that this would reduce the need to put up prices.

The taxpayers did not like this. There were strong protests from affected interests, notably from the hotel and catering industry, which, because of the growing number of visitors from abroad, was a big earner of foreign currency. The Conservatives attacked S.E.T. on the second reading of the Finance Bill, as a scheme certain to drive up prices, and so to increase the cost of living and stimulate demands for wage increases. They were also critical of the way in which manufacturers were to be forced to make an interest-free loan to the Government, because there would be a three-months' delay before the refund of the tax. The paper work involved in claiming the refund was complex, and would certainly be time consuming, they thought.

It was generally believed that this tax would be a short-lived one. But in spite of all the protests, the Government stuck to it.[1]

On 16 May 1966 the National Union of Seamen called a strike in support of their pay claim, and demand for a forty-hour week. This in fact meant a claim for payment at overtime rates for the very long hours inevitably worked while the men were at sea. The strike lasted forty-seven days, having been preceded by six months of negotiations. Its effects might have been much worse, had it not been for the use of air transport, and the fact that foreign-owned ships took over much of the work. There was not very much evidence of public sympathy with the seamen, and the dock workers did not join in. The Seamen's Union was badly led. Their pay and conditions probably were inadequate by the standards then common among other workers. Many of the shipping companies were old-fashioned and probably inefficient. On May 23rd the Government declared a State of Emergency thus enabling it to control ports, dock labour, food prices, etc. On June 8th the Union, led by Mr. Hogarth, rejected the interim report of the Court of Inquiry headed by Lord Justice Pearson. On June 16th Mr. Wilson announced a far-reaching inquiry into the shipping industry as a whole. On June 20th, in a statement in the Commons, he referred to '... the tightly knit group of politically motivated men who, as the last General Election showed, utterly failed to secure acceptance of their views by the British electorate but who are now determined to exercise back-stage pressures.' On June 28th he substantiated his charges and named eight Communists, some in the Union, some outside it, who, he said, aimed to destroy the Government's incomes policy.

In July 1966 there was a sterling crisis as a result of widespread speculation against the pound. Foreign bankers had, it seemed, little faith in the Government's economic policy. And the seamen's strike in May and

[1] In November 1967 the system of refunds, except for the development areas, was dropped. And in March 1968 S.E.T. was increased by 50 per cent.

June had an adverse effect on exports, and made it seem probable that there would, after all, be a deficit on the balance of payments at the end of the year.

The Government at this time rejected devaluation, although some of its economic advisers are thought to have pressed for it; and most economists seem to have felt that by July 1966 the case for it was overwhelming.

Instead, the Government decided on severe deflationary measures to defend sterling. Thus, the Bank Rate was raised to 7 per cent; there were various tax increases; unemployment was allowed to rise to 1–2 per cent; and a prices and incomes freeze was announced. Mr. Wilson was understandably anxious to demonstrate how safe he was. A spectacular economic measure like devaluation would be likely to damage his image as a responsible Leader and a good economist.

Already in 1965 the Government had decided to introduce an early warning system to compel unions to submit wage claims to the Prices and Incomes Board for adjudication. The Bill incorporating this system, to which the trade unions were bitterly opposed, had been published just before the General Election. Now, on 4 July 1966, an amended and strengthened Prices and Incomes Bill was published. And on July 20th, as a crisis measure, a prices and incomes standstill was announced. There would be six months of freeze on all wage increases; and this would be followed by six months of 'severe restraint'. There would also be a twelve months' freeze on price increases. This was to be a voluntary arrangement, but the Government announced that it was prepared, under Part IV of the Bill, to give the freeze statutory backing, if this proved necessary. On 12 August 1966 this Bill was duly passed into law.[1]

At first, it seemed that the measures of July and August were succeeding reasonably well. For 1966 as a whole, there was a 6 per cent expansion in exports, in spite of the damage done by the seamen's strike. However, in March 1967 a White Paper was published proposing new compulsory powers to enable the Government to hold the line against inflationary wage claims, until it would be safe to move back to the old voluntary system. These powers would, however, be reserve powers, which would merely enable the Government to ease the transition from a freeze to a controlled thaw. The necessary legislation came into force in August 1967, and gave the Government fresh powers to hold up pay increases during a twelve months' period of 'moderation'. It was hoped, though, that the Government could manage with a voluntary system, with the

[1] In October 1966 Part IV of the Act was brought into force after the ASSET case (Association of Supervisory Staffs, Executives and Technicians). ASSET had challenged the right of employers to withhold wage increases agreed before the freeze, and won a test case in the courts in September against Thorn Electrical Industries.

T.U.C. supervising wage claims, and the C.B.I. keeping a watch over price increases. In fact, the Government did not have occasion to use their delaying powers under the Prices and Incomes Acts until 29 January 1968.

By April 1967 it was thought possible to reduce the Bank Rate to 6 per cent; and the April Budget brought few changes. However, by the summer of 1967 the position had become much less encouraging, and it looked as if the modest recovery of 1966 was petering out. But Mr. Callaghan stated categorically in the House of Commons on July 24th that the pound would not be devalued. He said: 'Those who advocate devaluation are calling for a reduction in the wage levels and the real wage standards of every member of the working class of this country. . . . Devaluation is not the way out of Britain's difficulties.'

On Saturday 18 November 1967 the pound was devalued by 14.3 per cent, that is from $2.80 to the pound to $2.40 to the pound. The strains caused by the Middle East war, and the consequent oil embargo, and the dock strikes, had proved to be the last straw. Devaluation was accompanied by a raising of the Bank Rate to 8 per cent and a promise to cut defence and other public expenditure. Mr. Wilson, in a television broadcast on November 19th, said that devaluation would mean more jobs; but there must be a big shift to exports to seize the advantages that devaluation would bring. Imports must be cut back. 'We have the chance now to break out from the straitjacket of these past years.' He also said: 'this does not mean that the pound in your pocket . . . has been devalued.' Indeed, Mr. Wilson tried at first to present devaluation as a step forward, in a planned advance towards greater economic prosperity, rather than, as he had soon to admit, a defeat for the policy to which he and Mr. Callaghan had been totally committed. Mr. Callaghan resigned as Chancellor of the Exchequer on November 29th and was succeeded by Mr. Roy Jenkins.

The object of devaluation was to reduce the standard of living to a level that current economic reserves could support, and to give a much needed boost to exports. This might have been expected to happen because the whole purpose of devaluation was that the price of imported goods would rise; and the export industries would get a shot in the arm, since British exports would be cheaper on world markets, and thus more readily marketable.

Mr. Jenkins, the new Chancellor, immediately became the centre of political controversy when he published the Letter of Intent sent by Mr. Callaghan on November 23rd to the International Monetary Fund.[1] This outlined the steps the Government proposed to take to restore the balance of payments, and was seized on by Labour left wingers as proof that foreign bankers had now imposed stringent conditions on Britain, in return for an I.M.F. credit. Mr. Jenkins did his best to argue that a

[1] *Annual Register, 1967*, p. 507.

creditor making a loan would not unreasonably want to know how the loan would be used. The Government was merely explaining, in the Letter of Intent, what its policies would be, and this was not the same as agreeing to conditions imposed on it from outside.

In January 1968 further cuts in public expenditure amounting to £300m. in 1968 were announced. There were defence cuts, always palatable to Labour M.P.s though a source of alarm to the Tories. Other cuts were much less welcome to the Parliamentary Labour Party. They included the postponement of the raising of the school leaving age to sixteen for two years, till 1973, the reimposition of prescription charges, cuts in road building and a reduction in council house building.

By February 1968 it had become apparent that the T.U.C. wage vetting machinery would not be enough to hold back the tide of wage demands. The Government would probably have to introduce further incomes legislation, although it was feared that this might unite left wing Labour M.P.s and the T.U.C. against the Government.

On 22 March 1968 Mr. Peter Shore outlined the Government's new plans for control over prices and incomes. The ceiling on wages and salaries should be $3\frac{1}{2}$ per cent; and twelve months should be the minimum period between wage increases. The only exception would be genuine productivity agreements, and major reorganization of wage and salary structures, justified on grounds of economic efficiency. There would, it was stated, be eighteen months more of prices and incomes restraint, with provision for an extension of this period if necessary. Mrs. Castle, as Secretary of State for Employment and Productivity, took over responsibility for the Government's incomes policy.

The March 1968 Budget following up devaluation in November 1967 was a tough one. This had been expected. It was unfortunate that it was preceded by a consumer spending spree, which the new Chancellor ought, some people thought, to have prevented. On the whole, the Budget cuts were made by increases in indirect taxation, and there was no increase in income tax or surtax as, presumably, Mr. Jenkins did not think it politic to discourage any further the geese who must somehow be persuaded to go on laying the now not very profitable golden eggs. However, there was a special levy, for one year, on investment income. S.E.T., which had, in spite of all the furore it aroused, turned out to be a handy fund raiser, was stepped up by 50 per cent. In all, revenue was increased by £900m. per annum.

In May 1968 the new Prices and Incomes Bill was given its second reading. There were thirty-four Labour abstentions, and one Labour M.P. voted against the Bill.

The summer of 1968 was not very encouraging, and the Government gradually began to accept the fact that there was little hope of a balance of payments surplus until 1969. Internal consumer demand remained high as wage rates soared. All attempt at an incomes policy was abandoned. Imports, in spite of devaluation, remained at a high level. The economic situation was further complicated by external factors making for instability. The French franc, for instance, was over-valued, and the German mark under-valued.

In September 1968 the T.U.C. and the Labour Party Conference voted against the Government's incomes policy, even though a good many wage increases had been allowed, on the basis of productivity deals.

On 22 November 1968 Mr. Jenkins made an emergency statement in the House of Commons. A further £250m. a year would be levied in taxation since the very large tax increases in the April Budget had not had the anticipated effect of curbing consumer demand, partly, no doubt, because increases in wages and incomes had provided the consumer with the additional purchasing power required to meet the higher prices, including the higher costs of imported goods, as a result of devaluation.

By the beginning of 1969 the full impact of Mr. Jenkins' November measures began to sink in. Continuing economic failure, over, it seemed, a twenty-five-year period, but particularly since the early sixties, brought with it a sense of disillusion not only with the Labour Government, but now, it seemed, with politics in general. Devaluation had not brought the expected benefits. The Budget presented by Mr. Jenkins on 15 April 1969 was the third heaviest since the war. The two even heavier ones were also Labour Budgets, as Mr. Macleod, the Shadow Chancellor, pointed out. Mr. Jenkins's strategy was to restrain consumer demand, by a policy of wage restraint and by additional taxation. These two lines of attack would, it was hoped, keep imports down, and make the export drive seem more worth while, because manufacturers would not be tempted to cater to the easier home market. But the strategy did not seem to be succeeding. Gradually Mr. Wilson turned his attention in a big way towards the problems posed by wage inflation, and in particular the wildcat strikes which produced this; and the structure of the trade union movement, which seemed unable to control the mounting number of these strikes.

There was a certain inevitability about all this. Once the policy of full employment was accepted at the national level, as it had been by both the major political Parties after the end of the Second World War, it was no longer possible for any government, whatever its political complexion, to leave the trade unions to forge ahead and create havoc in the economy by making a series of *ad hoc* demands for wage increases which, however unreasonable they might be, the employers would be virtually powerless to resist. For full employment had enormously increased trade union powers. There was now no pool of unemployed whose perhaps cheaper labour could restrain union demands. Then, industry was becoming ever more capital intensive. The general interest of employers was, therefore, to avoid strikes at all costs, and, when necessary, to concede wage increases. If employers wanted workers, they had to play along with the unions; and as often as not that meant agreeing to escalating wage claims. But if wages were constantly pushed up, prices would have to follow or firms would simply be forced out of business. And, as prices escalated, the advantages of devaluation, with the boost it could give to the export industries, would be quickly lost. Thus, full employment seemed to necessitate an incomes policy. And an incomes policy seemed to require trade union reform before it could be made to stick.

It was not, however, simply a matter of convincing leading trade unionists of these inescapable economic facts of life. It was not a matter of convincing the leaders of individual unions, however large and powerful. For the fact was that by now power lay not with these men, but with the shop stewards, who, factory by factory, were able to bring work to a standstill by unofficial or 'wildcat' strikes. The Donovan Commissioners said that 95 per cent of industrial disputes were now in this category. Very frequently these strikes caused a chain reaction of stoppages in other factories depending, in so many cases, on component parts from the first striking factory; and not infrequently in quite other sectors of industry. Not only did leading trade unionists not understand national economic problems. Even when they did have some understanding they could do nothing because they were not, and perhaps had never been, masters in their own house. It was not that kind of house. By 1969 it seemed impossible to break away from the vicious upward spiral. Higher wages led to higher prices or to unemployment caused by the shedding of labour; or to bankruptcy. Higher prices in turn led to demands for still higher wages. And all the time, the poor, and those on fixed or semi-fixed incomes got poorer; and the demand for state hand-outs became more vociferous. All this made nonsense of Mr. Jenkins's or anybody else's fiscal and monetary policies. Mr. Wilson became more and more determined to break out of this vicious circle by tackling the threat posed to the national interest by the unions. The experiences of the years since 1964 had shown him that prices and incomes could not be dealt with except in the context of trade union reform.

In April 1965 the Donovan Commission on Trade Unions and Employers' Associations had been set up; in June 1968 it reported.[1] The

[1] Cmnd 3626. Its main proposals were as follows:
(a) Agreements on hours and conditions of work should be local agreements reached at company and factory levels. These should replace the existing system of industry with agreements reached by national trade unions and employers' associations, which had now virtually broken down. The old, formal system of collective bargaining had been replaced by an informal system of bargaining at the place of work. And actual pay now bore little relation to nationally negotiated pay rates. It would be better to recognize the de facto arrangements. So

main theme was provided by Professor Hugh Clegg of Warwick University, then a Fellow of Nuffield College, Oxford, and Mr. Allan Flanders, Senior Lecturer in Industrial Relations at Oxford. The dissentient voice was that of Mr. Andrew Schonfield. All agreed that there was need for a reform of industrial relations on the shop floor. In the Clegg view this should be achieved by voluntary agreements, the role of the state being confined to persuasion, and the law having no role at all. Mr. Schonfield, in his Note of Reservation, wished to go somewhat further. He wrote: 'The main report addresses itself to the immediate situation in British industrial relations and proposes a number of remedies which I heartily support. But it barely concerns itself with the long-term problem of accommodating bodies with the kind of concentrated power which is possessed by trade unions, to the changing future needs of an advanced industrial society.' The Donovan Commission recommended the setting up of a Commission for Industrial Relations. This was to work, by voluntary means, to bring order on the shop floor. No legal penalties were suggested, to give it teeth. This was not Mr. Schonfield's view. He wanted a legal framework for trade union activities, and penalty clauses for its disregard. He wrote: '... the deliberate abstention of the law from the activities of mighty subjects tends to diminish the liberty of the ordinary citizen and to place his welfare at risk.' Mr. Schonfield's was the minority view. But increasingly, it came to be the view taken by Mr. Wilson. It was also the view taken by Mrs. Castle, appointed Minister to the Department of Employment and Productivity (the new name for the Ministry of Labour) in March 1968. These two erstwhile stalwarts of the Labour left now prepared to engage in a struggle with the unions.

Since the Conservatives had in March 1969, before the report of the Donovan Commission was available, put out their policy statement on all this, in 'Fair Deal at Work', which went a good deal further than Donovan, it was necessary for the Wilson/Castle line to be drawn somewhere between Donovan and the Conservatives. On 17 January

---

these local agreements should be registered with the Department of Employment and Productivity.
(b) Urgent measures were needed to deal with unofficial strikes, which now constituted 95 per cent of all stoppages. Employers should be able to take civil action against them; but taking part in an unofficial strike should not be made a criminal offence.
(c) An Industrial Relations Commission should be set up to investigate problems in individual factories, and in whole industries.
(d) Workers should have statutory protection against unfair dismissal.
(e) Tory proposals regarding the legal enforcement of agreements were rejected.
(f) There should be considerable amalgamation of unions.

1969 the Wilson/Castle line was duly published in a White Paper entitled 'In Place of Strife'.[1] There were three main controversial clauses in this White Paper:

(1) Collective agreements would not be enforceable at law, but the Minister had powers to order a twenty-eight-day 'conciliation pause' on workers threatening an unofficial strike.
(2) The Minister could order trade unions to ballot their members before calling and official strike.
(3) An industrial board would be able to impose certain specified financial penalties for failure to comply with the Minister's order.

These proposals were supported by Mr. Jenkins, who by now saw his whole financial strategy as undermined by the irresponsibility of the trade unions.

The trade unions were soon bitterly opposed to the Government's policy, which, it came to be realized, constituted an attack not just on wage increases, but – a much more serious matter – on the methods by which these increases were achieved.

The background to this whole dispute is the fact that it was extremely difficult for a Labour Government to quarrel with the trade unions, for these dominated the Party Conference, and provided most of the money required for the Labour Party machine. The National Executive Committee of the Party Conference had the right to draw up the Party's programme, and to endorse candidates for the P.L.P. Any Labour Prime Minister would quickly run into serious difficulty if his government lost the support of the Party Conference and its N.E.C. Mr. Wilson did just this. And his position was further weakened by the fact that his Home Secretary, Mr. Callaghan, who was a member of the N.E.C., voted, as the unions' friend, against the White Paper sponsored by the Cabinet of which he was a leading member on March 26th in the N.E.C., where the White Paper was rejected by sixteen votes to five.

There were much more serious troubles to come, for Mr. Wilson found he had not only to take on the unions and the N.E.C. but also the P.L.P. and most of the Cabinet. The real trouble began on 15 April 1969 when Mr. Jenkins, in his Budget speech, announced the Government's intention to pass, in the immediate future, a short Industrial Relations Bill which would incorporate the policies set out in 'In Place of Strife'. Opposition to the Prime Minister mounted rapidly; and, if there had been a conventional method of getting rid of him without having a General Election, the Prime Minister might have lost his job. But there was not.

The alternatives, if a new trail was to be blazed in this regard, seemed to be a Cabinet revolt; or a back-bench revolt. It was rumoured that the

[1] Cmnd. 3888.

two rival candidates for the Prime Minister's job were Mr. Jenkins and Mr. Callaghan. But Mr. Jenkins was pledged to the support of the hated Industrial Relations Bill. And Mr. Callaghan probably did not have sufficiently wide support. A back-bench revolt also proved difficult to organize. Again, the Bill muddled the issues, for those most strongly opposed to Mr. Wilson were the middle of the road Labour M.P.s who had come into Parliament in 1966, and who, disgusted by the muddles and the failures, wanted to put Mr. Jenkins in place of Mr. Wilson. But Mr. Jenkins stood for the Bill; and this they were passionately determined to defeat. The issue was probably settled by Mr. Douglas Houghton, the chairman of the Parliamentary Labour Party, who did not, it seems, want any change in the leadership, but who did want the defeat of the Bill; and especially those clauses in the Bill which provided for penalties. It would be better, the thought now was, for the T.U.C. itself to handle the problem of wildcat strikes. Mr. Wilson was not unwilling to see a solution along these lines provided that the T.U.C. really did change its rules, to enable it formally to take a much tougher line than it had ever done in the past. But in the end, at a Cabinet meeting held on 17 June 1969, the Prime Minister had to abandon even this stand. The Chief Whip, Mr. Mellish, warned the Cabinet that he could not get the Bill upstairs to the safety of a committee; and he could not be responsible for it on the floor of the House. One by one Mr. Wilson's colleagues, including Mr. Jenkins, deserted, leaving only the Prime Minister and Mrs. Castle. In the end he had to abandon the Bill, and settle for a deal with the T.U.C., whereby, without altering any of their rules, they gave a 'solemn and binding undertaking'.[1]

The T.U.C. leaders, and especially Mr. Feather, the Acting General Secretary, were in a difficult position, in that they had to steer a middle course between, on the one hand, the danger that a later Conservative Government might legislate for much more far-reaching state control, if nothing had in the meantime been achieved; and the fear of the overmighty and now extremely powerful left wingers, as Jack Jones and Hugh Scanlon.[2] Even so, the T.U.C. leaders were in a very much stronger position than the Prime Minister.

The failures of Mr. Wilson were mounting rather ominously. He had in this one session, failed with his Prices and Incomes policy; failed with the Parliament Bill; and now, much more seriously, he had failed in his battle to bring the trade unions within the law, and thus make it possible to control wage inflation.

By the autumn of 1969 the general economic situation showed some improvement. The August trade figures, published on 11th September

[1] Nuffield Election Studies, D. E. Butler and M. Pinto-Duschinsky, *The British General Election of 1970*.
[2] Peter Jenkins, *The Battle of Downing Street*.

showed a trade surplus of £40m.; and the Treasury announced a £100m. surplus on the balance of payments for the second quarter of 1969. Mr. Jenkins was able to tell the Labour Party Conference in the autumn that the balance of payments was running at a £450 to £500 million a year surplus. The moderate up-turn in the economy was predictably matched by a moderate up-turn in the Government's rating in the opinion polls.

But by January 1970 there was again great anxiety because of the avalanche of wage claims in the post freeze pipeline. Mr. Wilson and Mrs. Castle, Secretary for Employment and Productivity, prodded by Mr. Aubrey Jones, chairman of the National Board for Prices and Incomes, did what they could. Mr. Wilson pointed out that one man's wage increase was another man's price increase. A 50 per cent wage increase all round would bring everybody back to square one, but with higher prices and thus in a less competitive position *vis-à-vis* the outside world.

The Government announced, in early 1970, its intention to introduce a Commission for Industry and Manpower, with wide powers to veto price increases and company mergers, and with advisory powers only over pay rises. The new Commission would absorb the work previously done by the P.I.B. Also in the pipeline was the new Industrial Relations Bill, which was supposed to be made up of a selection of proposals broadly acceptable to the T.U.C. as well as to the P.L.P.

From the beginning of 1970 the eyes of commentators were closely fixed on Mr. Wilson in an effort to guess his electoral strategy, and for this reason Mr. Jenkins's 1970 Budget was eagerly awaited. It might, and probably would, be the last in the life of this Government, for a General Election had to be held some time before April 1971, and it was thought to be most unlikely that Mr. Wilson would wait for as long as this. He would see it as desirable to choose some favourable moment between January 1970 and April 1971, preferably before the anticipated American recession; and certainly before the upheaval of decimalization in February 1971. Mr. Jenkins's April Budget might be expected to give some clues. It could not, it was generally felt, be a give-away Budget. The British electorate was now too sophisticated to be caught again by this one. Anyway, it was not in Mr. Jenkins's style lightly to subordinate the good of the economy to political whim. He had said, over and over again, that though much progress had been made since the summer of 1969, the time for reflation had not yet come. So it was bound to be a cautious Budget. He was known, also, to favour cuts in direct taxation, and increases in some indirect taxes. It was thought likely, therefore, to be a Budget which shuffled around existing tax arrangements, rather than a concessionary Budget.

Mr. Heath, in the pre-Budget period, was at pains to explain the Tory view of the improvement in the balance of payments in the last quarter of 1969. It was a matter for considerable relief, of course, but it was, he argued, to a large extent a consequence of external factors, and these alone would have led to a turn-about in the British balance of payments.

The Budget, when it came on April 14th, was a cautious one. As *The Times* leading article remarked on April 15th: 'The Chancellor has helped many people, but by small amounts.' So cautious was it that some cynics thought that there might well be a rather more give away Budget in the autumn, preceding a General Election. But it was also noted that the Finance Bill arising out of the Budget would be relatively small and uncontroversial, and so could be readily disposed of, if need be, before a June Election.

In some ways things looked good. But the continual and unchecked increases in wages and prices led many to dark foreboding. Lord Shawcross, a former Labour President of the Board of Trade, remarked on April 29th:

> The economy, if not being manipulated for electioneering purposes, is being allowed to run loose into an inflationary situation which may assist the Government in an early election, but will lead the country to renewed calamity if not arrested as soon as the election is over.... I am afraid now that if the underlying trends in our economy are not corrected in eighteen months or so, we shall be facing again the possibility of a further devaluation.

5 DOMESTIC AFFAIRS

The Labour Government of 1966–70 passed some important legislation and, as most governments, began consideration of changes which did not reach completion in its four years in office. Much of the legislation was not of a strictly Party nature. Social legislation in particular tended to cut across Party lines. So did issues associated with immigration from the Commonwealth.

Among the more important measures were:

a The Commonwealth Immigration Act of 1968
This was rushed through in February 1968. It was an attempt to halt the flow of Kenyan Asians holding British passports and now anxious to leave Kenya and come to the United Kingdom. When Kenyan independence was negotiated in 1963 it was then agreed that first-generation members of the Asian community should be given two years in which to take up if they wished, Kenyan citizenship. Those who did not do so could keep the United Kingdom citizenship they held before independence, and would be exempted from the restrictions imposed by the Commonwealth Immigrants Act of 1962. After independence all Kenyans born in Kenya, and with one parent born there, automatically became Kenya citizens. About 120,000 Kenyan Asians did not claim Kenyan citizenship, and

were thus possible candidates for migration to the United Kingdom. Many of these Asians had been traders in East Africa, and their very success made them unpopular with local Africans. The Kenya Government was not disposed to grant them trading licences. Once this was seen to be happening, and once the British Government began to question the possibility of accepting so large a flow of immigrants from one part of the Commonwealth at one moment of time, the trickle from Kenya became a flood of people anxious to get in before new legislation made it impossible for them to do so. The aim of the new Bill was not so much to cut down immigration from Kenya altogether as to arrange that the Kenyan Asians should, as it were, form a queue, so that not all of them came at once. A special allocation of 1,500 labour vouchers per annum was suggested, for those who held United Kingdom passports but who had no substantial connections with the United Kingdom by birth or parentage.

The background to the Bill as far as the United Kingdom went was the mounting uneasiness at the steady increases in the number of coloured Commonwealth residents in England. Although the number of work permits issued had dropped drastically between 1963 and 1967 (from 30,000 per annum to 5,000 per annum), the dependants of those already in England had increased from 26,200 to 52,000. And in those areas where immigrants were concentrated, tension was mounting.

There was a big outcry about this Bill. Mr. Macleod, under whose auspices the original promises to the Kenya Asians had been made, opposed it, as a breach of promise, on the part of the British Government. Assurances formally given should be honoured even when they became inconvenient, he argued. The Archbishop of Canterbury and other churchmen condemned it as a racialist measure; and thirty-five Labour M.P.s voted against the Bill as being a reversal of the traditional Labour Party policy over issues of race and colour. The Labour Party, they pointed out, had opposed the 1962 Immigration Bill, and had promised to repeal it. But the new Bill was passed.

b *The Race Relations Act*

The Bill was introduced and passed very shortly after the Immigration Act and was given its second reading on 23 April 1968. The intention was to eliminate racial discrimination in housing, employment, insurance and hotels. A Race Relations Board was set up; and special county courts were empowered to hear cases brought by local conciliation committees, although discrimination was not made a criminal offence. It was apropos of this Bill that Mr. Enoch Powell, now the leading prophet of doom on the increase in coloured citizens, remarked: 'Like the Roman, I seem to see the River Tiber flowing with much blood.' This remark, seized on by the press, resulted in his dismissal from the Shadow Cabinet.

The Tories moved a 'reasoned amendment' to the Bill, on its second reading, on the grounds that it would not effectively counter racial discrimination. The Bill was passed.

6 DEFENCE POLICY

In the four years from 1966 to 1970 Britain still possessed her nuclear force intact. The Polaris submarines had been, it is true, assigned to NATO; but their ultimate control was in British hands.

In July 1967 a supplementary Defence White Paper announced the withdrawal of all but a token force of British troops from the mainland bases in Malaysia and Singapore by the mid 1970s. The plan was that British forces would, in the meantime, stay in Hong Kong, the Persian Gulf and Gan; and a naval force would be maintained in the Indian Ocean. Big cuts were announced in Service manpower. But the level of the British contribution to NATO would remain the same. The general aim was to cut back on defence costs, except in the case of the defence of Western Europe.

Gradually, however, even this drastic pruning was seen as inadequate. In January 1968, plans to withdraw from the Far East were speeded up and it was announced that there would be a total British withdrawal from Malaysia and Singapore by 1971. No amphibious force would be left after all the bases had been closed. There would also be a total withdrawal from the Persian Gulf after the end of 1971.

The decision to withdraw from the Persian Gulf met with a good deal of criticism. The Foreign Office and the Ministry of Defence were known to be bitterly opposed to it, for it involved the breaking of treaty commitments, and was thought likely to endanger the political stability of the area, and thus the considerable British oil investments there. British oil came, to a large extent, from the Gulf area. And a large amount of sterling was held in the oil states. The foreign exchange cost of keeping British troops in the Gulf was only £9m. a year. Probably the decision was taken on political rather than on financial grounds, and should be seen against the background of the general Labour Party clamour against cuts in domestic and social expenditure. It is possible, also, that the Middle East war of 1967 may have contributed to the Government's decision, for this had demonstrated that Britain need not be wholly dependent on the Middle East for her oil supplies, and that, anyway, a British presence in the Gulf would not necessarily stop the closure of the Canal, or prevent an Arab oil embargo.

The White Paper of July 1968 provided for an increase in Britain's contribution to NATO, both in Europe and in the Mediterranean.

There was thus a very definite change of emphasis in British defence thinking. Europe and the NATO defence link was the number one priority. All other commitments could be drastically reduced.

7 FOREIGN POLICY

a *General*
There was a very marked shift in emphasis, towards Europe, in foreign policy generally, as well as in defence, during the period from 1966 to 1970. The Prime Minister had started off with a firm belief in the value of continuing Britain's peace-keeping role east of Suez, to fill a power vacuum, protect Britain's commercial interests, deter the Chinese from aggression, please the United States, and so on. But very soon the view grew that Britain's real interests lay in Europe and not east of Suez, or even with the Commonwealth. No doubt economic considerations were of paramount importance in persuading the Government to drop Britain's global role. And economic considerations perhaps best explain Mr. Wilson's conversion to the policy of entering the European Economic Community. But unfortunately Mr. Wilson's conversion was of no avail, and in 1968, the Community, led by the French, said *Non* for the second time. This left Britain in a dangerously isolated position. She was excluded from the mainstream of European economic development. She was becoming ever less credible as an ally for the United States, and her Commonwealth role was fast becoming a thing of the past.

b *The Anglo-American Relationship*
There were indications, in this period, that the old 'special relationship' was waning. When Mr. Wilson visited Washington in July 1966 the general impression he made seems to have been poor, although President Johnson personally paid him warm tributes. It is easy to understand that the old 'special relationship' with Britain looked less and less attractive to the Americans. The British attitude to American policy in Vietnam was seen as increasingly unsatisfactory. In June 1966 Mr. Wilson had clearly dissociated Britain from the extended American bombing policy, which involved the bombing of oil installations near Hanoi and Haiphong and, of course, the Americans resented this. The feeling in the United States was that Britain should, like Australia and New Zealand, have sent anyway a token force out to join the Americans, since Britain had obligations under the SEATO Treaty to defend South Vietnam. The British argument was that this would be unsuitable, since Britain was the co-chairman of the Geneva Conference and thus committed to a neutral role. She had, anyway, been heavily involved elsewhere in the area, especially in Malaya. Mr. Wilson's attempts to mediate between the United States and North Vietnam were resented; and were regarded, anyway, as a gesture designed to placate his own left wing rather than a serious peace move.

Britain's decision to leave Aden, and her subsequent decision to withdraw from the whole Persian Gulf area, and from the Far East, were strongly criticized in America. From 1962 onwards the Americans had been much opposed to any reduction in British commitments east of Suez, and especially in the Indian Ocean, which was one of the few areas in the world where America had no foothold. The thought was that, while America sustained NATO, and took care of Communist aggression in the Far East, the least Britain could do would be to use her residual influence as an old imperial power, to see that the Indian Ocean did not become a power vacuum. British possessions, or former possessions, were strung around this ocean. Britain had the contacts that the United States lacked. She must now make use of the links remaining from her imperial past, in the interests of present security.

Unfortunately some of Britain's imperial past was a present source of considerable embarrassment, both to her and to her allies. As a result of the Rhodesian dispute, for instance, British influence in Southern Africa had to be largely discounted. And the black African states to the north too, were unlikely to be at all obliging, even if the more extreme fears of Russian and Chinese influence could be discounted.

British trade with North Vietnam and with Cuba, although on a small scale, was a continual source of irritation to Americans. So America was probably as much disenchanted with Britain as vice versa.

President Johnson, in contrast to President Kennedy, was neither liked nor trusted in Britain. He seemed more impatient than most recent Presidents of advice or suggestions from his allies. He was more 'American' than President Kennedy. On the other hand, the American public had always had a propensity to identify the Labour Party with socialism, if not communism. On both sides of the Atlantic, therefore, the 'special relationship' seemed to make less good sense.

c *The Communist world*

In July 1966 Mr. Wilson visited Moscow. In February 1967 Mr. Kosygin visited Britain. Mr. Wilson found the Russians disconcertingly unyielding over Vietnam, and prone to make embarrassingly anti-German pronouncements.

A more encouraging development, however, was the endorsement, by the U.N. General Assembly, of the Nuclear Non-Proliferation Treaty in June 1968. This marked the conclusion of six years of negotiations, and of considerable opposition from near-nuclear countries such as Japan, India and Germany. The main provisions of the Treaty were as follows:

(1) The small powers signing it would be protected by the United States, the U.S.S.R. and Britain.
(2) The existing nuclear powers would agree not to give nuclear weapons to non-nuclear countries, or to help them in making nuclear weapons.

(3) Non-nuclear countries for their part would agree not to make or acquire nuclear weapons.

It was a step in the right direction. But the Treaty had serious limitations. Two of the five nuclear powers – France and China – refused to sign it. So did Japan. West Germany resented it, as it seemed to underscore her second-class status. To some extent it inhibited states from taking steps towards military nuclear status. But advances in civil nuclear technology were going on all over the world, and it was, of course, difficult to deprecate these. After the Russian invasion of Czechoslovakia in 1968 it looked as if the Non-Proliferation Treaty might, anyway, be one of those many treaties disregarded by its own signatories.

d *Europe*
The shift in British thinking from the global towards the European was a very pronounced one.
(i) *NATO* In 1966 the French announced the withdrawal of their forces from NATO. And between 1966 and 1968 there were talks on a reduction in NATO force levels, to meet changed conditions in Europe. Britain threatened, in 1967, to withdraw troops from Germany altogether if Germany did not meet the foreign exchange costs. However, in the Defence White Paper of July 1968, an increase in British contributions to NATO, on land and sea, was announced. And the Russian invasion of Czechoslovakia in August 1968 underscored the need for just such a move.

(ii) *The Common Market*[1] In April 1966, in the Queen's Speech opening the new Parliament, the Government announced its intention to try to negotiate entry into the E.E.C., provided that special British and Commonwealth interests could be safeguarded. Two Ministers were given particular responsibilities for this policy – Mr. George Brown, Secretary of State for Economic Affairs; and Mr. George Thomson, Chancellor of the Duchy of Lancaster, who was given responsibility for political relations with Europe.

The Speech from the Throne heralded a dramatic change in Labour policy. In 1961–3 the Labour Leadership had opposed Mr. Macmillan's attempt to join Europe, although there had always been some, and notably Mr. Jenkins, who had wanted to join. As late as 1964 Mr. Wilson was talking about not being willing to be 'dictated to by foreigners', etc. By 1966 a series of experiences had apparently persuaded Mr. Wilson to change his mind.

On economic grounds, the shock of a series of balance of payments and sterling crises had underlined the need for wider markets and greater financial and technical resources than Britain could provide by herself.

[1] See U. W. Kitzinger, *The Second Try: Labour and the E.E.C.*

There was increasingly seen to be a need for massive expenditure on research and development in, for instance, the aircraft and computer industries. Britain could not provide the capital herself. Nor could she, by herself, attract it.

The advantages of a market of 280 million people became even more alluring to the business world in general. EFTA had not proved to be a satisfactory grouping. And there were growing trade barriers between the EFTA countries and the E.E.C. Increasingly, economists and business men compared the low British growth rate with the startlingly higher growth rates of the E.E.C. countries. The short-term effects on the balance of payments and on agriculture, might, it was thought, be adverse. But the long-term outlook seemed perhaps promising.

The Commonwealth was no longer seen as a feasible alternative to Europe. There was a decline in British exports to Commonwealth countries, and in Commonwealth trade in general. Commonwealth countries were themselves finding new markets, for example Australia and New Zealand in Japan; and Nigeria with the E.E.C.

There was a very general feeling that the United Kingdom had been over-extended politically. A strong European rôle might well be preferable to a weak global rôle.

Meantime, Europe had begun to look more attractive to the Labour Leadership. The supranationalist idea, which they had always disliked, seemed to have been scotched by General de Gaulle – so entering Europe would be an economic union without much in the way of political overtones. Finally, and perhaps not least, Mr. George Brown was a fanatical pro-European.

There may possibly have been other considerations. It may be that the Prime Minister did not bother over much about the possibilities of failure, since one of his aims was to divert attention from the difficult home front by encouraging the public to think of a Brave New World elsewhere. It may also have seemed desirable to defuse Europe, as a political issue. It would not do to leave what might, at some future time, turn out to be a trump card, in Tory hands.

Be this as it may, on 10 November 1966 the Government announced its decision to investigate whether conditions existed which would make it possible for Britain to negotiate entry into the E.E.C. The subsequent debate in the Commons showed that there were fewer critics, on both sides of the House, than in the earlier Macmillan years from 1961 to 1963 when entry into Europe was first attempted. Mr. Wilson made it clear, when he spoke in the House, that he had no intention of weakening Britain's defence links with the United States and that there was no question of moving from an Anglo-American nuclear relationship to an Anglo-French one. In fact, he rejected any idea of a European nuclear force at all. His line was that foreign policy lay outside the terms of reference of the Treaty of Rome. However, in so far as foreign policy came into it, Europe, and not just Britain, should be closely linked with the United States. But there was no question of Britain joining a European federation, for the E.E.C. countries were not federated. The existing commitments were only in the economic field. Britain was, this time, fully prepared to accept the Treaty of Rome. There were a few outstanding problems to be negotiated, such as the necessity to safeguard New Zealand's interests; the common agricultural policy which it was difficult for Britain to accept because it would probably involve an increase in food prices; regional policies, Commonwealth sugar, and so on. As it turned out, however, these were not the difficult issues. The main problem was political: how to convince General de Gaulle that it would be in the interests of France for Britain to join.

There were clearly defined stages in Britain's second attempt at entry. In December 1966 an EFTA meeting in London approved the attempt to negotiate. And in April 1967 EFTA gave its all-clear. There was no question of unilateral British action; or of a disregard of her EFTA partners. Between January and March 1967 Mr. Wilson and Mr. Brown went on a round of visits to the capitals of the Six, ostensibly to see whether the conditions for entry existed, but, probably more importantly, to prove the sincerity of the British Government's commitment, and to bridge the 'credibility gap', for Mr. Wilson was inevitably seen as a very recent convert to the European idea, and his real intentions were still suspect in Europe – possibly with reason. During his talks, especially those with the French, he stressed British technological strength, and the value to Europeans of her technological co-operation. Mr. Brown says that although at first Mr. Wilson, who had been the leading anti-marketeer in the early sixties, was out just to explore the possibilities: 'Gradually our line got firmer and firmer, and by the time we had finished we had virtually decided to make our application. Then came a great battle in the Cabinet which ended with a majority decision in favour of applying to join.'[1]

On 12 May 1967 Britain put in her formal application. It was hoped that negotiations could begin in the autumn.

On May 16th, at a press conference, General de Gaulle in effect said *Non* – sooner and much more explicitly than anyone had expected. He said that he thought Britain was unready to join Europe, for both political and economical reasons. Her links were still primarily outside Europe – with her Commonwealth, and with the United States. For Europe to try to absorb her, and her EFTA partners would be to destroy the E.E.C.

Britain did not take this as the final answer; and Lord Chalfont was appointed to head British negotiations in Brussels. The Five strongly

---

[1] George-Brown, op. cit., p. 206.

supported the opening of negotiations. The General fell back on a series of delaying tactics.

In September 1967 the Commission's report on the British application recommended the opening of negotiations. But at the end of November, after the devaluation of the pound, General de Gaulle, at another press conference, made it clear beyond any possibility of doubt, that France would not negotiate. If the Five tried to impose British membership on France, that would mean the breaking up of the E.E.C., he said.

In June 1968, after the French riots and strikes, M. Couve de Murville became the French Prime Minister. This was the last nail in the coffin for he was, next to the General, the strongest opponent of British entry.

It is interesting to speculate on the real reasons for the French objection to Britain's entry. At different times, the General made the following points:

Sterling, with its role as a reserve currency, would be a heavy burden for the Europeans.

There was need for austerity and deflation in Britain, so that the British economy would be strong when Britain entered. She would otherwise bring her endemic financial and economic crises into the E.E.C., and the consequent difficulties would slow down growth in the other E.E.C. countries. The whole nature of the E.E.C. would change, with an influx of new members.[1] Britain was still seen by France as dependent on the United States. Britain would not give up this relationship, so the result would be a great extension of American influence, if not control, over European affairs. But probably the General's real objection, though never stated, was that Britain might come to rival France as the leader of Europe. In any event, Britain's second attempt to get into Europe failed, in the last analysis, for the same reason as the first – the personal hostility of General de Gaulle.

The tactics of the Wilson Government were probably mistaken. The thought seems to have been that Britain could get in all right, with the aid of the Five. But, unexpectedly, the Five attached more importance in the end, to the well-being of the E.E.C. than to Britain's entry, with all its imponderable problems. It was probably a mistake to count so heavily on support from West Germany. West Germany did, on balance, want to see Britain, and all the EFTA countries, inside the E.E.C. But her support was cautious. West Germany did not, at this time, want to damage her relations with France, for it was only with French diplomatic support, or so it seemed, that Germany could hope for reunification. And West Germany had various reasons for feeling rather cool towards Britain about this time, anyway. She resented British efforts over the nuclear non-proliferation treaty. She resented British threats to reduce

[1] The Rey Commission, reporting in September 1967, said that this was not so.

the strength of the B.A.O.R. She resented the circumstances of Mr. Kosygin's visit to Britain in 1967, and his anti-German remarks on this occasion.

In Britain, the failure was not taken too tragically. Pro-marketeers felt that Britain's entry was merely delayed. The matter would be brought to a successful conclusion when General de Gaulle had departed from the scene.

e *The Middle East*
In June 1967 the Arab-Israeli six-day war broke out. Britain's objective was to keep the Gulf of Aqaba open to world shipping, either with the help of the United Nations, or through the co-operation of maritime nations using the waterway, on the lines of S.C.U.A. in 1956. Speaking in the House of Commons, Mr. Wilson implied that force might be used to protect British interests in the Middle East if these attempts failed. In fact, it seemed fairly obvious that this was an empty threat. Britain attempted to take the initiative, but exerted no influence at all on events. The Suez Canal was closed, and an oil embargo was imposed by the Arab states which lasted until September 1967, in spite of a British military presence in Aden and Bahrain. However, events also showed that oil from the Middle East could be obtained, though at higher cost, from elsewhere.

In retrospect, it seems likely that the Middle East war contributed towards Britain's decision, in January 1968, to withdraw the British military presence from the Gulf by 1971. It was difficult, now, to argue that it was serving any very useful purpose.

8 THE COMMONWEALTH

a *Membership*
Four new members were admitted as independent states in 1966:
Botswana, formerly the High Commission territory of Bechuanaland, with a population of half a million.
Lesotho, formerly the High Commission territory of Basutoland, with a population of one million.
Both these new members were poor in resources and were, territorially speaking, so placed as to be heavily dependent on South Africa for trade and employment.
Guyana, formerly British Guiana.
Barbados. This small West Indian island was heavily populated, and rather precariously dependent on sugar and tourism. But its people were, by Caribbean standards, relatively sophisticated. And it had a long tradition of quasi self-government.

In 1968 *Mauritius*, in the Indian Ocean, joined these as an independent member of the Commonwealth, which now had twenty-six members, ten of them being African States. In 1967, following the break-up of the short-lived West Indies Federation, five small Caribbean islands ceased to be colonies and were given associated status with Britain. This arrangement combined political advance with continued external protection and assistance. Grenada, St. Vincent, Dominica, St. Lucia, Antigua and St. Kitts came in on these terms, at the wish of their political leaders but with the disapproval of the U.N. Committee of Twenty-four on Decolonization. The view there was that full independence ought to have been granted.

At first sight, it might seem that the Commonwealth family of states, some large and long-established, some new and small, some white, some black, some coloured, was indeed a going and growing concern. It is doubtful whether this was really so. There was at best an increasing indifference in Britain as to whether Commonwealth ties were maintained or not, and at worst, there were serious strains between Britain and many parts of the Commonwealth. Moreover it was difficult to avoid the conclusion that Commonwealth countries were increasingly, and probably correctly, viewed in Britain as a burden rather than an asset. Just as Britain was feeling the need to cut back on defence and foreign policy commitments, so, now, there was growing awareness of Britain's inability to carry the full burden of her Commonwealth commitments either.

The Commonwealth was coming to be viewed, not as an alternative to Europe, but as a millstone which might give General de Gaulle an excuse for keeping Britain out of Europe. There were, perhaps, more specific reasons for British discontents. The new Commonwealth countries in Africa and Asia had not retained British political and legal traditions as had the old white dominions. So the Commonwealth could no longer be regarded as a group of like-minded states. The Indo-Pakistan war had been a shock for which British opinion had been unprepared. Still more of a shock was the fact that these countries had finally turned not to Britain for an arbitrator, but to the U.S.S.R. The failure of the various federal schemes, such as the West Indian Federation, had resulted in the emergence of tiny little statelets, claiming 'equality' with India and Canada, and often the small new states were as vociferous in their criticisms of Britain as in their demands for her aid. Commonwealth Conferences were seen as occasions when pressures of all kinds could be put on British governments and this was resented. It seemed, increasingly, that the Commonwealth involved Britain in a series of obligations to Commonwealth countries, but that these countries recognized no reciprocal obligations to Britain.

One straw in the wind was provided by the increasing tendency to lump Commonwealth citizens in with other foreigners. Thus, when in January

1967 it was decided to raise fees for overseas students, who had hitherto been subsidized to the same extent as British students in British universities, Commonwealth students were treated on the same level as foreign students. The thought seemed to be that their claims on the British taxpayer were no more and no less.

Then, in 1967, the Fugitive Offenders Act was passed. In one way, this seemed a move forward. In the old dispensation, offenders from the Commonwealth could not claim political asylum, whereas aliens could. Now, Commonwealth citizens and aliens were put on the same footing, in that both could claim it.

The 1968 Immigration Act (see p. 205), however much it may have been justified, certainly went far in undermining the old conception of the multi-racial Commonwealth, all of whose citizens could look on the United Kingdom as their home.

b *Rhodesia*

Rhodesia was the most difficult and intractable of all of Mr. Wilson's Commonwealth problems. The hard fact was that sanctions had not worked. By one means or another oil got in; and Rhodesian exports got out.

At the Commonwealth Prime Ministers' Conference in September 1966 Mr. Wilson was under great pressure from the other African states to use force to bring down the illegal Smith regime. In the end, he got a three months' breathing space in which to try further negotiations.

Things did not, however, go well. In September 1966 the Rhodesian High Court, hitherto staunch for Britain, ruled that although the 1965 constitution was illegal, the Government was the *de facto* administration of the country, and that therefore the Courts should enforce its laws.

In December 1966 Mr. Wilson and Mr. Smith met on board the cruiser *Tiger* in the Mediterranean, to attempt to work out a formula for a new constitution and a return to legality. The prize seemed almost within the Wilson grasp when Mr. Smith said he needed the approval of his Cabinet before he could sign. After a day-long meeting of the Rhodesian Cabinet he said that he could not.

Following the rejection of the *Tiger* proposals, Britain applied to the U.N. in December 1966 for the imposition of selective mandatory sanctions. She withdrew all previous offers and said that there could now be no independence before majority rule (NIBMAR).

The Security Council approved a resolution requesting all member nations to ban the import and export of specified goods from Rhodesia, and, at the demand of the African states, this included oil. The Africans' demand for a blockade of the whole of the South African coastline was, however, turned down as impossible to enforce.

In April 1968, having reaffirmed that Britain would not use force, the Government put a new sanctions resolution to the U.N. Security Council, asking that all imports and exports should be banned; that Rhodesian passports should not be recognized; and that investments in Rhodesia should be blocked. These arrangements proved to be too much for the House of Lords, and by June 1968 the bipartisan approach to the Rhodesian problem had ended.

By September 1968 the Rhodesian High Court had given *de jure* as well as *de facto* recognition to the 'illegal' 1965 constitution. In October 1968 Mr. Wilson and Mr. Smith had further, and equally abortive, talks on H.M.S. *Fearless*.

It was a wretched issue from Mr. Wilson's standpoint. His early optimism that economic sanctions would force a Rhodesian surrender in a few weeks had been seen to be wholly misplaced. Talks and visits to Rhodesia and to Mediterranean warships got nowhere because Mr. Wilson was committed to the Six Points and NIBMAR; and Mr. Smith was committed to their rejection. Sanctions depressed the Rhodesian economy and increased African unemployment. African guerrilla activity increased, some of it infiltrating across the Zambesi from Zambia. South Africa and Portugal refused to co-operate in imposing sanctions, and it was obvious that the Smith regime, though inconvenienced, would not give up independence, especially after it had been accepted by the Rhodesian judiciary. Mr. Wilson had met his match in Mr. Smith, and it must have been obvious to him that his own Party, though concerned, felt helpless.

c *The Nigerian civil war*
Following an Ibo massacre in 1966, the Eastern Region of Nigeria, which was predominantly Ibo, attempted secession, under the name of Biafra. There followed the Nigerian civil war of 1967-8. Throughout this distressing period, the British Government gave unwavering support to the Federal Government, and continued to supply it with arms. Britain wished to maintain the integrity of the Nigerian state. The thought was that the splitting up of Nigeria into tribal statelets would be a disastrous backward step, which could have repercussions elsewhere in Africa. Further, if the British supply of arms was stopped, the Nigerian Federal Government would turn to the Russians for aid, and Britain would lose all her power to moderate in Lagos, both at that time and in the future.

d *The West Indies*
The smaller islands, left to their own devices since the break up of the West Indies Federation in 1962, now pressed for a new form of postcolonial relationship with Britain, as associated states. Each associated state would be fully self-governing in its internal affairs. Each island would

recognize the Sovereign, and would have its own Senate and House of Representatives and a Premier and Cabinet responsible to its Parliament. Britain would be responsible for defence and external relations. Either country could terminate the arrangement at any time.

Behind this arrangement was the thought that as these small islands could not seemingly federate with one another, the associated state arrangement might enable them to have the best of both worlds, in that they could be regarded as independent democratic states, but they need have no fears of take-overs from more powerful neighbours, since they would be under the protection of a powerful metropolitan state. Such resources as they had need not, therefore, be diverted into futile attempts to defend themselves against aggression.

Unfortunately, the process of fragmentation did not stop with the setting up of the new associated states. In 1967 Anguilla, with an adult population of 1,818, declared itself independent of St. Kitts-Nevis. Anguilla sought help from the United Nations. In the end it was agreed that a British official should administer the affairs of Anguilla for a time, while efforts could be made to restore her, in some new kind of relationship, to St. Kitts.

9 THE OPPOSITION

a *The Conservatives*

Grumbling continued in the constituencies about Mr. Heath's lack of leadership, lack of charisma, and his failure, in general, to get through to the country as an inspiring Leader and a credible alternative Prime Minister. He was no match for Mr. Wilson in the House; and he cut a poor figure on the television screen. But no contender emerged to challenge him.

In spite of the unpopularity of the Labour Government there was a lack of enthusiasm for the Conservatives. They made a negative impression on the public, and seemed to be content to rely on the general disillusion with Labour to get them back into office at the next Election.[1] By-election results reflected Labour abstentions rather than a positive turning towards the Conservatives. And, for those who cared to probe behind the scenes, it was not too difficult to see that Mr. Heath's team was deeply divided on most of the major issues of the time, whether on management of the economy, race relations, defence, or Rhodesia. Mr. Heath had not yet surfaced as a leader. He really had no clear public image at all. And too many in his own Party regarded him with scarcely veiled contempt.

[1] S. Brittan, 'Some Thoughts on the Conservative Opposition', *Parliamentary Quarterly*, No. 2, April 1968.

After the 1966 General Election Mr. Heath reshaped his Shadow Cabinet. The trend towards appointing younger men was marked. Thus, four senior ex-Ministers were dropped from the front bench – Mr. Selwyn Lloyd, Mr. Marples, Mr. Boyd-Carpenter and Mr. Sandys. Mr. Sandys was the last of the pre-war generation among leading Tories. Three of the four men dropped were well under sixty. But the policy seemed to be that, with the likelihood of four or five more years of opposition, a man with no prospect of office before the age of sixty-two might as well be dropped at once. Only two members of the new Shadow Cabinet were over fifty-five – Sir Alec Douglas-Home and Mr. Quintin Hogg. Most of Mr. Heath's new team had entered Parliament for the first time in 1959.

The Race Relations Bill, debated in the House between April and July 1968, provided the greatest test for Mr. Heath's Leadership since the crisis over the Rhodesian oil embargo in December 1965. The issue split the Party in three ways. The Shadow Cabinet was at first uncertain as to whether or not to oppose the Bill. Eventually it put down a 'reasoned amendment', having discovered the extent of back-bench opposition. It was on this occasion that Mr. Humphry Berkeley resigned from the Party. Perhaps a more serious blow was the abstention of Sir Edward Boyle, and twenty-four back-bench M.P.s. On the other side of the political spectrum, Mr. Enoch Powell had to be dismissed from the Shadow Cabinet after what seemed to be a flagrantly racialist speech on immigration on 22 April 1968. In July 1968, on the Bill's third reading, the Shadow Cabinet directed the Party to abstain from voting, since the Government had made some concessions to Opposition views, but forty-five Tory M.P.s none the less voted against the Bill. There was no doubt that Mr. Heath was finding it difficult to maintain Party unity and keep his team together. The tough leadership, the clear-cut political will, the certainty of touch, which were to characterize Mr. Heath as Prime Minister, in four years' time, were not revealed at all at this stage. He did not look in the least like an embryonic Prime Minister, and it was difficult to resist the conclusion that his election to the Leadership had been a great mistake for which the Tories were likely to pay heavily. But in fact, the Conservatives in Opposition were merely facing the disadvantages that all oppositions must face A political party in opposition is not tightly knit because divisions of opinion do not greatly matter. A Government can demand support, because without support it will fall. And, apart from this general threat, a Government has all kinds of ways of coaxing support from its followers. There are no corresponding sanctions available to a Leader of the Opposition. While there is some need for the Opposition Party to put forward attractive alternative policies to those of the Government, the longer it is in Opposition the more difficult it becomes for this to be done, for members of Shadow Cabinets do not have access to the necessary information, nor do they have the skilled civil service advisers to help them formulate their alternatives. Again, public discussions about alternative policies are all too likely to reveal divergencies within an Opposition Party, which the leaders would wish to withhold from the electorate. Also, premature discussion of alternative policies by an Opposition make it possible for the government in office to spike their guns, either by adopting some of the better ideas themselves, or by so arranging matters that their implementation can be seen to be impossible by the time the General Election comes. The real need, probably, is to have a team in the background, working out reasoned alternatives, which can then be released at the appropriate moment. This the Conservatives did, in the years from 1945 to 1951, to their very great advantage. The Labour Party in the fifties failed to do this. Probably the Conservatives did rather better in this regard, in the period from 1966 to 1970, than they were at the time given credit for. Mr. Barber's appointment at the Conservative Central Office in February 1967 was a very good move. And on 12 September 1967, Mr. Barber became the Tory Party Chairman, on the resignation of Mr. Edward du Cann.

b *The Liberals*
Liberal dreams of a massive revival were indefinitely postponed by the overwhelming Labour victory in the 1966 General Election. And in January 1967 Mr. Grimond resigned as Party Leader and was succeeded by Mr. Jeremy Thorpe. Mr. Thorpe was thirty-seven years old. He was a barrister who had been educated at Eton and Oxford. And he was a good deal more radical than any of the other Liberal M.P.s.

Since the war there had been two main Liberal strategies, both of which had now seemingly failed. There has been Clement Davies's strategy, which required Liberals to be seen as the Party of the expanding centre. This failed because the Labour and the Conservative Parties, instead of moving to the left and right respectively, converged on middle ground, from which the Liberals were thus excluded. The Grimond strategy had been aimed at a realignment of the left, which would have involved the creation of a non-socialist alternative capable of breaking the Conservative grip on the governmental machine. The presupposition here was of a split in Labour ranks, under the stress of their disappointed hopes of office. The old socialists would march off into the wilderness, and the new radicals into the Liberal Party. But, when Labour won the 1964 Election these hopes ended. The new Thorpe strategy now rested on the premise that Labour and Conservative policies had become indistinguishable, both being, in fact, conservative with a small c. The field was therefore open for a strong radical Opposition Party, able to harness to its own ends the discontents, which were felt in the outlying regions, about Whitehall. And presumably the thought was that the Celtic fringe regions would be a counterweight to the Young Liberals, who emerged, as a rather embarrassingly left wing group with neo-Trotskyist leanings, in 1966.[1]

Meantime, however, the emergence of the Scottish and the Welsh nationalists began to pose a possible though not as yet very serious threat to Liberal strongholds in Scotland and Wales.

[1] *Annual Register, 1966*, pp. 33-4.

EPILOGUE

The General Election of 18 June 1970[1]

The General Election held on 18 June 1970 seemed, at the time, a very unexpected ending to the turbulent years of Labour rule which began in 1964. The results, in the 630 constituencies, were as follows:

	Percentage of votes
Conservative seats 330 (as compared with 253 in 1966)	46.4
Labour seats 287 (as compared with 363)	43.0
Liberal seats 6 (as compared with 12)	7.5
There were 7 others.	

The average swing to the Conservatives was 4.5 per cent.

The Election was a very quiet one, and turn-out was, for the first time in thirty-five years, under 72 per cent.

It was unexpected in a variety of ways.

A June General Election had not been anticipated. Politicians had always thought of June as an awkward month if only because so many electors were by then away on holiday. And in this case, June was thought particularly unlikely because so many major Bills were by that time in the pipeline and could not be completed before the autumn. Then, it was thought that it would be awkward for a new government to take over in June, just as Parliament was getting ready for the recess and the country in general about to relax for the summer holidays.[2] More importantly, the polls, until the campaign actually got under way, gave rather uncertain indications of a Labour recovery. Then, finally, the April Budget hadn't seemed at all like a pre-Election Budget. It was almost as if the Chancellor was holding back a bit, so that there could be some popular pre-Election hand-outs in the autumn.

Why, then, did Mr. Wilson choose June? The onlooker can only speculate. Certainly, according to the polls, the tide had turned in Labour's favour. In June, Labour might just make it. By the autumn, however, the Government might expect to run into bad economic trouble. Mr. Wilson seems also to have feared that the Conservatives would use the summer recess to deploy their large financial resources to make trouble for the Government; and in this they would, as ever, be assisted by the international banking world. Moreover if the Government did wait till October and then found itself in trouble, no options

[1] See D. E. Butler and M. Pinto-Duschinsky, op. cit., and *The Polls and the 1970 Election*, ed. Richard Rose.

[2] In fact it was not. On the contrary it was a great advantage to the new Ministers to have a long quiet summer, undisturbed, to work themselves into their new departments.

would be left open, for it was firmly believed that the troubles caused by decimalization would make an Election early in 1971 highly undesirable for Labour.

It may be tempting to think that a June Election was just one of Mr. Wilson's hunches, and that his colleagues, had they known about it in time, might have restrained him. This, however, was apparently not the case, and at least the inner Government circle knew of his plans and supported them. The desperate dash for victory in June was a collective decision.

At first it looked as if Mr. Wilson's hunch had been right. However, Lord George-Brown has remarked, in his memoirs, on the fact that many Labour Party constituency workers warned that their impressions did not tally with the opinion poll results.[1] After the start of the campaign all the five polls taking regular samples showed Labour as having a large lead. There was only one hesitant verdict, the other way, by the Opinion Research Centre, taking an eve-of-poll sample. The outcome seemed a foregone conclusion, and the only worthwhile speculation was on the size of Labour's majority.

Why did the polls go so very wrong? They had been reasonably right, for a long period of time, in their forecasts on by-elections and local government elections. The pollsters themselves have suggested a variety of possible reasons. One of the more plausible is that there was a swing to the Conservatives in the last week, which came too late to be measured in the polls. The O.R.C. was the one poll which indicated a small Conservative lead in its eve-of-poll sampling. It was the last poll taken, and this perhaps does lend some plausibility to this theory. But of course it poses another question. What explanation can there be for the swing against Labour in the last week? The publication of a bad set of trade figures may conceivably have made some electors more receptive to Conservative warnings of economic troubles to come. On the B.B.C. *Panorama* programme on June 1st, Lord Cromer, a Tory supporter, and Governor of the Bank of England from 1961 to 1966, and Lord Kearton, a leading industrialist who was a cautious Labour supporter, discussed what they saw as the very difficult economic situation. Certainly this TV performance must have given rise to uneasiness, for these two prophets of doom did, presumably, know what they were talking about. Then most people seem to have felt that Mr. Heath's last performance on TV was good, and Mr. Wilson's rather bad. But it seems difficult to believe that much importance can be attached to this. Mr. Heath was surely too far behind Mr. Wilson, in his public image, to have caught him up and overtaken him, in one short twenty-minute set-piece.

The 'hot vote' theory also seems plausible. According to this view, hot votes like hot money, come and go, often for quite insubstantial reasons.

[1] George-Brown, op. cit., p. 262.

This was a fact that the pollsters failed to take account of. Thus, declared intentions two and three weeks before the Election bore no necessary correlation with how people might cast their votes when the day came. This volatility was a new factor, which in itself requires explanation. Over the past decades the British electorate had been remarkably stable in its voting habits. There is, of course, no way of knowing for certain but some suggestions may be explored.

There was very little, it seemed, to choose between the two Parties, as far as their policies went – less, perhaps, than ever before. Trade union reform; education; selectivity in welfare hand-outs; Rhodesia; east of Suez; the Common Market – whatever the issue, it seemed difficult to detect a clear difference of policy. This meant that switching was relatively easy, as it didn't have to imply conversion to a different set of political principles.

Such political issues as there were were of too sophisticated a nature to be understood by the ordinary elector. No one could feel great confidence in his own views on the E.E.C. when top-level economists were divided, and when politicians, and even the Leaders of the political Parties, seemed to shift their ground continually. Thus the real issues could, in the nature of the case, not be matters for meaningful public debate. This may partly account for the fact that the electorate seemed more interested in betting on the polls than on issues of policy between the Parties. In a way, it was a very unserious Election. Politicians, too, seemed increasingly mesmerized by what the pollsters said the people thought. It hardly seemed worth waiting for the final votes to be counted. It is difficult to resist the conclusion that all too much weight was coming to be placed on this ersatz kind of democracy. It was as well that the bubble was pricked in 1970.

There could, of course, have been some attempt at debate. One of the weaknesses of the Wilson campaign was, it was afterwards thought, the total absence of this. Where Mr. Heath tried to make reasoned speeches, Mr. Wilson tended simply to rely on 'dropping in' and 'chatting', without advance notice.

Possibly the pollsters took insufficient account of the difference between the two Party machines. The Conservatives had, for instance, 400 full-time agents as against Labour's 160. The Tory Election fund was £2.3m.; Labour's was £500,000. Mr. Heath's style was to decentralize and to rely on what he knew to be a good and efficient Party machine. A serious attempt was made to try to find out, by private polls on special issues, what were the electorate's view. The Conservatives had always been better at organizing and getting out their vote. Mr. Wilson was handicapped not only by the relative lack of Party funds, but also by his own conviction that he could do it all better by himself. This was the arrangement that he preferred. A powerful organization at Transport House might rival 10 Downing Street, and that would never do. But it is difficult to see how much difference all this made, in that the swing to the Conservatives was so uniform. Labour did no better in constituencies with a high turn-out than in the low turn-out ones.[1]

Another curious feature of this Election was that it was, more than any other General Election since the war, a contest between two men – Mr. Wilson and Mr. Heath. And, whatever else may have been in question, there was no possible doubt that Mr. Wilson was generally regarded as the more adroit politician. Mr. Heath was not well known; not well liked; and few thought him very able. Even in the days when the Conservatives had had their largest leads against Labour, in 1968 and 1969, Mr. Heath had trailed far behind his Party. He was certainly not a popular figure with the electorate at large. He was not even a popular figure in his own Party. No group of Conservatives felt, it seemed, enthusiastic. To the working-class Tory he seemed cold and arrogant; to the middle- and upper-class Tory he seemed a bit of an upstart. He had acquired expensive tastes – like yachting and the Albany. But he was not one of them. He was not good on telly, and was generally unloved. A dull, cold, proud, unconvincing upstart. But he won.

[1] The swing to the Tories was nearly uniform. In no part of the country was it less than $2\frac{1}{2}$ per cent, or as much as $6\frac{1}{4}$ per cent.

BIBLIOGRAPHY

Abrams, M. and R. Rose, *Must Labour Lose?*, Penguin, 1960
Attlee, C. R., Earl, *As it Happened*, Heinemann, 1954
Beer, S. H., *Modern British Politics*, Faber and Faber, 1965
Bevan, A., *In Place of Fear*, MacGibbon and Kee, 1961
Bevins, R., *The Greasy Pole*, Hodder and Stoughton, 1965
Brown, R. Douglas, *The Battle of Crichel Down*, Bodley Head, 1955
Bulmer-Thomas, I., *The Growth of the British Party System*, Vol. II, John Baker, 1965.
Butler, D. and J. Freeman, *British Political Facts 1900–1968*, Macmillan, 1969
Butler, Lord, *The Art of the Possible*, Hamish Hamilton, 1971
Butt, R., *The Power of Parliament*, 2nd edn., Constable, 1969
Camps, M., *Britain and the European Community 1955–1963*, Oxford University Press, 1964
Camps, M., *European Unification in the Sixties*, Oxford University Press, 1967
Churchill, R., *The Fight for the Tory Leadership*, Heinemann, 1964
Crick, B., *The Reform of Parliament*, 2nd edn., Weidenfeld and Nicolson, 1968
Crossman, R., *Labour in the Affluent Society*, Fabian Tract 325, 1960
Daalder, H., *Cabinet Reform in Britain 1914–1963*, Oxford University Press, 1964
Dalton, H., *Memoirs: Vol. III High Tide and After*, Muller, 1962
Diebold, W., *The Schuman Plan: A Study in Economic Cooperation 1950–1959*, Praeger (for Council on Foreign Relations), 1959
Dow, J. C. R., *The Management of the British Economy 1945–1960*, Cambridge University Press, 1968
Dowse, R. E., 'The Parliamentary Labour Party in Opposition', *Parliamentary Affairs*, Vol. 13, No. 4
Eden, The Rt. Hon. Sir Anthony, Lord Avon, The Eden Memoirs. *Full Circle*, Cassell, 1960
Epstein, L., 'Partisanship in the Suez Crisis', *Studies in British Politics*, ed. Richard Rose, Macmillan, 1969
Epstein, L., 'The Nuclear Deterrent and the British General Election of 1964', *Journal of British Studies*, Vol. II, 1966
Gelman, N. I., 'Bevanism: A Philosophy for British Labour', *Journal of British Politics*, 1954
George-Brown, Lord, *In My Way*, Gollancz, 1971
Gott, R., 'The Evolution of the Independent Nuclear Deterrent', *International Affairs*, April 1963
Hanna, A., *The Story of the Rhodesians and Nyasaland*, Faber and Faber, 2nd edn., 1965

Hamson, C. J., 'The Real Lesson of Crichel Down', *Public Administration*, 1954
Hansard Society, *Parliamentary Reform 1933–1960*, Cassell, 1961
Harris, R., *Politics without Prejudice*, Staples Press, 1956
Harrison, M., *Trade Unions and the Labour Party since 1945*, George Allen and Unwin, 1960
Haseler, S., *The Gaitskellites 1951–1964*, Macmillan, 1969
von Herwerth, H., 'A German View', *International Affairs*, October 1963
Hoffman, J. D., *The Conservative Party in Opposition*, MacGibbon and Kee, 1964
Howard, A. M. and R. West, *The Making of the Prime Minister*, Jonathan Cape, 1965
Hunter, L., *The Road to Brighton Pier*, Arthur Barker, 1959
Ingham, K., *A History of East Africa*, Longmans, 1965
Irving, C., *Scandal 63*, Heinemann, 1963
James, R. R., *Ambitions and Realities: British Politics 1964–1970*, Weidenfeld and Nicolson, 1972
Jenkins, P., *The Battle of Downing Street*, Knight, 1970
Jones, G., 'The Prime Minister's Power', *Crisis in British Government*, ed. W. J. Stankiewicz, Collier-Macmillan, 1967
Kilmuir, Earl of, *Memoirs: Political Adventure*, Weidenfeld and Nicolson, 1962
Kirkman, W., *Unscrambling an Empire: A Critique of British Colonial Policy 1956–1966*, Chatto and Windus, 1966
Kirkwood, K., *Britain and Africa*, Chatto and Windus, 1965
Kitzinger, U., *The Second Try: Labour and the E.E.C.*, Pergamon Press, 1968
Knapp, W., *A History of War and Peace 1939–1965*, Oxford University Press, 1967
Lee, J. M., *Colonial Development and Good Government*, Oxford University Press, 1967
Loewenberg, J., 'The Transformation of Labour Party Policy since 1945', *Journal of Politics*, 1959
McKenzie, R. T., *British Political Parties*, 2nd edn., Heinemann, 1955
McKenzie, R. T., 'Policy Decisions in Opposition', *Political Studies*, Vol. V, No. 2, 1957
Mackintosh, J. P., *The British Cabinet*, 2nd edn., Stevens, 1968
Macmillan, H., Memoirs, Vol. I 1914–1939 *Winds of Change*, Macmillan 1966
Vol. II   1939–1945 *The Blast of War*, Macmillan, 1967
Vol. III 1945–1955 *Tides of Fortune*, Macmillan, 1969
Vol. IV   1956–1959 *Riding the Storm*, Macmillan, 1971
Vol. V   1959–1961 *Pointing the Way*, Macmillan, 1972
Vol. VI   1961–1963 *At the End of the Day*, Macmillan, 1973

Mansergh, N., *Documents and Speeches on Commonwealth Affairs 1952–1962*, Oxford University Press, 1963

Martin, L., 'The Bournemouth Affair', *Journal of Politics*, 1960

Medlicott, W., *Contemporary England*, Longmans, 1967

Moran, Lord, *Winston Churchill: The Struggle for Survival 1940–1965*, Constable, 1966

Morrison, H., *An Autobiography by Lord Morrison of Lambeth*, Odhams, 1960

Northedge, F. S., *British Foreign Policy 1945–1961*, George Allen and Unwin, 1962

Nuffield Election Studies:

McCallum, R. B. and A. Readman, *The British General Election 1945*, Oxford University Press, 1947

Nicholas, H. G., *The British General Election of 1950*, Cass, 1951

Butler, D. E., *The British General Election of 1951*, Macmillan, 1952

Butler, D. E., *The British General Election of 1955*, Cass, 1955

Butler, D. E. and R. Rose, *The British General Election of 1959*, Macmillan, 1960

Butler, D. E. and A. King, *The British General Election of 1964*, Macmillan, 1965

Butler, D. E. and A. King, *The British General Election of 1966*, Macmillan, 1967

Butler, D. E. and M. Pinto-Duschinsky, *The British General Election of 1970*, Macmillan, 1971

Nutting, A., *No End of a Lesson*, Constable, 1967

Pelling, H., *A Short History of the Labour Party*, Macmillan, 1961

Punnett, R. M., 'The Labour Shadow Cabinet 1955–1964', *Parliamentary Affairs*, 1964

Robertson, T., *Crisis: The Inside Story of the Suez Conspiracy*, Hutchinson, 1965

Rodgers, W. T., ed., *Hugh Gaitskell, 1906–1963*, Thames and Hudson, 1964

Durant, H., 'Voting Behaviour in Britain, 1945–1966', *Studies in British Politics*, ed. R. Rose, 1966

Rose, R., ed., *The Polls and the 1970 Election*, University of Strathclyde, Survey Research Center Occasional Paper No. 7, 1970

Sampson, A., *Macmillan: A Study in Ambiguity*, Allen Lane, The Penguin Press, 1967

Schlesinger, A., *A Thousand Days: John F. Kennedy in the White House*, Deutsch, 1965

Shinwell, E., *The Labour Story*, Macdonald, 1963

Shonfield, A., *British Economic Policy Since the War*, Penguin, 1958

Sparrow, G., *R.A.B. Study of a Statesman: The Career of Baron Butler of Saffron Walden*, Odhams, 1965

Thomas, H., *The Suez Affair*, Weidenfeld and Nicolson, 1967
Vincent, J. R., 'The House of Lords in the Macmillan Era', *Parliamentary Affairs*, 1966
Watkins, A., *The Liberal Dilemma*, MacGibbon and Kee, 1966
Watts, R. L., *New Federations*, Oxford University Press, 1966
Wheeler-Bennett, J., *John Anderson, Viscount Waverley*, Macmillan, 1962
Walker, P. Gordon, *The Cabinet*, Cape, 1970
Williams, F., *A Prime Minister Remembers*, Heinemann, 1961
Willson, F. M. G., *The Organisation of British Central Government, 1914–1964*, ed. D. N. Chester, Allen and Unwin, 1968
Wilson, H., *The Labour Government, 1964–1970: A Personal Record*, Weidenfeld and Nicolson and Michael Joseph, 1971
Woolton, the Rt. Hon. Earl of, *Memoirs*, Cassell, 1959
Worswick, G. D. N. and P. H. Ady, *The British Economy in the Nineteen Fifties*, Clarendon Press, 1962
Younger, K., *Changing Perspectives in British Foreign Policy*, Chatham House Essays: 7, Oxford University Press, 1964
Youngson, A., *The British Economy, 1927–1957*, Allen and Unwin, 1966
Youngson, A., *Britain's Economic Growth 1920–1966*, Allen and Unwin, 1967

The following journals have provided useful articles:

The Journal of British Studies
The Canadian Journal of Economics and Political Science
The Economic Journal
Encounter
Foreign Affairs
International Affairs
Parliamentary Affairs   Hansard Society
Parliamentary Quarterly
Journal of Politics
Midwest Journal of Political Science
Political Science Quarterly
Political Studies
Public Administration   Royal Institute of Public Administration

Index

Abadan, 21
Abrams, M., 147
Accra riots, 95
Acheson, Dean, 47
Aden, 143–4, 214
Adenauer, Konrad, 85
African Affairs Board, 51
age of majority, 193
Agricultural Act, 1953, 34
Alexander, Earl, 25
Algeria, 46, 87
All African People's Conference, 140
Amory, Heathcoat, 70, 76, 109
Anderson, John, 28n.
Anglo-Egyptian Treaty, 1954 86
Anglo-Iranian Oil Company, 17
Anguilla, 21, 218
Antigua, 215
Anzus Pact, 38
Arab-Israeli war, 214
Arab League, 45
Arab nationalism, 36
Army Bureau of Current Affairs (A.B.C.A.), 12n.
Asquith, H. H., 25
ASSET, 196n.
Assheton, Ralph, 18
Astor, Lord and Lady, 113
Aswan High Dam, 86–7
Atomic Research Centre, Harwell, 79
Attlee, Clement, as deputy to Churchill, 13; and the Cabinet, 71; and extremists, 59, 60; and foreign affairs, 14, 16; and leadership of the Party, 57; and nationalization, 15, 34; and nuclear weapons, 60, 79; the Parliamentary Labour Party and the unions, 56; retires, 101
Australia, and Japan, 46; and Malaysia, 166; and SEATO, 48; trading agreements, 49
Austria, 39, 77

Austrian Peace Treaty, 1955, 83

Baghdad Pact (CENTO), 43, 45, 58, 82, 86, 99, 132
Bahrain, 214
Balogh, Professor, 162
Banda, Dr., 97
Bank of England, 15
Bank Rate, 30, 32, 76, 121, 122, 161, 196, 197
Barbados, 214
Barber, Anthony, 220
Basutoland, 170
Beadle, Sir Hugh, 171
Bechuanaland, 170
Beeching Report on the Railways, 125, 131–2
Benn, Anthony Wedgwood, 119, 182, 185
Berkeley, Humphry, 219
Berlin, 85, 136
Berlin Conference on Austria, 1954, 39
Berlin Declaration, 1957, 85
Bevan, Aneurin, becomes Shadow Foreign Secretary, 102; gains seat on N.E.C., 60; hatred of the Tory Party, 16; and the left wing, 57–8, 59–61; and nuclear disarmament, 81; and Party Leadership, 101; resigns over health charges, 17, 25
Bevanism, 57–8, 59–61, 65
Beveridge, Sir William, 14n., 15
Beveridge Report, 14, 15
Bevin, Ernest, 14, 16
Biafra, 217
Birch, Nigel, 70, 76
Blue Streak missiles, 133, 134
Blundell, Mr., 141
B.O.A.C., 131
Botswana, 214
Bottomley, Arthur, 171

Bournemouth Conservative Association, 72
Boyle, Sir Edward, 76, 92, 111, 219
British Caribbean Federation Act, 1956, 100
Brooke, Henry, 78, 111, 181
Brown, George, 58, 223; and the E.E.C., 210–11; as Foreign Secretary, 182–3; and Party Leadership, 150, 151, 151n.; and re-nationalization of steel, 163; resigns as Foreign Secretary, 183–4, 186; as Secretary for Economic Affairs, 158, 162
Brunei, 143
Brussels Treaty, 41
Buchanan Report on Town Planning, 125
Budgets, 1952, 31–2; 1953, 32; 1955, 32, 64, 76; 1956, 76; 1959, 76; 1961, 121; 1962, 122; 1963, 122; 1965, 161, 162; 1966, 194; 1967, 197; 1968, 188, 198; 1969, 202; 1970, 204–5
Buganda, 142–1
Bulganin, Nikolai, 83
Bunyoro, 142–3
Burma, independence, 49
Butler, R. A. B., 14, 25, 173; as possible Prime Minister, 112, 114, 115, 116; becomes Home Secretary, 69; becomes Lord Privy Seal, 67; 1953 Budget, 32; 1955 Budget, 32, 64; and the Central African Federation, 141; and economic liberalism, 30; 1959 Election, 107; and floating the pound, 76; and immigration, 126; and post-war Conservative policy, 19; and selection of Prime Minister, 68, 70–1; and Suez crisis, 90, 91
by-elections, 1945–50 government, 15; 1951–55 government, 62, 72; 1955–1959 government, 67; 1959–64 government, 110–11, 151; 1964–66 government, 160, 178, 180; 1966–70 government, 189, 218
Byers, Frank, 62

Cabinet committees, 28
Caffery, Jefferson, 44
Callaghan, James, 1966 Budget, 194; as Chancellor of the Exchequer, 158, 162, 183; and devaluation, 197; as Home Secretary, 183; and the Parliamentary Committee of the Cabinet, 193; and Party Leadership, 150, 151, 151n.; and the trade unions, 189, 202, 203; as a 'threat' to Mr. Wilson, 186
Cambodia, 47–8
Campaign for Nuclear Disarmament (C.N.D.), 81, 102, 148
Canada, trading agreements, 49
capital punishment, 78–9, 164
Castle, Barbara, and 'Bevanism', 60n., 61; and the 'fundamentalists', 146; and incomes policy, 203, 204; and the trade unions, 201–2; as Minister for Overseas Development, 158; as Secretary for Employment and Productivity, 184
CENTO (Baghdad Pact), 43, 58, 82, 86, 99, 132
Central African Federation, 50–2, 96–7, 139, 140–1
Ceylon, independence, 49
Chalfont, Lord, 212
Chamberlain, Joseph, 15
Chamberlain, Neville, 13
Cherwell, Lord, 28, 29
Chiang Kai-shek, 40, 47, 83
China, Britain and, 39–40; Britain recognizes, 38, 40; claims Quemoy and Matsu, 82; and North Korea, 46–7; and the Nuclear Non-Proliferation Treaty, 209; and Vietnam, 36, 47, 167, 168
Chou En-lai, 168
Christmas Island, 37
Churchill, Lord Randolph, 15, 20, 116
Churchill, Sir Winston, 18, 24; and Britain in Europe, 40; and the Cabinet, 71; domestic policy, 19; and Eden's attitude to America, 26–7, 39; 1945 Election, 11, 12–14; health, 25–6; housing policy, 24;

and the Industrial Charter, 20; and nuclear deterrents, 36, 39, 79–80; post-war speeches, 20; resigns as Prime Minister, 64; and Soviet Union, 39; and trade unions, 33
Civil Service, 193–4
Clegg, Hugh, 201
C.N.D., 81, 102, 148
Cole, G. D. H., 69
Common Market, 85, 134, 145, 191; Commonwealth and, 77, 125, 145–6, 170, 211, 215; Labour's opposition to, 150, 169, 187; Macmillan reopens negotiations, 109, 121, 123–5, 135; negotiations opened, 1957, 77; Wilson attempts entry into, 208, 210–14
Commonwealth, and the E.E.C., 77, 125, 145–6, 170, 211, 215; 1951–55 government and, 48–54; 1955–59 government and, 94–100; 1959–64 government and, 138–46; 1964–66 government and, 169–73; 1966–70 government and, 214–18
Commonwealth Immigration Act, 1962, 126–8, 146, 156, 164, 205
Commonwealth Immigration Act, 1968, 205–6, 216
Commonwealth Party, 1945 Election, 11
Commonwealth Prime Ministers' Conference, 1960, 145
Commonwealth Secretariat, 169–70
Communist Party, 1945 General Election, 11; 1966 General Election, 181
comprehensive schools, 163
Compton, Sir Edward, 190
Concorde project, 131
Conservative Party, election of Leader, 174–6; 1945 Election, 11–14; 1950 Election, 16, 19; 1951 Election, 18–21, 23–5; 1955 Election, 64–5, 66; 1959 Election, 106–8; 1964 Election, 153–6; 1966 Election, 180–1; 1970 Election, 222–5; in opposition, 18–22, 173–7, 218–20; in office, 25–8, 66–70, 108–18

Conservative Party Conference, 1946, 19: 1950, 24; 1963, 114
Conservative Research Department, 19
Constantinople Convention, 1888, 45, 86
constituencies, M.P.'s and their, 72–3
Constitutional Amendment Act, 1957, 97
constitutional issues, 1951–55 government, 28–30; 1955–59 government, 70–4; 1959–64 government, 118–20; 1964–66 government, 159–60; 1966–1970 government, 189–94
Council of Europe, 123
County Council elections, 1965, 159
Cousins, Frank, as a 'fundamentalist', 146; influence on the unions, 102; as Minister of Technology, 158, 182; resigns, 186
Couve de Murville, Maurice, 213
Creech Jones, Arthur, 100
Crichel Down case, 29–30
Cripps, Sir Stafford, 16, 59
Cromer, Lord, 223
Crookshank, Harry, 25, 27
Crosland, Anthony, as Secretary for Local Government and Regional Planning, 185
Crossman, Richard, and 'Bevanism', 60n., 61; and the 'fundamentalists', 146, 147; and housing, 164; as Minister for Social Services, 184; and Parliamentary committees, 190
Crowther Report, 129
Cuba, British trade with, 209; 1962 crisis, 136
Cyprus, 45, 70, 98–9, 138, 144, 167
Czechoslovakia, 209

Daalder, Hans, 91, 116
Dalton, Hugh, 11, 17, 18; and Hugh Gaitskell, 101, 102; loses seat on N.E.C., 60
Davies, Clement, 62, 220
Davies, Harold, 168
Deakin, Arthur, attacks 'Bevanism', 60
death penalty, 78–9, 164

Index

Declaration of Intent on Productivity, Prices and Incomes, 161
defence policies, 1951–55 government, 35–7, 45; 1955–59 government, 79–81; 1959–64 government, 132–4; 1964–66 government, 165–7; 1966–1970 government, 207
Defence White Paper, 1957, 81
De Gaulle, Charles, and Britain's entry to E.E.C., 85, 109, 121, 125, 134, 135, 169, 211–14
Delamere, Lord, 52
Denmark, 77
Denning Report, 113
Department of Economic Affairs, 159
devaluation, 32, 160, 187–8, 196, 197
Devlin Commission on disturbances in Nyasaland, 97
Dien Bien Phu, 47
Dilhorne, Lord, 111, 115
Disraeli, Benjamin, 15, 20
domestic affairs, 1951–55 government, 32–5; 1955–59 government, 77–9; 1959–64 government, 125–32; 1964–1966 government, 162–5; 1966–70 government, 205–7
Dominica, 215
Donnelly, Desmond, 163
Donovan, Lord, 159, 164, 200
Douglas-Home, Sir Alec, 28, 112, 158, 219; and the 1964 Election, 154–5; becomes Foreign Secretary, 109, 110; as Prime Minister, 115, 116, 117–18, 154; resigns as Leader, 175; and Rhodesia, 171; becomes Secretary of State for Commonwealth Relations, 67
Driberg, Tom, and 'Bevanism', 60n., 61
du Cann, Edward, 174, 220
Dugdale, Sir Thomas, 29, 30
Dulles, John Foster, Anthony Eden and, 26, 38–9, 47, 48, 82; Suez crisis, 38–9, 87, 88, 92, 93; support for France in Vietnam, 47, 48

'East of Suez', Britain's role, 166–7, 208

Eccles, Sir David, 111
economic issues, 1951–55 government, 30–2; 1955–59 government, 74–7; 1959–64 government, 120–5; 1964–66 government, 160–2; 1966–1970 government, 194–205
Eden, Sir Anthony, 25, 26; and Britain in Europe, 41, 42; Churchill and, 26–7; and the 1955 Election, 64; Foreign Office, 26, 27; and John Foster Dulles, 26, 38–9, 47, 48, 82; and the Korean war, 47; and nuclear deterrents, 39; as Prime Minister, 26, 27, 64, 66–8, 70–1; and Sudan, 45; Suez Crisis, 72, 86–94; and Vietnam, 47
education, 129–31, 163
EFTA, 77, 124, 125, 160–1, 211–13
Egypt, 36, 39, 43–5, 86–90, 94
Eisenhower, Dwight D., 92, 92n., 133, 135
elections, *see* by-, general and local government elections
Elizabeth II, Queen, 28
EOKA, 98
Europe, Britain and, 40–2, 83–6, 137–138, 169, 208, 210–14
European Defence Community, 123
European Economic Community, 85, 134, 145, 191; Commonwealth and, 77, 125, 145–6, 170, 211, 215; Labour's opposition to, 150, 169, 187; Macmillan reopens negotiations, 109, 121, 123–5, 135; negotiations opened, 1957, 77; Wilson attempts entry into, 208, 210–14

Far East, 46–8
Farouk, King, 44
Feather, Vic, 203
Flanders, Hugh, 201
food rationing, 32
foreign policy, 1945–51 governments, 14–15, 17, 21; 1951–55 government, 37–48; 1955–59 government, 81–94; 1959–64 government, 135–8; 1964–66 government, 167–9; 1966–1970 government, 208–14

Formosa, 38, 40, 47, 82–3
France, and the Algerian problem, 46, 87; Anglo-French relations, 77, 85, 137; and Britain's entry into the E.E.C., 213, *see also* de Gaulle, Charles; and Indo-China, 47–8; nuclear weapons, 209; and SEATO, 48; Suez Canal, 44; Suez Crisis, 87–90; and unification of Europe, 41, 42; U.S. opinion of, 84–5; and West Germany, 40, 85; withdraws troops from NATO, 210
Freeman, John, 17, 25
Friend, Major, 72
Fugitive Offenders Act, 1967, 216
Fulton, Missouri, 40
Fulton Committee on the Future of the Civil Service, 119, 193–4

Gaitskell, Hugh, and 'Campaign for Democratic Socialism', 149–50; as Chancellor of the Exchequer, 59; death, 150; and the E.E.C., 124; 1959 Election, 107, 108; imposes N.H.S. charges, 17, 34; and nuclear weapons, 80; as Party Leader, 57, 101–2, 103–4, 150; and the 'revisionists', 146–7; and Suez Crisis, 88, 93
Galbraith, Thomas, 112, 112n.
Gallup polls, 11, 16, 66, 154
Gambia, 170
Gan, 207
General Agreement on Tariffs and Trade, 41
General Elections, 1945, 11; 1950, 16, 19, 25; 1951, 18, 23–5, 33; 1955, 33, 64–6; 1959, 106–8; 1964, 153–6, 173, 177; 1966, 180–2; 1970, 186, 222–5
George VI, King, 28
George-Brown, Lord, *see* Brown, George
Germany, East, 39, 40, 84
Germany, West, and Britain's entry into E.E.C., 125, 213–14; and British troops in NATO, 210; and nuclear weapons, 137, 166, 169; rearmament, 35, 58, 60; reunification of Germany, 84–5; and unification of Europe, 40–2

Ghana, 49, 95, 140
Gibbs, Sir Humphrey, 171
Gibraltar, 21, 167, 172–3
Glubb, General, 67, 86
Gold Coast, 95
Gollancz, Victor, 79
Gowers, Sir Edward, 78
Greece, and Cyprus, 98
Greenwood, Anthony, 158, 170
Grenada, 215
Griffith, James, 52, 101
Griffiths, Peter, 156
Grimmond, Joseph, and coalition with Labour, 62, 158, 177; 1966 General Election, 181; and regionalism, 156; resigns as Party Leader, 220
Guillebaud Committee Report on the Railways, 125, 131
Gunter, Ray, 186
Guyana, 214

Hailsham, Lord, 219; as possible Prime Minister, 112, 114, 115, 116; and the 1957 public relations campaign, 107; renounces peerage, 119–120; responsibility for the North-East, 121
Hall, Sir Robert, 75
Hancock Commission, 142
Hare, John, 116
Head, Anthony, 90
Healey, Denis, 58n.; as Defence Secretary, 165; and sale of arms to South Africa, 184
Heath, Edward, 71; attacks 1965 Finance Bill, 161–2; and the balance of payments, 204; as Chairman of Advisory Committee on Policy, 174; and the E.E.C., 124, 125; 1966 General Election, 180, 181; 1970 General Election, 186, 223–5; as Lord Privy Seal, 110; as Party Leader, 175–6, 218–20; and the 1968 Race Relations Bill, 219; and

Index

resale price maintenance, 128; and Rhodesia, 176-7; as Secretary for Industry, Trade and Regional Development, 121
Herbison, Margaret, 183, 186
Hill, Charles, 111
Hogarth, 195
Hogg, Quintin, *see* Hailsham, Lord
Hola Camp incident, 98, 140
Homicide Act, 1957, 78-9
Hong Kong, 40, 167, 207
hospitals, 129
Houghton, Douglas, 203
House of Lords, 73-4, 119-20, 188, 191-3
housing, 24, 33-4, 78, 129, 163-4
Hussein, King, 46, 86

Ibn Saud, 46
immigration, 126-8, 164-5, 205-6
incomes policy, 161, 196-204
India, 45, 49, 127, 170-1, 215
Indo-China, 36, 47-8
Industrial Charter, 1947, 19-20, 33
International Monetary Fund, 41, 76, 121, 161, 197
Iran, 17, 22, 25, 42, 43
Iraq, 43, 99
Iron and Steel Nationalization Act, 1951, 15, 24
Ismay, Lord, 28
Israel, Suez Crisis, 87-90, 93; Arab-Israeli War, 214
Italy, 41, 42
Ivanov, Captain, 113

Jamaica, 138
Japan, and Britain, 46; and Indo-China, 47; U.S. policy towards, 46
Jay, Douglas, 124, 183, 186
Jenkins, Roy, 1968 Budget, 188, 198; 1969 Budget, 202; 1970 Budgets, 204-5; as Chancellor of the Exchequer, 183, 197, 199-205; and the E.E.C., 124, 210; as Home Secretary, 182; and the Party Constitution, 148; as a 'threat' to Mr. Wilson, 186

Johnson, Lyndon Baines, 208-9
Jones, Aubrey, 161, 204
Jones, Jack, 203
Jordan, 46, 86
Joseph, Sir Keith, 111

Kabaka, 142
Kaesong, 47
Kaldor, Nicholas, 161, 194
Kashmir, 170
Kearton, Lord, 223
Keeler, Christine, 113, 129
Kennedy, John F., 111, 133, 135, 137, 207
Kenya, 49, 141-2; immigration into Britain, 141, 205-6; independence, 138, 141; Mau Mau, 50, 52-4, 97-8, 141
Kenya African Union, 52
Kenyatta, Jomo, 52
Keynes, Lord, 69
Kilmuir, Lord, 16, 27, 92, 93, 111
King, Cecil, 188
Kitchener, Lord, 44
Koestler, Arthur, 79
Korean War, 16, 17, 18, 23, 25, 30, 32, 34, 39, 46-7, 48
Kosygin, A. N., 171, 209, 214
Krushchev, Nikita, 83, 136, 155

Labour Party, 1945 Election, 11, 12-14; 1950 Election, 16; 1951 Election, 23-5; 1955 Election, 65-6, 100-1; 1959 Election, 106-8; 1964 Election, 154-6; 1966 Election, 180-1; 1970 Election, 222-5; in office, 14-18, 157-9, 182-9; in opposition, 54-61, 100-4, 146-51; Party Leadership, 57, 150; Shadow Cabinet, 60n., 74; and the trade unions, 54-7
Labour Party Conference, 1952, 60; 1953, 60; 1955, 101, 103; 1957, 81; 1959, 146; 1960, 148; 1961, 150; 1963, 151; 1965, 159; 1966, 187; 1968, 199; 1969, 204
Laos, 47-8
League of Empire Loyalists, 139

Index

Leathers, Lord, 25, 28, 29
Lennox-Boyd, Alan, 90
Lesotho, 214
Liberal Party, 61-2, 151-2, 177-8, 220-1; 1945 Election, 11; 1950 Election, 16; 1951 Election, 24, 25; 1955 Election, 66; 1959 Election, 106, 107; 1964 Election, 155, 156; 1966 Election, 180, 181; 1970 Election, 222
Life Peerage Act, 1958, 73
Lloyd, Selwyn, becomes Chancellor of the Exchequer, 109-10, 111; 1961 Budget, 121; dropped from Shadow Cabinet, 219; as Foreign Secretary, 67, 70; becomes Minister of Defence, 67; and Suez Crisis, 90; and the pay-pause, 122
local government elections, 1963, 113; 1967-69, 185, 189
Longford, Lord, 183, 186
Lubbock, Eric, 110, 151
Lyttleton, Oliver, 25; and Central African Federation, 50-2; and colonial constitutional development, 53

McCarran-Walter Immigration Act (U.S.), 126
McCarthy, Joe, 85
MacDonald, Ramsay, 54
Mackintosh, John P., 90
Maclay, John Scott, 111
Macleod, Iain, 25, 176; and Lord Home as Macmillan's successor, 115, 116; and Kenya Asian immigration, 206; on Labour Party, 199; leads Conference on Kenya, 141; as a rival to Mr. Macmillan, 112; and Uganda, 142
MacMahon Act, 1946 (U.S.), 36-7, 80
Macmillan, Harold, 20, 21, 25; African tour, 138; and the Cabinet, 72; becomes Chancellor of the Exchequer, 67; and Churchill's health, 26; economic affaiirs, 210; and the E.E.C., 121, 123-5; 1959 election, 107, 108; becomes Foreign Secretary, 67, 67n.; and J. F. Kennedy, 135-6; as mediator between East and West, 83, 109, 135, 136-7; as Minister of Housing, 24, 33-4, 69; and nuclear weapons, 133-4; as Prime Minister, 68-70, 71, 108-17; selects successor, 114-18; and South Africa, 109, 144, 145; and the Suez Crisis, 90, 91, 92, 93; and the U.S., 133-4, 135-6
Maher, Ali, 44
Makarios, Archbishop, 70, 98, 144
Malawi, 21, 138, 141
Malaya, 143
Malaysia, 139, 143, 166, 207
Malta, 99, 138, 167
Mantoux, Etienne, 93
Marples, Ernest, 219
Marsh, Richard, 182, 185
Mathu, 52
Matsu, 82
Mau Mau, 50, 52-4, 97-8, 141
Maudling, Reginald, 1963 Budget, 122; as Chancellor of the Exchequer, 110, 111, 112; and the Common Market, 77; as Deputy Leader, 176; and EFTA, 124; and the 1964 Election, 155; and Party Leadership, 175-6; as possible Prime Minister, 113, 114, 115, 116
Mauritius, 215
Maxwell Fyfe, Sir David, 25
Mayhew, Christopher, 167
Mboya, Tom, 97
Mellish, Bob, 203
Middle East, 42-6, 86-94, 207, 214
Mikardo, Ian, 60n., 61, 146
Mills, Sir Percy, 111
Ministry of Overseas Development, 159, 169
Ministry of Technology, 159
Mollet, 90
Monckton, Sir Walter, 25, 33
Monckton Commission on Federal Constitution, 97, 140-1
Monmouthshire, Conservative policy on, 20
Montello Island, 36

Moran, Lord, 25-6, 27
Morocco, 46
Morrison, Herbert, Deputy Leadership, 60; and 1951 Election, 17, 25; foreign affairs, 17, 18, 21, 23, 59; loses seat on N.E.C., 60; and the Party constitution, 148; and Party Leadership, 57, 101
Mountbatten, Lord, 165
Moussadeg, Dr. Muhammad, 42
Müller, Dr., 184
Munster, Lord, 142
Murder Act, 1965, 164

Nahas Pasha, 44
Nassau Agreement, 1962, 133-4
Nasser, Gamal, 38, 45, 86-9, 92, 93
National Campaign for the Abolition of Capital Punishment, 79
National Economic Development Council, 120, 122, 123
National Economic Plan, 1965, 160n., 162
National Health charges, 17, 34, 56, 59, 128-9, 161, 165
National Incomes Commission, 121-2
National Service, 81
National Union of Seamen, 195
nationalization, 15, 19, 24, 34, 65, 146, 163
NATO, 41-3, 58, 81, 84-6, 132-4, 148, 165, 169, 207, 209, 210
Neguib, Colonel, 44, 45, 86
New Zealand, 38, 46, 49, 125
Newsom Report on Secondary Education, 125, 130-1
Nicolson, Nigel, 72
Nigeria, 21, 49, 138, 142, 217
1922 Committee, 72
Nkrumah, Kwame, 95, 140
Nobel, Michael, 111
Noel-Baker, Francis Edward, 81, 91
North Borneo, 143
Northern Ireland, 21
Norway, 77
Nuclear Non-Proliferation Treaty, 1968, 209-10
nuclear weapons, 36-7, 79-80, 102, 132-3, 136, 137-8, 148-9, 165-6, 169, 207, 209-10
Nutting, Anthony, 89, 92
Nyasaland, 50-1, 96-7, 140-1
Nyerere, President, 142

Obote, Milton, 143
O.E.E.C., 42
Ombudsman, 154, 190
Opinion Research Centre, 223
Orpington, 151

Pakistan, joins CENTO, 43, 215; immigration into Britain, 127; independence, 49; and the Kashmir question, 170-1; membership of Commission governing Sudan, 45; and SEATO, 48
Panmunjom, 47
Paris Agreements, 41
Parkin, Ben, 129
Parliamentary Commissioner, 154, 190
Parliamentary Committee of the Cabinet, 193
Parliamentary Committees, 190-1
Pearson, Lord, 195
Peart, Fred, 184-5
Peerage Act, 1963, 119-20
Perham, Dame Margery, 140
Persian Gulf, 166, 167, 207, 209
Philippines, 48
Pineau, 90
Polaris missiles, 133, 134
police, 131
Poole, Lord, 71, 107, 115, 116
Portugal, 77, 172, 217
Powell, Enoch, and hospital expenditure, 129; and immigration, 206; increase in N.H.S. charges, 128; and Party Leadership, 176; resigns over 1958 Budget estimates, 70, 76
Prices and Incomes Act, 1966, 182-3, 196
Prices and Incomes Act, 1967, 185
Prices and Incomes Board, 159, 161, 196
Profumo, John, 112-13

Index

Quemoy, 82

race relations, 164–5, 206–7
Race Relations Act, 1965, 164
Race Relations Act, 1968, 206–7, 219
Race Relations Board, 164, 206
Rachmann, Peter, 129
Rachmanism, 129
Radcliffe, Lord, 112
Radcliffe Committee, 75
railways, 131–2
Rapacki, 85
Redmayne, Martin, 115
regional planning, 121
Rent Act, 1957, 77–8, 129, 154, 163
Rent Act, 1965, 163–4
resale price maintenance, abolition of, 126, 128
Rhodesia, Northern, 50–1, 96–7, 140–1
Rhodesia, Southern, 49, 50–1, 96–7, 140–1, 171–2; declares UDI, 176–7, 216–17
Rhodesia Sanctions Order, 191
Road Transport Nationalization Act, 24
Robbins Report on Higher Education, 125, 130
Rose, R., 147
Rosebery, Lord, 27
Royal Commission on Capital Punishment, 78
Royal Commission on Police, 131
Royal Commission on Trade Unions and Employers' Associations, 159, 164, 188, 200–1
Russia, *see* Soviet Union

St. Aldwyn, Lord, 115
St. Kitts, 215, 218
St. Lucia, 215
St. Vincent, 215
Salisbury, Lord, 25, 27, 67, 68n., 70, 90, 176–7, 191
Sandys, Duncan, 219
Sarawak, 143
Saudi Arabia, 46, 86
Scanlon, Hugh, 203
Schonfield, Andrew, 201

Schuman Plan, 1957, 123
Scotland, Conservative policy on, 20; nationalism, 21, 221
Scottish Nationalists, 221
SEATO, 38, 43, 48, 58, 60, 132, 166, 167, 208
Secret Treaty of Sèvres, 1956, 90
Selective Employment Tax, 194–5, 198
Senegal, 170
Sharpeville shootings, 144–5
Shawcross, Lord, 11, 205
Shinwell, Emanuel, 17, 101
Shore, Peter, 183, 184, 198
Short, Edward, 184
Sidki Pasha, 44
Sierra Leone, 138
Silverman, Sydney, 79, 168
Simonds, Lord, 25, 27
Singapore, 143, 166, 167, 207
Skybolt missiles, 133, 134
Smethwick, 156
Smith, Ian, 171–2, 216–71
Smuts, General, 144
Soames, Christopher, 181
Soskice, Sir Frank, 182
South Africa, 109, 140, 144–6, 170, 172, 184, 216, 217
South Arabia Federation, 139, 143–4
South-Eastern Regional Study, 211
Soviet Union, Anglo-Soviet relations, 39, 82, 83, 136–7, 167, 169, 209–10; invasion of Czechoslovakia, 209; and the Middle East, 86, 89, 92, 94; nuclear weapons, 80, 132, 133, 165; and the Test Ban Treaty, 136; and Vietnam, 168, 169; threat to Europe, 35, 37, 40; and West Germany, 84
Spain, 172–3
Sparrow, Gerald, 91
Stalin, Josef, 35, 39
Stansgate, Lord, 119
Steel, David, 178
Stewart, Michael, 160, 183
Stonehouse, John Thomson, 145
Strachey, John, 80
strikes, 65, 75, 195, 200
Sudan, 44–5

Index

Suez Canal, 17, 43–5
Suez Canal Company, 86
Suez Canal Users Association (S.C.U.A.), 87
Suez crisis, 38–9, 67, 68, 71–2, 76, 82, 86–94, 99, 102
Suez Group, 45
Swaziland, 170
Sweden, 77
Switzerland, 77
Syria, 86

Tanganyika, 52, 138, 142
Tanzania, 21, 138
taxation, 76, 122, 161, 181, 194–5, 199
Territorial Army, 166
Test Ban Treaty, 1963, 135, 136, 137
Thailand, 48
Thomson, George, 210
Thorneycroft, Peter, 70, 76, 111, 181
Thorpe, Jeremy, 220
Trade Disputes Act, 1927, 33
Trade Disputes Act, 1965, 164
trade unions, 33, 34, 54–7, 102, 149–150, 199–203; Royal Commission on, 159, 164, 188, 200–1
Treaty of Rome, 1957, 77, 85, 123, 212
Trinidad, 100, 138
T.U.C., 33, 120–1, 122, 159, 162, 185, 197, 198, 199, 203, 204
Tunisia, 46
Turkey, 43, 44, 45, 98

Uganda, 52, 138, 142–3
unemployment, 76, 196, 199–200
United Nations, 16, 17, 98, 139, 144, 173, 191; Committee of Twenty-four on Decolonization, 215; Security Council, 38, 40, 44, 88, 91, 94, 216–17
United States, Anglo-American relations, 26, 35, 37–9, 82–3, 93, 135–6, 168–9, 208–9; and Britain 'East of Suez', 166; and Britain in Europe, 38, 40, 41, 82, 123, 124; and European colonial rule, 96; and the Far East, 46–7; nuclear weapons, 80, 133, 136, 137–8, 165; and

SEATO, 48, 208; and the Suez Canal, 44, 45; and the Suez Crisis, 87–9, 92, 93; and Vietnam, 167, 208–9; and West Germany, 84–5
U.S.S.R., *see* Soviet Union

Vassall, William, 112
Verwoerd, Hendrik, 145
Vietnam, 36, 47–8, 159, 167–8, 187, 208–9
Virgin Islands, 170

Wales, Conservative policy on, 20; nationalism, 21
Walker, Patrick Gordon, defeat at Smethwick, 156; as Foreign Secretary, 158, 160, 165; and the Leyton by-election, 159–60; as Secretary for Education, 183, 184
Ward, Stephen, 113, 129
Watkinson, Harold Arthur, 111
Webb, Sidney, 55n.
Welensky, Sir Roy, 97, 141
Welsh Nationalists, 221
Welsh Office, 159
West India Royal Commission, 1939, 99–100
West Indies, 99–100, 126, 127, 139, 170, 215, 217–18
West Indies Federation, 99–100, 139, 170, 215, 217
Western European Union Scheme, 1954, 41
Wilson, Harold, and the Arab-Israeli war, 214; and 'Bevanism', 60n., 61; Cabinets under, 158, 182–5, 193; defence policy, 165–6; devaluation, 196, 197; and the E.E.C., 208, 210–213; and the 1955 Election, 100–1; and the 1964 Election, 155; and the 1966 Election, 180–1; and the 1970 Election, 186, 222–5; enters Shadow Cabinet, 60; foundations of new policies, 109; and the House of Lords, 191–12; incomes policies, 202–3, 204; as Prime Minister, 157–159, 185–9; and Party Leadership, 150–1, 151n.; resigns over Health

charges, 17, 25; and Rhodesia, 172, 216–17; and the unions, 200–4; and the U.S.S.R., 209–10; and Vietnam, 168–9, 209
'Wind of Change', 109, 138–9
Woolton, Lord, 18–19, 25, 27, 28, 29, 64, 116

World Bank, 87
World War II, 10–13, 38
Wyatt, Woodrow, 163

Zambia, 138, 141, 217
Zanzibar, 138
Zurich, 40